"By way of deception, thou shalt do war."

~From: *Proverbs 24:6*

Thus saith the Lord God:
Behold, I will stretch out my hand…
And they shall know that I am the Lord,
When I shall lay my vengeance upon them.

~From: *Ezekiel 25*

"When I stand before you here, Judges of Israel, to lead the Prosecution of Adolf Eichmann, I am not standing alone. With me are **six million accusers**. But they cannot rise to their feet and point an accusing finger towards him who sits in the dock and cry, "I accuse." For their ashes are piled up on the hills of Auschwitz and the fields of Treblinka…

~From*: Israeli Attorney-General Gideon Hausner's opening speech at Eichmann's trial, Jerusalem, April 1961.*

Contents

Author's Note

Although I have written over a dozen historical novels, writing this novel, *Six Million Accusers*, was the hardest of all. During the whole period that I was working on this book, that is, writing and editing it, in front of me was a picture, one of the iconic Nazi pictures today, that is, the picture of Adolf Eichmann in his smart SS-*Obergruppenführer* uniform (see back cover). In it he looks out, and under his Nazi cap, complete with its Death's Head badge, this smug and smooth-faced Nazi is wearing a sneering smile as if to say, 'Here I am and see what I have achieved so far.'

This picture was taken in 1942, the year that he attended the infamous Wannsee Conference that took place in Berlin in January of that year. This was the meeting where the top Nazis met to establish the official party policy of genocide and how it was to be carried out. It was here that Eichmann was given the responsibility of co-ordinating all the different Nazi and transport organizations and ensure that this the murderous Nazi war-machine could work more efficiently. It would smoothly transport all the Jews and others who were to be caught up in the Nazi net from their place of capture to the many concentration camps that were spread around Europe like cancerous spots on a body. Eleven million(!) Jews were to be transported to their deaths, as well as hundreds of thousands of Gypsies and Soviet Russian prisoners-of-war. This was the essence of the 'Final Solution to the Jewish Problem.' Conducting this vast orchestra of trains, time-tables, 200,000 railway workers and the millions of hapless victims was Adolf Eichmann. He was answerable only to Hitler and Himmler.

And if the murder of six million Jews and the wiping out of their communities and the hundreds of years of Jewish culture in Poland, Hungary, Russia and elsewhere wasn't enough, Eichmann was also responsible for the speedy and efficient transportation of thousands of others who were considered enemies of the Third Reich. These included homosexuals, people with disabilities, political prisoners, Catholic clergy and outspoken intellectuals as well as thousands of captured enemy soldiers and airmen.

When I used to teach about the Holocaust in high-school, in order to make the horrific scale of the terrible statistic 'six million Jews (and others)' more realistic, I would ask my students to imagine this figure as sixty-six Rose Bowl, California, stadiums or Wembley stadiums, London all packed to capacity standing in line. *This* was what six million people looked like. In addition, I told my students that Eichmann and the Nazis were responsible for the deaths of three to four times that incredible number of people, all in a cold-blooded and industrial manner.

Adolf Eichmann was the evil mastermind who was responsible for designing and arranging this vast organization. He worked mainly behind the scenes from 1941 until the war in Europe came to an end in 1945. He was never held accountable for his crimes as he escaped from Europe and fled to Argentina. It was only fifteen years later that he was caught and brought to Israel, the land of the people who had suffered most at his hands. If this book sheds some light on how this heinous man operated and eventually paid for his crimes, then the writing of it will have been worth it.

I hope I have succeeded and will be pleased to receive your comments, positive or otherwise, at: dlwhy08@gmail.com or at: www.dly-books.weebly.com

D. Lawrence-Young
Jerusalem, Israel - May 2014

Prologue

Sunset in Buenos Aires. The old 203 bus rumbled around the corner and a grey nondescript-looking clerk stepped off at the bus-stop almost opposite his house. At the end of a long day at the office, he was looking forward to see his wife and three sons. But he was never to see them again. As soon as the bus was out of sight, two men standing by the roadside pretending to fix their car, grabbed him. Like a bundle of rags, they threw him into the back of the car and covered him with a heavy blanket.

Ordered not to cry out, he was forced to lie down as he was whisked off to a distant safe-house.

The team responsible for kidnapping Adolf Eichmann, one of the chief planners and executors of the "Final Solution to the Jewish Problem," had waited fifteen years and had travelled thousands of miles to do this. I was a proud member of that team.

Chapter One
From Germany to Palestine

My name is Haim, Haim A. The name, Haim, rhymes with 'climb.' As you read these pages you'll see why I don't tell you my family name, It's still a secret, and that's one of the things that happens to you when you work for the Mossad, the Israeli secret service. You learn to keep your mouth shut.

I was named Haim after my grandfather who was killed fighting in the Polish Legion during the First World War. This unit, led by Josef Pilsudski, fought for Polish independence. Later, when the country achieved independence, Pilsudski became the country's first president.

From several old, tattered sepia colored photographs I saw that my grandfather was a large man with a powerful face, piercing eyes and a large black handlebar moustache; and in some of the pictures, he was carrying a rifle. In most of these pictures he is surrounded by a group of similar proud rifle-carrying soldiers. I have only one photograph of him with my grandmother. She is seated in a large wicker chair and he is standing erect behind her with a protective hand on her shoulder.

This photo was taken immediately after their wedding. They are both smartly dressed: he in a dark suit and tie, and she in a white dress. Both of them are looking at the camera with frozen faces, shocked and shy. They were probably wondering what the future held in store for them. In those days you didn't smile at the camera, especially when your photo was being taken as a studio portrait.

Unlike most Jewish families at the beginning of the twentieth century who had many children, my grandparents had only two. Two sons named Avraham and David. Avraham died when he was five of typhus during one of the several outbreaks which plagued our town during this period. After this tragedy, my grandparents decided not to have any more children so David, my father, was now their only son, the son of a successful grain merchant.

12

Naturally my grandfather wanted my father to enter his business and he even had a large sign engraved in brass saying 'Haim Polachek and Son' on his office door, but my father was not interested in joining the business. He preferred working with his hands rather than with a pen, paper and a calculator. He loved taking all sorts of mechanical devices apart and seeing if he could rebuild them. Therefore, it was not completely unexpected when one day he announced that instead of going into the business with my grandfather he would open his own auto-repair shop. Nothing made him happier than getting his hands on an old engine, greasy and rusting, and returning it to its original condition, as an immaculate, working machine. He did not enjoy the business aspect of running his shop and that he left to Rosa, my mother. Luckily I inherited my love of mechanics from my father, and this was to stand me in good stead later on.

But I'm getting ahead of myself so I'll go back to the beginning of my story. I was born in Breslau, an important German town on the River Oder. In 1945 after the Russian army had overrun it, it was renamed Wroclau and became a major town in west Poland. Breslau had had a checkered history, having been ruled in the past by the various Bohemian, Prussian and German authorities.

Since 1854 it had also had an important Jewish Theological Seminary but the Nazis had destroyed this in 1938. Perhaps the two most famous people linked to this town were, the composer, Brahms, who wrote one of his overtures there and the First World War flying ace, Manfred von Richtofen, However, when I was born it was part of Germany.

Until I was ten my life was pretty carefree. I went to the local school and was one of the fifteen Jewish pupils there. Apart from the occasional anti-Semitic remark shouted out by an overgrown Catholic lout called Gregor, I had no problems and got on well with almost everyone there. I was a good student in math and languages and fairly good at sport. I did not like learning literature and considered the time spent on it wasted. I enjoyed studying the more dramatic parts of history: the kings and queens and the various battles that had been fought in Europe, but was not really interested in the political and military situations that had caused these hostilities to break out. It was the action and the personalities involved that really interested me.

And because Breslau was near the Polish border I also learnt Polish from hearing it spoken in the streets as well as from some of my father's customers. I also learnt Hebrew, the religious Hebrew of the Siddur and the Bible. I had to attend the local *cheder* which was set up in an old house ten minutes' walk from my own. I did not like going there and, in fact, the only thing that kept me attending regularly was that my two best friends, Yossele and Avrum also studied there.

Little did I know then that my knowledge of Hebrew, German and Polish, to say nothing of a smattering of Yiddish, would later equip me for taking part in the greatest adventure of my life.

But then when I was ten, my life began to change. Gregor and some of his friends began shouting out more and more anti-Semitic remarks to me and my Jewish friends. And then one day after school, a group of them grabbed hold of me and six year-old Motti Goldstein and made us pull down our pants so they could laugh at the evidence of our circumcision. When my other Jewish friends in the school heard about this we agreed to confront Gregor and tell him that if he or his friends dared to do this again or continue shouting out his stupid anti-Semitic remarks we would beat him up. For a few weeks nothing happened. Then one day, Motti's twin brother, Baruch, was given the same 'pants pulling-down' treatment.

We, ten angry Jewish kids, marched up to Gregor again to teach him a lesson, but he must have got wind of this. When we found him, he had surrounded himself with a dozen similarly built louts who laughed in our faces when we approached them. There was nothing we could do. We were outnumbered and out-muscled. And besides, some of them were holding large wooden sticks. It was very humiliating. We had no choice but to turn round and get out of the schoolyard as quickly as possible. From then on life in school became increasingly brutal and nasty.

If a Jewish student answered a teacher's question correctly, then you would hear loud whispers, "Of course he knows the answer - he's Jewish." But if one of us got the answer wrong you'd hear remarks like "Stupid Jew," or "Ignorant pig" in a voice just loud enough for everyone else in the class to hear. And what made this situation worse was that none of our teachers did anything to stop this. They just ignored it.

And this didn't happen only in the classroom. It also happened on the football pitch. Tackling the Jewish players became especially violent and often the non-Jewish kids would add an extra kick in the shins or elsewhere 'for fun.' Jewish students known to be good players were now left on the sidelines and mocked. "You don't know how to play" and "You cheat" were some of the milder insults.

As time passed, the whole school body, principal, teachers and students, would assemble in the school hall to hear talks about German heroes from the country's medieval past or from the Great War of 1914-1918. We were taught to sing the Horst Wessel song, the Nazi anti-Communist marching song named after the SA Storm Troopers Division unit. Its first lines were:

The flag on high! The ranks tightly closed! The SA march with a quiet steady step.

Comrades shot by the Red Front and reactionaries March in spirit with our ranks…

Then we had to raise our arms in a stiff and straight Nazi salute. My Jewish friends and I refused to do this and so we were beaten up after school on more than one occasion. During one of these beatings one of my teachers happened to walk past.

"What are you boys doing?" he called out.

Reinhart, a heavy-set student shouted, "We're teaching the Jewish pigs a lesson on how to become good Germans."

"*Gut*, good," he smiled and walked off, leaving Reinhart and his thugs to punch and kick us as they saw fit.

"Huh, that will teach you not to sing and salute," they said leaving our bloody faces in the dust. "Next time you'll pay respect to the Nazi party or we'll have to 'educate' you Jewish scum again."

They kept their word. Any time there was an assembly and we refused to salute or sing the Horst Wessel or any other Nazi song we would get a beating in the schoolyard at the end of the day. No teacher ever came to our defense and our bruised and bloody Jewish faces became a regular feature of the classroom.

Every time I came home my mother would wash my face, hands and knees and cry as she cleaned up the worst of the cuts.

"Can't you just salute and sing the songs, maybe just quietly?" she asked, trying to persuade me to accept the situation. "And then maybe they'll stop doing this."

My father, standing behind her, would shake his head sadly. Later he showed me how to duck and to use my fists. His help must have paid off, for one day I got the upper hand and knocked out one of my attackers for a minute or two. For two weeks I was left alone but then it started again. This time it was much worse. This time Gregor, Reinhart and their mates decided to use wooden sticks and metal pipes instead of their fists. That night my mother did not cry. She was speechless when I staggered through the front door and saw my bloody face and half-closed eye. All she could do was hold up her hands to her tear-stained face and murmur," What happened? What have these *goyim* done to you? What will become of us?"

The answer came one week later. Early one morning, my parents and myself, each of us carrying two suitcases and wearing a knapsack, made our way to the local railroad station to begin our long journey to start a new life in a distant country. It was called Palestine and it was controlled by the British.

Of course, I had heard about Palestine before. I had heard about its sunny days and endless blue skies, and where the land was covered with orchards full of orange trees. There, the Jews were strong and lived a full and free life and did not have to worry about the Horst Wessel song or about getting beaten up by jeering Nazi thugs. I had heard that some of these brave Palestinian Jews lived in cities called Tel-Aviv and Haifa while others lived on collective settlements called kibbutzim.

After a day's work in the fields, these pioneers would spend their time sitting around campfires singing patriotic songs in Hebrew or dancing circular dances called the hora. We heard that it was an idyllic life and much better than the one we were fleeing from in Nazi Germany.

Sometimes we heard or read about Arab attacks on Jews and Jewish property. These included the attack on Tel Hai when eight Jewish defenders were killed or the anti-Jewish rioting that broke out at Nebi Musa, but these reports did not deter us from leaving home. I remember the night before we left, my mother's brothers looking at the bulging suitcases and knapsacks stacked in the corner of our front room and laughing at us.

"Tell me, why are you leaving?" Yitzhak had asked. "This Adolf Hitler and his Nazi hooligans will come and go. You forget, David, we're living in the twentieth century. The days of the pogroms are over, at least in Germany."

"That's right," his brother, Ya'acov, added. "Just think what we Jews have done for Germany. Think about Einstein and Moses Mendelssohn, the philosopher."

"Yes, and Felix Mendelssohn, the composer."

"Right, and at least two Nobel prize-winners, Meyerhoff and Ehrlich, and you want to leave all this and live in some desert country far away? You must be crazy."

"He's right, David. And think about the last war. Didn't we fight for Germany? Didn't over twelve thousand of us die to save the Fatherland?"

But my father was not convinced. "Look at Haim's face," he said. "He comes home almost every day now looking like that. No, believe me, this madman called Hitler is here to stay, and if you don't leave soon like us, you will regret it."

Unfortunately my father's prophecy became true. After the war was over I learned that my two uncles and their families had been rounded up in the spring of 1940, taken to the local forest outside the town and brutally murdered.

But as for me, it was the beginning of an adventure. We caught the train as planned, and after a journey that seemed to take forever, we stopped at the border with France. Our papers were checked and stamped by a Nazi-saluting official and then we continued our journey south. After three days and several changes of trains we arrived in Marseilles. There I remember sitting around with my mother guarding our luggage while my father disappeared to arrange the rest of the journey to Palestine. He returned two hours later holding a bunch of stamped documents, a wide grin spread over his face. *"Noss'im, noss'im-* we're going," he smiled, using the little Hebrew he knew. "We're off to Palestine and a new life."

Soon after this we joined up with another two German-Jewish families and made our way to the ship that was riding at anchor in the harbor.

"My family told my father he was *meshuggah* – crazy for leaving Germany," I told Moses Jung, one of the other boys.

"Yes, that's what happened in our family," my new dark-haired friend replied. "They said that life for the Jews where we lived in Berlin was good and that this Hitler fellow would never do to the Jews what he's been promising. Stop worrying, they said. He won't be here for long."

"That's right," Simon Gertler added. "Our friends said the same in Hamburg. They tried to persuade us that these brown and black shirted mobs are just a passing phase. Just like those militias that started up after the war in 1918. Just a lot of noise and marching, my father said."

However, it was not until some time later that we learned that all we had seen and heard in our last few months in Germany was not merely "a lot of noise and marching" and that this "Hitler fellow" was here to stay. However, by the time I had learned this, I was a student at a kibbutz school in the Jezreel Valley in the north of Palestine.

It did not take me long to learn Hebrew and my previous experience of learning Biblical Hebrew in *cheder* stood me in good stead. Soon I was speaking more Hebrew than German or Polish.

My parents, however, continued speaking more German and Polish and the change in life-style was difficult for them than it was for me. This was especially true for my father. From being the proud owner of his own auto-repair shop he now worked as a mechanic in a local garage performing the simpler tasks he had done when he had first started. To his disgust, his boss would not allow his new employee to carry out any of the more complicated jobs that came into the workshop. However, although he often complained to my mother that his knowledge and experience were not being exploited, he was pleased to have left Germany, especially as we began to hear more and more about the attacks on the Jews there and their property. These grim reports began to filter out of Germany and we heard more and more of them repeated as more German and Polish refugees arrived in Palestine. They all looked like we had on our arrival: pale-faced and carrying their suitcases, but pleased to have escaped the increasing violence that was now becoming part of everyday life back in Berlin, Hamburg and Warsaw.

"But the trouble is," most of them said was "that we are just the lucky few who were able to see what was happening back home now. Most of those who have remained don't really believe that this situation will last, like the attacks on the Jews and the synagogues and the shops."

I remained in the kibbutz school until I was fifteen in November 1938, that is, until a few days before I heard about the *Kristallnacht* attacks. This was a pogrom in which the Nazis killed over ninety Jews and sent thirty-thousand to concentration camps. At the same time the Nazi authorities incited the local population to burn and loot many synagogues in Germany and Austria.

But while this was happening in Europe, I was becoming quite proficient in speaking, reading and writing Hebrew. I'd also learned to become a skilled mechanic working in the kibbutz garage.

There I learned to take car and tractor engines apart and even to reassemble them again without having any extra nuts and bolts left behind on my work-bench!

Then, one day quite unexpectedly, and soon after I had heard about the Kristallnacht attacks I was asked to go to the center of Tel Aviv where I was to meet a man in a café on Dizengoff Street. I was told to carry a rolled-up copy of *Ha'aretz* in my left hand and if someone asked me,"*Bnei Noah*?" – the sons of Noah? I was to reply, "Shem, Ham and Yapheth." He would be my contact man.

I must say that I was quite surprised by this cloak-and-dagger stuff and thought it was all exaggerated but it all worked out as planned. I met the man in a small café on Dizengoff Street. He glanced at my newspaper and then ushered me into a gloomy room at the back of it. We sat down and when we shook hands and I introduced myself as "Haim," he just told me to sit down.

He did not tell me his name, but ordered two coffees. Then without wasting any time he asked me about my political opinions and how I thought we Jewish Palestinians should deal with the British as well as with the Arabs who were attacking our settlements, buses and trains.

"We should fight the Arabs," I replied, "and do everything we can to make the British leave and let us rule our own country."

"You mean, have an independent Jewish country – not one that is part of the British Empire?" the unknown dark- haired man in a short-sleeved shirt asked me.

"Yes, that's exactly what I mean, but I don't think the British will want to leave here in a hurry."

He made no comment but then asked whether I knew how to use a rifle and a pistol.

"Of course. All the men on my kibbutz do. We have to carry them when we go out on guard duty or when we work in some of the more distant fields."

He seemed pleased with my answer and then asked me which languages I spoke.

"I'm completely fluent in Hebrew and not too bad in German, Polish and Yiddish," I replied. "I can speak some English although my reading and writing need some improvement," I added.

"Do you know any Arabic?"

"A bit. Just some very basic stuff. I can't read it although I do know what the numbers look like."

He smiled to himself and scribbled a few notes down in a small notebook.

"All right, young man," he said, standing up to shake my hand after half an hour. "It's very possible that we'll be in touch with you in the near future. But in the meanwhile, do not say anything about this meeting. It never happened. Do you understand? You do not mention it to your parents or your friends or anyone else. Is that clear?"

I nodded.

"Good." And suddenly he was gone. I rushed outside to see where he had disappeared, but all I could see were the crowds on Dizengoff Street; the people were strolling along, looking in the shop windows or sitting at the pavement cafes. The continuous flow of feet and faces had swallowed him up completely.

That was my introduction to the *Irgun* – the National Military Organization. From then until I enlisted in the British army's Palestine Battalion my life was one of contrast – a contrast of public and secret activities. I became a Jewish Dr. Jekyll and Mr. Hyde. I left the kibbutz and by day I worked as a humble mechanic in a small, scruffy garage on the border between Tel-Aviv and Jaffa. But when the sun went down – usually seen as a fiery ball sliding into the Mediterranean – then I would meet my fellow-*Irgun* members and attend secret sessions and learn how to become a useful and effective member of the organization. Some nights we would learn how to strip down pistols and rifles and then reassemble them in record time. On other nights we would learn about explosives and how to make and set booby-traps. These were to be used against the British soldiers whom we saw as the representatives of their government's policy, a policy, which advocated the hated White Paper. This document stated that the British authorities would allow only fifteen thousand Jews to enter Palestine per year for each of the next five years. Fifteen thousand per year! By now the Nazis were growing stronger and stronger. Now, probably hundreds of thousands of Jews were desperate to escape Hitler's expanding Nazi-controlled Europe and all the British would do was to allow a few thousand Jews find safety in Palestine. No wonder we hated the British so much.

Sometimes when we weren't keeping an eye on the British soldiers stationed in Tel-Aviv, we had meetings, which consisted of lectures and discussions. These usually dealt with what was happening in Palestine and Europe. We also discussed how we would run the country when we were independent, that is, after we had chased the British out. What would we call our new country?

Israel? Judea? New Judea? New Palestine? Those were heady and exciting days. We would sit around half the night drinking endless cups of coffee discussing these and other ideas and then go home to snatch a few hours' sleep before returning to our regular places of work the next day.

Most of our meetings, which were held in different houses and cellars every night, ended with us singing our hymn, which included the following dramatic words:

Unknown soldiers are we, without uniforms,
Around us but darkness and death,
We have joined the army for life,
Only death will relieve us from the ranks...

Of course we didn't sing it as loudly as we wanted because we were always aware that there were people who did not approve of our activities. Given the chance, they would have reported us to the authorities.

Of course, what made all this more exciting for many of us was that it was the first time that some of us boys had our first close contact with girls. This added more spice to our meetings. Who was going out with whom, and how did you treat your new girl-friend and how did she treat you?

Did you tell the others that you were going out with Ruthie, Sarah or Rachel? Did you hold hands with her in public? Did you kiss her on the cheek or did you dare to kiss her on the lips? Did you meet for a chat and a hurried kiss only after the organization's meetings were over or did you take her to the cinema? And what did you do or say when you discovered that your girl friend had 'betrayed' you when she said, "I can't see you tonight because I have to help my mother at home,"when in fact she was really meeting someone who, up to now, you had thought was your best friend?

When you wanted to distract a British patrol on the Tel-Aviv seafront, or follow them, did you put your arm around the girl's waist and pretend you were a young couple out for an evening walk, or did you walk past the cafés side by side holding hands? Life then was tense and exciting and full of questions.

Many of these questions were political. The main issue concerned our relationship with the British who many of us saw as conquerors of our country. This question became even more problematic after the war broke out in Europe in September 1939. Twenty years earlier, the British had received the Mandate from the League of Nations to run Palestine but now they were fighting Nazi Germany and its Axis partners.

"But don't you see, if we help the British now or, at least, not try and hinder them, we'll be encouraging them to stay here forever?"

"Not true. First of all we must co-operate with them because they are fighting the Nazis. Can you imagine what will happen if

Hitler or Mussolini succeed in invading this country? There'll be another *Kristallnacht* and concentration camps all over the place."

"Ah, come on, you're exaggerating. That'll never happen. They'll never reach here. No, my friend, we must do all we can to get the British out of here, and the quicker the better."

But then in the summer of 1940 many of our members who were still unsure what should be done about the British had their minds made up for them. German and Italian warplanes started bombing Tel-Aviv and Haifa and killed well over one hundred people. Suddenly the war was brought to our doorsteps. These attacks convinced me and many of my friends in the *Irgun* that from now on we had to listen to David Ben-Gurion, the left-wing Zionist leader, when he proclaimed that, "We should fight the White Paper as if there's no war, and fight the war as if there's no White Paper."

One week later, after several long nights of discussion and soul-searching I, together with six of my best friends, enlisted in one of the British army's Palestine battalions. This is not the time nor place to tell you in detail what we did except to say that I drove British army trucks – 'lorries' they called them – in Egypt, North Africa and Malta. I took part in the fighting in the north of Italy at the River Senio. I remember feeling very proud when Winston Churchill, the British Prime Minister, in September 1944 announced that from then on our Palestine Battalions would now combine to form the five thousand-man Jewish Brigade. Many of us asked ourselves why he had waited so long to come to this decision, while others said that after Churchill had learned about what the Nazis had done at Auschwitz and other extermination camps, he felt he should repay the thousands of Jewish soldiers who were fighting in the Allied armies.

One of the actions that I can give you a few more details about is what I was doing towards the end of the war.

At the end of 1944 I was approached by two Jewish Brigade officers, Meir Zorea and Haim Laskov. They took me aside one evening while we were resting in a camp near the old fortress in

Imola and asked whether I would be willing to join a special unit whose aim was to secretly kill Nazi officers who were still living in northern Italy and Austria.

"Why me?"

"Because we know about your background in the *Irgun* and your record as a fighter." "And you can also speak German."

"When do we start?" I replied immediately. I had seen how the few Jews who had escaped from the camps looked and had heard their terrible stories at first hand. I needed no time to think about joining this secret unit. The time for revenge had come. No-one should be allowed to treat us Jews the way the Nazis had done and get away with it.

Zorea and Laskov shook my hand and told me not to repeat this conversation to anyone, not even to my best friends, Uri Cohen and Yossi Gold.

"How do you know about them?" I asked.

"We know," Zorea smiled, tapping the side of his nose as he walked away.

I admit it was hard not to tell my closest buddies about this conversation, but you can imagine my surprise when, on the night of my first action, I found both Uri and Yossi standing there waiting for me in a British jeep by a small, abandoned building in the woods. We were all wearing British Military Police uniforms.

"I didn't know you'd be here," I said. "I was told not to tell you anything about this."

"They said the same thing to us," Uri said.

"Who? Lieutenant Zorea and Laskov?"

"Yes. They said this business was very hush-hush and nobody needed to know what we were doing."

"And do you know where we're going tonight?" I asked.

"No, but I guess we'll know soon. Zorea and Laskov are heading this way."

A few moments later the two officers, together with Sergeant Carmi, told us to get behind the wheels of the three waiting jeeps and then we set off. Apart from a brief *"Shalom,"* there were no greetings and our instructions were equally brief. "Drive in the direction of Ravenna until you get to Cotignola and then stop there. Just make sure you stay within the speed limit and watch out for pot- holes in the road."

We arrived at the small village of Cotignola after half an hour and stopped outside an isolated farmhouse. The two officers and Carmi left the jeeps and told us to wait but to keep the engines running. They returned ten minutes later leading a German SS officer in uniform. If I remember, he held the rank of a SS *Sturmbannführer* – an SS major. His wrists were tied behind his back and he was ordered to get into the back of my jeep. He found this hard to do as apart from a boot to his rear by Sergeant Carmi, he was given no help. As soon as he was settled in the back, we drove off to a nearby wood which surrounded a small lake. Again, following instructions, I stopped, turned off the engine and the headlamps and helped to pull the quaking SS man out of the back of the jeep.

Laskov asked me to use my German and ask him details about his name and rank. When he had replied, Zorea told me to ask him to give me the names of other SS officers who were living in the area. "Tell him that if he says he doesn't know anything, threaten him with your pistol and if that doesn't work, hit him in the stomach."

"Just don't touch his face," Carmi added. "We want him to talk. Tell him that if he gives us a few names, we may spare his miserable life."

By now the SS major was a trembling wreck. There was no need to threaten him with any violence at all. As soon as I asked him for the necessary details, he couldn't tell me fast enough.

"Tell him to slow down. I can't write that fast," Zorea said, recording everything that this past member of the 'Master race' was now spitting out in a desperate effort to save his life.

"Will you let me go now?" he pleaded after he had finished giving away his fellow officers.

"Huh! What's a promise to a Nazi worth?" Zorea said, and took out his service revolver.

"Just look at him," Uri cried out, holding his nose. "He's wet himself."

It was true. The Nazi's fear had caused him to urinate inside his sharply creased uniform trousers. We saw a dark patch spreading rapidly over the front of his trousers. Then Zorea stepped in front of the major and replaced the gag around his sweating face. Then he looked straight into the German's eyes.

"In the name of the Jewish people, in the name of the thousands, if not millions that you Nazis have murdered in cold blood, you have been condemned to die. The Jews will have their revenge."

The major tried to wriggle away but it was impossible and too late. Zorea fired one shot and the black-uniformed SS major fell to the muddy ground like a sack of potatoes, writhed for a moment or two and then was still. For a moment there was silence and then from somewhere in the forest we could hear an owl hoot.

We bound his legs with wire and then tied a sack of rocks around his waist and threw him as far as we could into the lake. It was only after the bubbles had stopped coming up to the surface did we turn around and walk back to our waiting jeeps and silently drive away.

We and other squads were to repeat this act of revenge tens, maybe hundreds of times over the next few months. None of the squads kept any records of who or how many were killed. This was a secret and would remain one forever.

Each time we carried out such an action we always felt the same: pleased that we Jews had carried out some sort of justice and revenge, but frustrated and unsatisfied that we had not done enough. All we had done was to rid the world of those who had claimed that they had merely carried out orders. Those who had actually given the orders, the leaders who had been responsible for the Holocaust, it seemed to me, had got away with their crimes, scot-free.

Chapter Two
Ruthie and Ein Hamidbar

In the summer of 1946, together with hundreds of other 'brigadiers,' I was put on a troop carrier to be sent back to Palestine. The British had disbanded the Jewish Brigade in June 1946 after only two years. The War Office in London was not pleased that the Brigade's men had been using British military supplies for housing, feeding and helping the Jews in Europe who had survived the Nazi concentration camps. The British were also annoyed that the Brigade had also been using its trucks to transport these survivors to ports in Italy and elsewhere and then helping them sail to Palestine where they hoped to start a new life.

The British government and the army felt that they were between the hammer and the anvil, the devil and the deep blue sea. On the one hand there were the Jews who wished to escape from the bloody events of Europe and start afresh in Palestine while, on the other, the Arab countries were putting enormous pressure on the British to prevent them from allowing the thousands of Jewish refugees from arriving in Palestine. They claimed that these new Jewish arrivals were reinforcing the Jewish community that had already settled there in a land which they, the Arabs, felt was really theirs.

In the end, the British government, led by the Foreign Minister, Ernest Bevin, surrendered to the powerful Arab oil interests and decided not to allow any more unfortunate Jews to sail to and settle in Palestine.

Thus it was that late in the summer of 1946 I found myself on a Royal Navy transport ship sailing into Malta's impressive harbor at Valletta en route to Palestine. We were destined to land at Haifa but had been told to stop in Valletta in order to deliver some much needed supplies to the British garrison there. During the war the Nazi air-force, the Luftwaffe, had bombed the 'island fortress' and many of the harbor's buildings and installations were in serious need of repair. As part of our final duties as British army servicemen, we received orders to help with the unloading of these supplies and as a result were to remain in Valletta for over a week. While at first this looked as if it were to be a frustrating experience, it also meant that this was the place that I first met my wife-to-be. Her name was Ruthie Goodman and she was one of the several ATS drivers who had arrived there on the transport ship before mine.

One evening while I was leaning over the rail looking at the twinkling lights surrounding Valletta's Grand Harbor I heard Ruthie ask another ATS girl in English if she knew where there was a café near the harbor where she could buy a good cup of coffee. "Yes, I know what you mean," the ATS girl said. "This army stuff they call coffee is terrible. Anyway, I know there's a place on St. Ursula Street near the Victoria Gate, but I'm too tired to go there tonight. Sorry. I'm just about to go to my cabin and turn in for the night. So, I'll see you in the morning. G'night."

And saying that, she gave Ruthie a pat on the shoulder and turned around to walk off in the direction of her cabin. Until today I still don't know what made me suddenly walk up to my future wife and say, "I know where that café is, the one that your friend was talking about. If you don't mind going for a coffee with a soon-to-be retired Jewish Brigade sergeant, I'll show you where it is. Oh, by the way, my name is Haim."

Maybe it was the twinkle in her dark brown eyes and maybe it was because, despite her ATS uniform, she looked exciting and full of life, a sharp contrast to the feelings of frustration and boredom that I'd been experiencing over the past few days. I had not been needed to help with the unloading of the supplies but had been spending my time playing endless games of pontoon or chess or just looking over the sides of the ship.

She looked at my Brigade shoulder flash with its gold Star of David badge on a blue and white striped background, smiled and said, "O.K, Haim the brigadier, I'll let you take me there – but there's one condition. That you let me pay for myself."

I bowed and said," Very good, my lady," and she put her arm

30

through mine and we made our way down the gangplank off the ship. Ten minutes later we were sitting face to face in a small dimly- lit café, which had a good view over the harbor.

Now I had a good chance to look at her. Her hair was dark brown and curly and some of the curls had escaped from under her uniform hat to curl upward like delicate tendrils. This made her look less formal even though she was wearing her well-cut regulation hat, jacket and skirt. Her sharp brown eyes reflected the light of the candle on the table between us and its flickering flame seemed to make the small dimples on either side of her mouth dance about. When I told her that her face seemed to be moving and changing all the time, she laughed and kicked me lightly under the table.

"That is no way to speak to a lady," she said.

"Then I am terribly sorry, milady," I replied, taking her hand. "I most humbly apologize," and I bowed slightly from the waist, speaking formally to cover up my embarrassment. "I was just trying to say that your face looks most interesting. That's all."

"Why? Is it boring when it's not in candlelight?"

"Oh no. Not at all. But tell me," I hurried on in order to change the subject. "What are you doing on a Royal Navy ship in Malta? Are you also going to Palestine?"

"What do you mean going to? I'm returning there. I was born in Palestine."

"So why are we speaking in English?" I asked and from then on we continued in Hebrew. "I'm from Ein Hamidbar. It's a small kibbutz about twenty kilometers south-west of Beersheva in the northern Negev. Not many people have heard of it. Have you?"

"Not really, except that I've heard it has an interesting archaeological site near it."

"That's right," she smiled. "But anyway, you asked me what I was doing here. I joined the ATS three years ago. At first I was posted to the Royal Signals where I worked as an English-

Hebrew translator but then I became bored and put in for a transfer."

"To what?"

"I wanted to be a driver but they wanted me to work with the military police. I said I didn't want that and repeated my request to become a driver."

"And they listened to you?"

"Funnily enough, they did. I told them that I had learned how to drive tractors and light trucks on the kibbutz and since the army is always in need of drivers, I became a driver. I was taught to drive lorries up to five tons."

"So you know all about Bedfords and AEC Matadors?"

"Of course. And also about the American Dodges and Chevrolets. My favorite was the Dodge WC-58."

"The one they called the 'Command car?'"

"Yes," Ruthie replied, wiping some cake crumbs off her chin. "It was a heavy vehicle but easy enough for me to drive. Sometimes though, I did drive the heavier stuff like the Bedford five-tonners."

Suddenly I started laughing.

"What's so funny, Mister Brigadier?" she asked.

"It just occurred to me: I asked you out on the spur of the moment and here we are sitting in a café, drinking a decent cup of coffee for a change and talking about British and American army lorries. Now isn't that romantic?"

For a reply, she kicked me softly under the table again.

"So what did you do while I was valiantly driving around Italy?" she asked when we had both stopped laughing.

"Me? I was in the Jewish Brigade and took part in the fighting near the River Senio." I decided not to tell her about my involvement with the revenge squads at this point. If we became friendlier, then maybe I would tell her later.

She noted that I was holding back and quite naturally put her soft hand on mine and asked me to tell her more about my time in the army. I told her something about my experiences in Egypt and North Africa and how I'd been part of the forces that had driven Rommel and the German army out of Libya and Tunisia. Then I told her about being transferred to Malta and how we had had to kick our heels there for a while before moving north to be retrained for combat duties in Italy.

"Ah, so that's how you know about this café," she said. "And who did you come here with last time? An army nurse from London? Another ATS driver from Palestine? All homesick for mummy and daddy?"

Despite the flickering candle-light she must have seen me blush and put her hand on mine again. "Don't worry," she said softly. "I was just kidding. You have the right to come here with whoever you want to."

"To tell you the truth," I said. "The last time I was here was with three of our own lads, Yossi, Danny and Baruch."

She noted I was suddenly looking sad. "What's up?" she asked quietly.

"Yossi was killed when we were fighting in the north of Italy and Danny was also badly wounded there. He trod on a landmine and lost both of his legs."

We all had stories like that and however many times we remembered and told them, it didn't become any easier. These were friends who had been to school with us, who had trained with us and then had experienced all the good and bad times we'd shared over the past few years. No doubt Ruthie had similar stories but I didn't want to ask. If she did want to tell me, then she would do so in her own good time.

Just then I looked up and saw that her eyes were wet and glistening. A couple of tears were flowing down her smooth cheeks.

"I'm sorry," I said, offering her a handkerchief. "I didn't mean to make you cry. It's just that Yossi and Danny were really good friends of mine."

"No, no. It's not that," she replied. "it's just that you brought it back to me that one of the girls in our unit, an American volunteer from New York, also stepped on a landmine and was killed in the north of Italy near Pontebba. Her name was Judith and she was one of my best friends. She even taught me how to fix engines, when they got stuck, and how to clean plugs and filters."

We sat there together for a minute or two thinking of our friends who were no longer with us.

Suddenly the sound of smashing glass and metal jerked us out of our grim memories of the past. "What's that?" Ruthie asked, swiveling her chair around to face the door.

We got up and rushed outside. A few yards down the street a British army jeep was standing there wedged into a lamppost, the front end crumpled up. Steam and smoke were pouring out over the engine like a cloud and hot water was pouring out from the smashed radiator. The driver was slumped over the steering wheel, his head jammed between the wheel and the cracked windscreen. His helmet was between him and the passenger seat, hanging off the gear shift. The passenger next to him was half-lying out of the front door moaning, "My head, my head."

Ruthie ran toward the jeep and I followed her.

"I know some first-aid," she said as I caught up with her. "Maybe I can do something for them."

"Don't worry, we'll take care of them," two nurses in Queen Alexandra uniforms said as they came up from behind us. "We were also in the café when we heard the noise."

Later we heard that the driver had been drinking to celebrate his or his passenger's birthday. But whatever the cause of their crash, it was the end of our meeting in the café and talking about our war experiences.

Feeling somewhat subdued we walked back to the ship and after saying that I'd like to see her again we parted company for the night.

We were not to meet again until the day she came aboard my ship before we set sail for Haifa. "Where have you been?" I asked as I saw her heave her kit-bag into a space on the forward deck. "I've been looking for you."

She smiled and pushed a dark brown curl out of her eye. "I've been ashore working in the stores, making lists and checking that everything was where it was supposed to be. They called up four of us ATS girls and we had to sleep in the navy hostel by the..."

"Oh good," I interrupted. "I was hoping you hadn't left on the ship that left two days ago. Are you free to go ashore to that café again before we set sail?"

She nodded and ten minutes later we were back in the Victoria Gate café. This time we talked about our families and where we lived. I told her about my German background and how my father had been foresighted enough to predict what Hitler had been planning for the Jews.

"We didn't have that problem," she said. "My grandparents came on aliya about fifty years ago. For them it was a combination of escaping pogroms and fulfilling the *mitzvah,* the religious commandment of living in the Holy Land."

"But you're not religious, are you?"

"No, not really. I mean, I like the *hagim*, the festivals, and my mother lights candles on Friday night, but I don't go to synagogue every Shabbat or things like that. You should know what it's like on most of the kibbutzim. They tend to regard the *hagim* as agricultural festivals rather than religious ones."

"Yes, it's like that on my kibbutz as well. And didn't you want to study?" I asked next.

"What is this?" she smiled. "The Spanish Inquisition?"

"No? Just my native curiosity."

"Well, yes, I do want to study. As a matter of fact, I'd like to study English lit. I really love English poetry and Shakespeare's comedies. I really like the way he plays with words in them. And what about you? Do you want to study?"

"Me? I want to learn mechanics or engineering. But for the time being I can still see myself working as a greasy mechanic in our kibbutz garage, fixing cars and tractors. I plan to return to my kibbutz when I get back."

"Maybe," she asked, her eyes lighting up, "you could come and work in the repair-shop on my kibbutz."

And that is exactly what happened. A month after arriving home I moved to Ruthie's kibbutz and became a mechanic and general fix-it man there. Apart from repairing the Fordson and John Deere tractors and various pieces of agricultural equipment, I also learnt to work on irrigation pipes and to weld great sheets of corrugated iron which were an important part of the kibbutz's defense system.

And we really needed these defenses because in May 1948, a few days after Ben-Gurion had declared independence for the new State of Israel, the Egyptian army attacked us. Their aim was to wipe us off the map and then continue north to take over Tel-Aviv. For them we were just a nuisance to be got rid of on their drive north.

It was therefore essential for our kibbutz and for the others in the northern Negev such as Yad Mordechai, that we put up the stiffest resistance we could. And so began one of the most dangerous chapters in my life. By day I was working in the repair-shop and by night I would join the others on guard duty. We spent the clear starry nights waiting for the Egyptian army which we knew would have to pass through our kibbutz on their way north.

"What are we going to do?" a young kibbutz member asked. "We're only a few dozen men here, and out there," and he pointed out to the deceptively quiet desert surrounding us, "is the whole Egyptian army. Shouldn't we retreat? You must know the old saying, He who runs away, lives to fight another day."

"We don't have another day," I said, looking south through my binoculars. "We have no choice. We have to stop the Egyptian army here and now, or at least slow them down until our other forces get here from the north."

"You mean, buying time?"

"Exactly," I said picking up my ex-British rifle where it was leaning against the side of one of our newly-dug defense trenches.

Nothing happened that night but on the following day one of our armored columns reached the kibbutz and evacuated seventy children to a safer kibbutz in the north. This was not before time.

The next day the first Egyptian fighter planes flew over the kibbutz and started strafing the central communal area which included the children's rooms, the school, the dining-room and the members' houses. Fortunately no-one was killed as the dining-room and the school were empty but several members were wounded by shrapnel and flying glass. After that there was an eerie silence and we all wondered what would happen next.

"I don't like being here like a sitting duck," Avi, a friend of mine in the garage, muttered that afternoon once we had swept the broken shards of glass out of the dining-room. "It's not the fighting that worries me, it's the waiting and hanging about that get on my nerves. That, and wondering how my two kids are doing."

I agreed with him even though I had no children to worry about. "Well, I'm sure we'll know soon enough what the Egyptians are planning. I'm sure that attack earlier wasn't the first one they've got planned for us.

I was right. Two hours later huge, rolling clouds of yellow-brown dust warned us that the Egyptian army had arrived. Almost as soon as we saw these clouds billowing in our direction, high- explosive shells started landing on the kibbutz. At first they landed on the outer defenses but soon the Egyptian artillery managed to pinpoint our central buildings – the dining room, the office block, the laundry and the bakery.

"Look! The dining-room's been hit!" someone yelled. "I hope no-one was in it."

"No, they're all in the underground shelter," came a shouted reply just as our water-tower collapsed and came crashing down with a deafening noise, showering huge chunks of concrete over a wide area.

Then just as suddenly as the shelling started, it stopped, leaving us wondering what would happen next. The only sound that broke the silence was a light breeze and the moaning of two members who were lying in a trench, bleeding and bruised where their defense shelters had fallen in on them.

We waited for another attack, but nothing happened. "Is that it?" someone asked.

"I doubt it," I said. "But I think it's because the Egyptians don't like fighting at night." And it was true. The rapid sunset was a sign for the enemy to break off for the day but it still meant that we had to remain on full alert during the night in case some of them tried to mount a sneak attack.

During the lull I ran over to one of the underground shelters that had been turned into a first-aid station where Ruthie was working as a medic. As soon as I entered I saw that the front of her blouse and British army trousers were spattered with blood.

"What's up? Are you…?"

She wiped the back of her hand across her forehead leaving a bloody smear above her eyes. "No," she half-smiled at seeing me. "This blood is from lifting the wounded up onto the table. Daniel and Yigal. We had to clean them up. They'll be all right in the morning, but they were pretty bloody when they were carried in earlier. Anyway, what's going on out there? All we heard down here was the shells and the sounds of smashing glass."

"I'm not sure," I said reaching out for a chipped mug of coffee. "I've heard that the Egyptians have bypassed a couple of kibbutzim but we are in their way. Someone said there's over two thousand of them, combined infantry and artillery."

"Two thousand!"

"Yes," I nodded. "To our hundred and fifty."

"So we don't stand a chance," Ruthie said quietly. "Maybe we'll be able to hold them off for a day or two, but that's the most."

"Well, if we can hold out for that long, then the *Palmach* shock-troops will have enough time to get here and reinforce us."

"Why can't they send them now?" she asked angrily. "It's now that we need reinforcements, not when we've been over-run."

"Because the radio reports said they're all tied up in the north and center."

"Well all I can say is it's a good thing we got the children and babies out of here in time. I hate to think what would have happened if they'd have still been here."

"Me too. And thanks for the coffee. I needed that. But I've got to get back now." I gave her a quick kiss and rushed back to my trench.

That night as I was catnapping I was woken up by a sharp tap on the shoulder.

"Haim, wake up! Some of us are going to sneak out and see if the Egyptians have left any guns and ammo behind in the dark. Come."

Like silent cats on the prowl half a dozen of us eased our way through our barbed wire defenses to search for enemy weapons and ammunition. We were running low of ammunition and knew that every bullet was important. Half an hour later we were back with a dozen rifles and a few boxes of ammo. We were hoping to find something more serious, such as sub-machine guns, but had no such luck. All we could do for the rest of the night was to take turns at guard-duty and wait for the next day's attack which we were sure would happen.

It did. As before, the enemy presence was heralded by rolling clouds of yellow-brown clouds of dust mixed with the dirty exhaust smoke of their light tanks and armored vehicles. Despite all our dire predictions we managed to hold them off for a few days even though by the end of the week there was not one building on the kibbutz left standing. They had all been smashed up, big or small: houses, cowsheds and workshops. Huge gaping holes and trailing wires and lengths of iron showed where the enemy shells had scored direct hits. Finally, after three days of artillery shells crashing, buildings collapsing and wounded men screaming, some units of the *Palmach* arrived to reinforce us. By then we were all completely exhausted. We could grab only the odd hour or two at night to sleep, that is, when we weren't sneaking out beyond our defenses to look for more enemy weapons. On the third night we were lucky. In addition to finding some twenty rifles lying near their fallen soldiers, we found three machine-guns and the necessary boxes of ammo to go with them.

The day after this the Egyptians opened fire upon us again, this time with even greater numbers of men and armored vehicles. Now it really was a do or die situation. We knew we could not expect any more reinforcements and just had to stand our ground whatever happened. The fighting and the shelling lasted all day and it was only at sunset that they retreated leaving our smashed up buildings looking even worse, if that were at all possible. All the land around the center of the kibbutz was pockmarked like the surface of the moon and not one single garden or flower-bed remained unscathed. As the noise of the shelling and the cracks of rifle-fire ceased we became aware of the smell of burnt cordite and gunpowder. During the day we had been too busy to notice, but now in the tense silence of the night we could smell the stench of war.

After a nervous night in which we knew we were in no position to hold out for more than one more day, we waited for the morning attack. It never came. Nor on the following day or the days after that.

"We were too hard a nut for them to crack," the *Palmach* commander said after a week's tense waiting. "They won't be back again."

"How do you know?" asked Motti, a tall skinny kibbutznik whose left leg was now freshly bound in plaster.

"Other *Palmach* units attacked them from the rear where they were least expecting it and now they've retreated to the border."

Naturally this news was greeted with loud cheers and someone found a bottle of cheap red wine to celebrate our victory. It was only later that we learned of the scale of our success. Over four hundred Egyptians had died while we had taken a light tank, an armored car and dozens of rifles as booty. However, in contrast to our joy of holding out, we were saddened by the price we had had to pay for it. Five of our men had been killed and seven had been seriously wounded. It was only after the cease-fire that we could send them north where they would receive proper treatment.

Physically the kibbutz looked like a wreck – a collection of smashed mounds of rubble, brick, wood and concrete, the sites of where our buildings once stood. We knew we would rebuild it all, but it was still depressing to think that all the buildings we had built with such love and pride had all been reduced to nothing.

"Not really nothing," Avi said to me the day after we heard that the enemy had retreated, "We did save the road to Tel-Aviv, and the underground shelters stood up to it all." I looked around at the pot-holes and piles of concrete. "I suppose you're right, but what a terrible price we paid," I said, thinking of those who had been killed and of all the rebuilding we would have to do

But for me, in the middle of this sad and desolate picture, a bright light shone. One month later I married Ruthie and we moved into our new home – a khaki British army tent. Despite our tough situation, other kibbutz members did us proud and organized a memorable celebration for us.

Somehow enough flour was found to make us an impressive wedding-cake and enough bottles of whisky and schnapps – plum brandy – were found to improve the celebrations. Moshe, a tubby kibbutznik, played his accordion and we had a long drawn-out sing-song around a camp-fire that lasted far into the night.

Owing to the situation and the urgent need to rebuild some of the main buildings before the winter started, Ruthie and I had only a one-day honeymoon before we were both back at work. The fighting in the War of Independence was over by the middle of 1949 and the various cease-fire agreements were signed soon after.

From then on, life continued peacefully enough, that is, if you didn't count the occasional Egyptian terrorist infiltration attacks as the kibbutz grew and expanded.

And so did my own family. By the time I was back home from playing my part in the Suez Campaign in the fall of 1957, Ruthie and I had three children. The first was named David after my father; his sister, Sara, named after Ruthie's grandmother joined him two years later, and little Yossi, named after my best friend who had been killed in Italy, made up the threesome two years after that.

I was now a respected and respectable member of the kibbutz and was constantly in demand to repair vehicles and agricultural equipment and both Ruthie and I were also busy sitting on various committees within the kibbutz. We felt very pleased, perhaps a little smug at how the way our life had turned out and with what we had achieved in a relatively short time. I remember thinking one day as I was fitting a new fan-belt on to a John Deere combined harvester that in comparison with what I heard from other friends, my own life was calm and peaceful. Little did I guess that evening that a phone-call from Tel-Aviv would disturb the tranquility of my life for a good few years.

Chapter Three
A Meeting at Bella's

"Haim, Haim, come over to the office," Moshe called out as I was walking back to my house. "There's someone on the phone for you from Tel-Aviv. He wouldn't give me his name or say who he was. All he said was that it was important that he speaks to you personally."

Wiping as much grease off my hands as I could on a rag in my pocket, I followed Moshe into the office and took the phone from him.

"*Shalom*. Is that Haim from Kibbutz Ein Hamidbar?" a deep voice asked.

"Yes, and who am I talking to?"

"Please tell me your identity number."

"Who am I talking to?" I repeated.

"I'll tell you in a minute. Now please tell me your ID number." I gave him the six-digit number and waited.

"Thank you," the voice said. "Now tell me, what is your father's name?"

"David."

"And your mother's name?"

"Rosa."

"And where did you live before you moved to Ein Hamidbar?" I told him.

"Thank you." The deep voice sounded satisfied with my answers.

"Now please tell me who I am talking to," I asked for the third time feeling rather mystified by all this cloak-and-dagger stuff.

"My name is Aleph and I work for a government agency."

"Oh," I said, wondering which agency but at least understanding now the reason for his secretive behavior.

"And what do you want from me?" was my next question.

43

This was followed by a few muffled whispers at the other end of the line and then he coughed and continued. "Can you come to Tel-Aviv next Monday and meet me there?"

"Yes. When and where?"

"You know Bella's café near the central bus station?" "Yes."

"Right. Then be there at two o'clock next Monday afternoon. Is that all right?"

"Fine, but how will I know you or how will you know me?" "Do you have a blue short-sleeved shirt?"

"Of course," I replied "All the men on kibbutz have shirts like that. They're usually worn as work shirts."

"Good. Then wear that and make sure you have three pens clipped in the front pocket. Three pens. Is that clear? "

I said it was.

"*Todah rabah* – Thank you," and he hung up leaving me holding the phone and wondering what I'd let myself in for.

That evening, once Ruthie and I had put the children to bed, we sat outside on the porch - "the best part of the day" I always called it – and I told her about the phone-call I'd received from Aleph.

"What do you think he wants?" she asked as we looked out toward the fields where ten years earlier Egyptian tanks and artillery shells had almost wiped our kibbutz off the map.

"I don't know. Maybe it's connected with what I was doing when I was in the Jewish Brigade."

"Like what? You were just a humble sergeant then, not a general or anything like that."

"Yes and no," I replied, putting my mug of coffee down on the small wicker table next to me. Then I told her of the rôle I had played in the revenge squads and how we had 'eliminated' as many Nazis as we could lay our hands on.

She sat there, silent and stunned, her hands to her mouth. It was the first time I had told her about this aspect of my army career.

"And is there any proof that you were involved in this?" she asked very quietly as though she thought that someone might overhear us. "Did you keep any documents or lists?"

"No. We never kept any records so that no one could ever charge us. Obviously we didn't want the British to know and we certainly weren't going to tell them or any of the Allied Occupation forces about it either. At times we had a hunch that they knew what we were doing because they never did anything about it."

"So now we'll just have to wait and see until you've had your chat with the mysterious Mr. Aleph next Monday to see what he wants."

The next Monday afternoon found me in Tel-Aviv. I had arrived at the bustling central bus station at half past one, earlier than I had planned. One of the kibbutz members had given me a lift in the kibbutz garage's somewhat dilapidated 'Sussita' car.

As we drove into south Tel-Aviv via the backstreets of Jaffa my driver patted the dashboard affectionately. "See," he said, "you did a good job in repairing this old jalopy. We got here without any problems. Now where do I let you off?"

I pointed to a busy side street leading to the bus station. The whole area was crowded with soldiers in all sorts of uniforms, shoppers and people rushing to and from where the noisy buses were standing by their platforms. The whole place was a cacophony of sound and a mixture of smells of fruit, spices and diesel smoke.

"Let me off over there, near that space by that fruit stand," I said. "You'll have room to stop for a minute without everyone hooting at you like crazy."

He did so and I got out. I slammed the door and he drove off shouting, "Good luck" although he didn't know what he was wishing me good luck for. Neither Ruthie nor I had told anyone about the phone-call from Aleph. All I had done was to change the work roster so that I would be free for this meeting.

I walked along the crowded street, the noise of the stallholders and the traffic shocking me; I was used to the winds of the Negev and the rustling of the trees on the kibbutz. And the smell! It was nothing like what I was used to. I was used to smelling the desert dust or our herd of two hundred Frisian cows, not this overpowering mixture of food, spices and diesel fumes.

I was just thinking along these lines when I looked at my watch and saw that it was almost two o'clock. And there I was, standing outside Bella's café in my blue short-sleeved shirt with my three pens clipped neatly in my front pocket.

I stood there for a minute wondering which one of the people sitting there drinking coffee or eating falafel was Aleph. Was he tall or short? Fat or thin? Did he look like an army man or a typical pale-faced government clerk?

Suddenly I felt a tap on the shoulder. I whirled around to hear a voice ask, "Haim? Ein Hamidbar?"

"Er, yes," I muttered. He must have been watching me for a minute as I had been waiting and yet I hadn't noticed him. He must have been partly hidden behind a billboard a few yards away from Bella's.

"Come," he said, guiding me to a quiet table at the back of the café. "We'll be able to talk here without being disturbed. Is that OK with you?"

I nodded my agreement and pulling up a chair I put down my newspaper on the side of the table.

"Now let's get down to business, but first I'll order some coffee," and he went to the bar to place his order. While he was there I looked at him carefully. He was the sort of person who would blend into any Israeli street scene. He was wearing a pale grey shirt, beige trousers and had a bland but slightly suntanned face under straight light brown hair. The only thing that stood out about him were his sharp and intelligent dark brown eyes.

He came back to the table holding a tray bearing two cups of coffee and two portions of apple cake. After we had started on the coffee and cake he leaned his chair in toward me. I did the same.

"First of all," he began, "I'm sure you've guessed my name isn't Aleph, but what it really is, is irrelevant at the moment, so we'll just leave it as Aleph, at least for the time being, OK?"

I nodded.

"As I told you on the phone," he continued. "I work for a government agency and we're looking for people fluent in various European and Arabic languages. We also want people who have served in the army, that is, in combat units. This I believe includes you."

I nodded again.

"According to our records, you are fluent in German, Polish, Hebrew and English. Is that right?"

"Almost," I said, wondering which government agency he was working for. "My Hebrew and German are fluent, my Polish is a bit rusty and my English is not bad except that my wife tells me that I have a typical Israeli accent when I speak it. But I can read and write it without any problems."

"And your Arabic?"

"It's street Arabic," I replied. "Arabic that I picked up during my army service and from what I've learned from the Beduin who come to the kibbutz to have their tractors repaired. I can manage in the markets but I can't read and write it. I can recognize the numbers, but that's about it when it comes to reading."

"Any other languages?"

"A bit of French and a few phrases in basic Spanish."

"And what about your army service?"

I was sure he knew all about that but that he wanted to know how much I would tell him. I told him how I had served with the Palestine battalion and the Jewish Brigade and how I had taken part in the fighting in North Africa and Italy.

He didn't say anything but then asked, "Didn't you end up as a second-lieutenant?"

"No," I replied guessing that he was checking me out to see if I was telling the truth. "I finished the war as a sergeant but then was promoted to lieutenant in the infantry when I joined the Reserves here."

"Didn't you serve in the south, in the Negev near where you live?"

"Yes, usually, although sometimes my unit was sent north to the Syrian border as well."

"I see." He seemed pleased with my answers and then leaned back to call for some more coffee from a passing waiter. "I presume you do want another?" he asked.

"Yes, it's thirsty work answering all your questions."

He smiled for the first time that afternoon. "Don't worry. The government is paying for your coffee and cakes, that is, it's all coming out of your taxes."

The waiter returned a few minutes later and while he was putting the cups on the table we sat there without saying anything.

"Now tell me something about yourself," Aleph said, once the waiter was out of earshot. "Your family, your health, what you do on the kibbutz, your likes and dislikes. Stuff like that."

I answered him telling him the facts about my life in the order he had asked me. I also told him that the kibbutz had once sent me to America for a few weeks to learn about John Deere tractors and agricultural equipment. This, I said, had been good for my knowledge in mechanics and also for my English. This trip and my friendship with some of the American volunteers on the kibbutz meant that I tended to speak English with an American accent.

"In your repair shop do you deal only with the mechanics, the engines and the like or also with electrical problems?"

"With both, although I prefer the mechanics to the electrics. Why?"

He shrugged and then asked, "How are you with weapons: rifles and pistols?"

"I guess I'm pretty good with them," I replied. "Every so often, as part of our defense program on the kibbutz, we go down to the firing-range to stay in practice."

"With pistols and rifles?"

I nodded and then added. "I normally use a Czech pistol – nine millimeter. That's my favorite."

He nodded and remarked, "I prefer the American Smith and Wesson or the British Webley Mark IV." Then he grinned and added, "I 'forgot' to return mine to His Majesty after the British left this country in 1948 but they don't seem to have noticed."

He was silent for a minute as though he were thinking about the fighting that we had both been involved in during the War of Independence. Then he faced me. "Do you have any idea why I've asked to meet you here today?"

"No," I said carefully. "But I suspect that it's something in connection with my past career in the Jewish Brigade."

Keeping his face perfectly expressionless, Aleph asked, "And what part of that career would that be?"

I decided to play dumb. I didn't want to mention the part I had played in the revenge squads.

I wanted to know if he would refer to it. He did.

"How many Nazis did you kill?" he asked quietly.

"I don't know. We didn't keep any records, but I guess my unit killed about thirty before the British disbanded the Brigade and sent us back to Palestine."

"Good," he said. "Thirty fewer to deal with. Thirty who didn't escape from the punishment they richly deserved. It's just a shame that hundreds, if not thousands of other Nazis got away with what they did. But I am digressing. By the way, do you want another coffee?"

"No thanks. I don't want to die of caffeine poisoning but if you want another, then I'll have an orange juice."

He ordered two more drinks and once the waiter had moved away he leaned toward me again.

"It's like this," he began stirring his coffee. "We're looking to make up a team to catch some specific enemies of the state. I'm not at liberty to tell you who they are at this stage or where they're living right now. But we are now scouting out for people who have the right background and have certain talents."

"You mean speaking foreign languages?"

"Yes, and other skills. And those who speak the languages must know them well. Not just high school level."

"So in other words, you are interested in my knowing German and Polish?"

"Yes, possibly." It was clear that he was not going to commit himself to anything.

"And what other skills?" He had aroused my curiosity.

"Your knowledge of mechanics for example and, of course, your army background. It's obvious you've been trained to carry out difficult orders especially as you trained in the British army. And then, as an officer…"

"Yes, in the Reserves," I reminded him.

"True," he said. "But no matter. You're also used to taking on responsibility and giving orders yourself. That's important to us. The ability to think on your feet and to be able to adapt and change if the situation calls for it."

I looked at him straight in the eye. "How do you know so much about my army career? All I told you was that I served in the Palestine Battalion and the Brigade as well as in our own army."

He looked straight back at me. "Believe me, Haim. We know. That's what we're paid for. Do you think I would have arranged to meet you here if I hadn't learned something about you beforehand?"

"Who is 'we'? You keep talking about 'we this' and 'we that.'"

Half-smiling, he tapped the side of his sharp nose with his finger. "Don't worry about that. If you join us, you'll find out soon enough. Just understand that I'm working for a government agency and everything we do is for the security of the state."

"Though not necessarily within the state."

"That possibility does exist but, as I said before, I'm not at liberty to tell you any more at the moment."

"So what was the point of this meeting?" I asked feeling somewhat exasperated at receiving so little information in return, especially after a three hour journey up from the kibbutz and knowing that I had another three hour journey to get back home.

He smiled, but this time, a little sheepishly. "So I could meet you and form an opinion of you. It's not enough just to see a photo of you or read about you in our files."

"I see. And do I pass the test?"

As before, he didn't give me a satisfactory answer. "Maybe," he shrugged. "If so, we'll be in touch with you in the near future."

"And when will that be?"

He shrugged again. "As I said, in the near future. By the way, how do you feel about working abroad for the government?"

"For a long period of time? Remember, I'm a married man with three kids."

"No, say two to three months at a time."

"It's a possibility. The kibbutz has sent me abroad in the past for training purposes. Also I went to the States for a few weeks to work as a counselor in a Jewish youth camp in upstate New York."

"And your wife wouldn't object?"

"Not if it wasn't for more than, say, three months. Besides, I wouldn't want to be away from her and the family for any longer either."

"Good. That sounds fine." And saying that, he put out his hand to say goodbye. "Well, *shalom*, Haim. If we think we can use you, we'll be in touch."

"Any idea when? Within a week? A month?"

"Soon. And by the way," he added, looking very serious. "This conversation never took place. You know what I mean? You're not to tell anyone about it. Not even your wife."

"But she knows I came to Tel-Aviv today."

"Fair enough. But don't tell her what we talked about. And if anyone else asks what you were doing in Tel-Aviv today, and I know that everyone knows everyone else's business on a kibbutz, tell them you were looking for something for the garage or visiting an old army buddy. Is that clear?"

Just as I was just about to say something he knocked my newspaper off the table as though by accident. I bent down to pick it up and when I stood up again, Aleph was gone.

"Well, of all the nerve," I thought and then I laughed to myself. What a simple trick. He had managed to disappear and make it look as natural as possible. Now, as I set off for the central bus station I had the long journey home to digest that afternoon's meeting.

Chapter Four
A Meeting in Germany

Nearly two thousand miles north-west of Bella's café two well-dressed academic looking gentlemen were sitting in a quiet corner in a motel restaurant overlooking the A3, the Cologne-Frankfurt autobahn. They were Dr. Felix Shinar and Dr. Fritz Bauer. Dr. Shinar was the Head of the Reparations Mission in West Germany and Dr. Bauer was the Public Prosecutor for the West German province of Hesse.

"You've had enough coffee?" Dr. Bauer asked. "Would you like another slice of this apfelstrudel?" His heavy jowls sagged on the side of his square face as he pushed his graying hair back off his forehead.

"Fritz, stop fussing over me like a Polish mother and let me hear the news that you've brought me here for. I'm sure it's much more important than your apfelstrudel, and besides, I can buy perfectly good strudel back home in Tel-Aviv."

"*Ja, ja*," Bauer said and leaned forward to tell his guest one of the closest kept secrets in West Germany. He looked around and then waiting for a moment he faced Shinar and said quietly, "Adolf Eichmann, that Nazi murderer, *y'mach sh'mo*, may his name be blotted out, has been located. We know where he is."

"Adolf Eichmann! Are you sure?"

"*Ja*, very sure. He's in Argentina."

"That's where many Nazis escaped to."

"*Ja, ja. Das ist rechts* – that is correct."

"And what are you going to do about this?" Shinar asked, hardly daring to believe what he had just heard.

"I'm not sure," Bauer said slowly. "I must admit that since learning about this piece of information I've been in a dilemma. On the one hand, I am a German citizen and a civil servant, and that passing such information to a foreign country with whom we do not have full or normal diplomatic relations may be seen by many people as treason." The Public Prosecutor paused for a moment thinking of what he would say next.

"But?"

"But the reason I am telling you this is that I do not know if we, the West Germans, can really rely on our judicial system to bring this top ex-Nazi to justice. And in addition, what I do know and what I am sure of is this: I know that I cannot count on our embassy in Buenos Aires to have him returned here to West Germany to be put on trial either. And that is one reason that I am telling you all this now. The other reason comes from my own background, who I am and what happened to me during the war."

"You mean being a Jew who was persecuted by the Nazis and being forced to flee to Denmark?"

"I see you've been doing your homework," Bauer smiled. "Yes, you're right, but not before the Nazis forced me to resign from the civil service and then stuck me in one of their accursed prisons for nine months. But, I must say, I was luckier than most. For some reason which I do not understand even today, they released me and I fled to Denmark. But then my luck ran out because…"

"The Nazis invaded Denmark in April 1940."

"Exactly. So they put me back in prison for a while and then when I was released I fled to Sweden which was neutral and managed to stay out of the war."

"And that's where you worked with Willy Brandt publishing that Social Democrat magazine."

"Felix, I am impressed. You really have been doing your homework," Bauer smiled. "How did you know that?"

Now it was Shinar's turn to smile. "We Israelis have to know a lot of things that happen or happened outside our little country. But please continue."

Bauer shrugged. "There's not much to add. After the war was over, I came back here, picked up the pieces and now I am the Public Prosecutor here in Hesse – a humble public servant."

"Ah, don't be so modest, Fritz. You've made quite a name for yourself prosecuting several Nazi war criminals as well as winning the slander trial against that right-wing scum, Otto Remer. But, Mr. Humble Public Prosecutor, you haven't asked me here to talk about the past. Tell me more about Adolf Eichmann. How did you find out where he's living? What's he doing today?"

"So here's the story," Bauer said, leaning forward again. "And like many such stories, Eichmann's hiding place was disclosed completely by accident. I doubt whether the person who did so even realized that he had done so."

"Do you know who that person was and how he knew?"

"*Jawohl*. It was Eichmann's own son. Nikolas Klement."

"His son? And why did he give his father away? And why did he call himself Klement? To disguise himself?"

Bauer held up his hand. "Slowly, Felix. One question at a time. Listen carefully and I will tell you everything." It was clear that Bauer was about to enjoy telling his story and that he knew that he had a very interested audience. Felix Shinar, one of the most important Israeli diplomats in West Germany, pulled his chair closer to the little round table, pushed his coffee cup aside and leaned in closer than before.

Bauer coughed to clear his throat and began. "This story starts as a love story, or something like that. It began several thousand kilometers west of here, in Argentina. A young girl called Sylvia Hermann was going out with a young man in Olivos, one of the poorer suburbs of Buenos Aires and…"

"And the young man's name was Nikolas Klement," Shinar couldn't help himself from interrupting.

"*Ja, ja*, that is correct."

"And she phoned you up or wrote to you to tell you that she'd found out where the Eichmann family was hiding," Shinar added.

"Felix, do you want to hear my story or not? But yes, my friend, in a way you are right. But be patient, for there are many details which you should know. So let me continue." Bauer took a sip of his coffee which was cold by now, grimaced, and then continued.

"So as I was saying, Sylvia Hermann was going out with Nikolas Klement, or Nick, as she called him. But whenever they met, it was always in her house, never his. They both spoke German and so all their conversations were in that language."

"Even though they were both brought up, I assume, in Argentina."

"*Ja*. Anyway, one evening, Sylvia invited Nick home for a meal, and like so many emigrants, they started talking about their backgrounds who they were, where they lived, how they arrived in Argentina and so on."

"So, Sylvia was German, as well?"

"*Ja, ja*. Her father, Lothar Hermann, was half-Jewish and in 1936 the Nazis imprisoned him in Dachau for his Socialist activities. While he was there, he was severely beaten up, so much so that when he came out he was almost blind."

Shinar said nothing There was no need. He had heard many such stories before.

"Then," Bauer continued, "like me, he was lucky enough to be released and he also fled the country. But unlike me, he fled to Argentina. He did this after *Kristallnacht* in November 1938 when the Nazis carried out a major pogrom and…"

"Yes, Fritz, I know all the details about that. Please continue with your story."

Bauer did so. "So, as I said, Sylvia's father fled to Argentina with his non-Jewish wife and managed to keep his Jewish identity a secret. So that was the situation when our German Romeo met his Argentinian Juliet. Now imagine the scene. They are all sitting around the table in the Hermann household, no doubt eating vorscht and sauerkraut and then young Nick starts boasting that his father had been a very high-ranking Nazi officer during the war. Sylvia's father kept very quiet and didn't react to this. Then Nick starts quoting his father and said that it was a shame that the Nazis hadn't finished off all the Jews during the war."

"He actually said that?"

"*Ja*, he did, but let me continue. Then after that, without any connection to what I have just said, Sylvia and her family moved to Coronel Suárez. This is a small village several hundred kilometers south-west of Buenos Aires. Then one day in April 1957, Sylvia was reading an article to her father out of the Argentinian-German newspaper, the *Argentinisches Tageblatt*. Now remember, her father, Lothar, was almost blind and she was reading an article about a Nazi war crime trial that was being held here, in Frankfurt. The article published all sorts of details about the Nazi on trial and that it also mentioned that one of the chief Nazis who had worked very closely with Hitler and Himmler was still missing."

"Adolf Eichmann."

"Exactly. Then Sylvia suddenly thought of her past boy-friend and what he'd said that night about the Nazis and his father and how all the Jews should have been finished off. Then Sylvia told this to her father. She also told him said that Nick had said at one point that his mother had remarried after the war but that she didn't know if Nick's father was still alive. She added that none of her meetings with Nick had ever been at his house and that she had never seen his father. However, she did remember Nick saying he was proud that his father had been an important Nazi. He had even told her that during the war, they had moved around Europe and had lived in several different countries. One of them, he said was Hungary and that was in 1944."

"This is sounding better and better. Please continue."

"And there's more to come. As I said, Sylvia had told her father that she had never been invited over to Nick's house while they had been going out and even now, she didn't know his full address. Just the suburb where he lived in Buenos Aires."

"That sounds a bit fishy."

"*Ja*, that's what Sylvia and her father thought, especially as Sylvia was still writing to Nick, but using someone else's address as the link."

"Now that really sounds fishy. Since when do young people today write to each other through a third party? We've moved on from the times of Romeo and Juliet, haven't we?"

Bauer shrugged. He had no answer to that one.

"So leaving that aside," the prosecutor continued, "or maybe because of it, Lothar Hermann became even more convinced that his daughter's former boyfriend was the son of Adolf Eichmann. He felt he had to do something about it and…"

"So what did he do? Contact the German embassy in Buenos Aires?"

"No, no. That's the last thing he wanted to do. He was sure that if he did that they would warn Eichmann that someone was on his trail. Remember, there were dozens if not hundreds of ex-Nazis in Argentina after the war. The Argentinian ruler, President Perón, had encouraged them to emigrate to his country as he wanted to exploit their scientific and engineering skills."

"That's right," Shinar nodded, then he added, "And also because he believed in Fascism."

"That's also right. Anyway, Lothar decided he wouldn't get any help from the German embassy so he wrote a letter and sent it to the judicial authorities here in Frankfurt. From there they forwarded it on to me."

"So that is why you asked me to join you here drinking coffee and eating strudel at the expense of the good citizens of Hesse. To tell me all about this."

Bauer smiled for a moment and said, "Yes, my friend, you're right and…"

"Wait a minute," Shinar said, holding up his hand. "You've just told me that a half-blind ex-German lawyer and his young teenage daughter have claimed they know where Eichmann lived, but what you haven't given me is any proof of this. As you said, there are hundreds of ex-Nazis in Argentina, how do you know that this specific one is Adolf Eichmann?"

"Patience, Felix. I was just coming to that. But before I continue, do you want any more to eat and drink?"

"Yes, please. Just another cup of coffee. I'll forgo the strudel this time. I'm beginning to put on weight," and he tapped his slightly bulging waistcoat.

Bauer ordered more coffee and when the waiter had retreated to the bar, he continued. "Shortly after our office in Frankfurt had passed Lothar's letter on to me I asked one of our chief prosecutors to obtain all the information he could find on Eichmann and his wartime activities. Once he had done so, he was to forward it on to me as quickly as possible – reports, photos, addresses, contacts, the lot. I told him it was for the Argentinian authorities and I must say, my man did a very thorough job."

"But you didn't send it to them, did you? Like Lothar Hermann, you suspected they wouldn't do anything about it, right?"

"Exactly. I was sure that the police were working hand-in-glove with the Nazi emigrés there, so I sent this information to Hermann and asked whether he could find out the address where this man who he thought was Eichmann lived - assuming he was still alive, of course."

Shinar leaned forward in his chair. "And did he find the address and was Eichmann still alive?"

"Wait a minute, Felix. You know, for a diplomat you are very impatient. Now let me enjoy telling you a good story." He took a sip of his coffee, looked around and continued. "So at this point, Lothar, who had never told his daughter about his past before, told her and soon after that the pair of them decided to play detectives and see if they could find out where Nick Klement and his father, if he really existed, lived.

"Apparently they took the train to Buenos Aires and went to the suburb of Olivos where, as far as they knew, the Eichmanns lived. Sylvia had hoped that she would bump into Nick in the street, because as you know, in these poorer neighborhoods people often spend a lot of time outside wandering around the streets, chatting and gossiping."

"And?"

"They had no such luck. No Nick and no father. But then their luck turned. Sylvia bumped into an old friend who knew where Nick lived and so off they went, complete with the somewhat blurred photos I had sent them."

"Which of course they kept hidden."

"Of course. Then our pair of Sherlock Holmeses decided to push their luck. Leaving her father to wait for her at a nearby bus-station, Sylvia went off to the Eichmann house and told the woman who opened the door that she was a friend of Nick. She said she had come to Buenos Aires for a visit and had decided to visit her past boyfriend for old times'sake."

"And the woman bought this story?"

"Of course. Why not? It sounded quite plausible, no? A pretty girl turns up and says she wants to meet her old boyfriend – what's wrong with that? So the woman invited her in and served her coffee and cakes while Nick's brother, Dieter, told her that Nick was out but that he would be back within the hour."

"And was Eichmann, Adolf, I mean, there?"

"Wait a minute, Felix. I'm coming to that." Bauer picked up his cup of coffee, drained it and leaned over to face Shinar.

"While our young heroine was drinking coffee and being nice and sociable, a man wearing glasses and about fifty years old came into the room."

"Eichmann!"

"*Jawohl, mein Doktor*! She said he was a bit bent over but he said he was pleased to meet her. 'Are you Herr Eichmann?' she asked. Apparently he didn't answer so she asked if he was Nick's father."

"And he said he was?'"

"No. He said he was Nick's uncle and then Sylvia decided to drop this line of questioning and changed the subject of conversation to tell them about her recent successes in school and how she wanted to study foreign languages at the university. Then she asked Nick's 'uncle' if he knew any foreign languages and he said that he had learned a few bits of French during his army service during the war. Then, according to what Lothar wrote to me, they were all having a pleasant chat over coffee and cakes when Nick entered. Naturally he was very surprised to see her there and immediately asked her how she had found out where he lived."

"And she said through a mutual friend."

"Exactly. Then the 'uncle' said everything was fine when she asked if she had done anything wrong. Apparently they didn't suspect anything and the pleasant chit-chat was resumed. Soon after, Sylvia said she had to leave for the bus station and Nick said he would accompany her there. On the way she asked him why he had called his father 'uncle' and Nick said that it was merely a sign of respect and it was nothing more than that. Luckily for her he didn't wait for her bus to arrive so she was able to pick up her father…"

"Who must have been as nervous as hell," Shinar guessed.

"I'm sure of that," Bauer agreed. "Anyway, she told him everything what she had seen and heard and that she was sure now that the man there was really Adolf Eichmann. *Y'mach sh'mo* – may his name be blotted out."

"I'll say Amen to that," Shinar added just as fervently. "And now I suppose, it will be my duty to inform my superiors in Tel-Aviv and Jerusalem what you have told me."

"Of course. That's why I asked you to come here. You must tell Ben-Gurion and Isser Harel of your secret service what I've just told you as soon as possible. We don't want to lose him again. Twelve years have passed since the war finished and this monster is still free. I am telling you, I'm counting on you to tell them of the importance of this news. I know we have had alleged sightings of him before, by those two Nazi hunters, Tuvia Friedman and Simon Wiesenthal, but this report, even though it's come from a half-blind lawyer and his teenage daughter, sounds the most reliable one I have heard up to now," Bauer said, standing up. "Shinar, remember, I'm counting on you."

Shinar stood up, shook hands and the long conversation was over. Dr. Fritz Bauer left the restaurant leaving Shinar half-hidden behind a newspaper. Then five minutes later, Shinar left and made his way to his own office.

Later that afternoon he made a short telephone call to Dr. Walter Eytan, another German-born diplomat who was now working as the Director-General of the Israeli Foreign Affairs Ministry in Jerusalem.

Chapter Five
Enter the "Mossad"

The phone rang on my desk, and feeling somewhat annoyed at being disturbed while reading the latest report on terrorism, I leaned over to answer it.

"Harel? Isser Harel," the voice at the other end asked.

"Yes, who is it?"

"Walter Eytan. I just wanted…"

"Ah, Walter, I didn't recognize your voice. You sounded agitated, not like your usual calm and collected self."

"You're probably right; it's just that I've just received some important news which I must tell you about. No, I can't tell you over the phone. I must see you personally. When will you be free?"

"In an hour. So how about coming over to my office then?"

"No, I'm afraid that's not possible. I have to leave for an embassy function in five minutes.

How about this afternoon?"

"All right. Will five o'clock be convenient?"

Eytan said it was and rang off leaving me wondering what news was so urgent that the Director-General of our Foreign Affairs Ministry insisted on coming over to my office to tell me personally.

At precisely five o'clock, my secretary showed him into the office. As I had learned to expect from him, he was as punctual as ever.

"It must be your German background," I gently mocked him as he took a seat and sat down facing me over my cluttered desk. I put the anti-terrorism report aside and asked him to tell me his urgent news. He didn't need a second bidding.

"Adolf Eichmann is alive and is hiding out in Argentina," he said. "And I have his exact address right here," and he pulled out a piece of paper from the inner pocket of his well-tailored jacket.

"That's it?" I asked. "That's why you insisted on coming over here personally, to tell me you know where Adolf Eichmann is hiding?"

"That's right. Don't you realize that now we know this, maybe we'll be able to catch him and put him on trial?"

I sat there quietly waiting for him to continue.

"Isser, aren't you excited?" the usually calm diplomat asked. "Don't you realize what all this means? I thought you would be over the moon when I told you. This latest information is much better, much more reliable than what Simon Wiesenthal and Tuvia Friedman have given us."

I continued sitting there quietly as he continued.

"I know they've come up with all sorts of photos of people and places so far, but none of it has proved to be useful. Come, Isser," he said running his hand back over his receding hairline, "aren't you excited about this, at all? Listen, for a dozen years we've been looking for this monster and now we've received some really positive information. Just look at that note. He's hiding out somewhere in the back end of Buenos Aires and now we know where."

I didn't say anything but looked at him carefully. I must admit he did look somewhat disappointed at my lack of enthusiasm. If I had to describe him at that moment, I would have said that he looked like a small boy who had been promised a holiday and then had it taken away from him at the last minute. In order to buy a few moments while I considered what I was going to say to him, I leaned over and stirred my glass of tea. Then I began.

"Walter," I said. "It's like this. As you know, this is a small country with a small security and defense budget. Not small by our standards, but small in comparison with the United States or any European country. In addition, we have many enemies; some inside the country but many more outside. As the head of the secret services, my job is to stretch my budget as far as I can and see what I can do with it. From what I can see, I do not have the money to catch Adolf Eichmann. That's it, plain and simple. I have enough financial problems dealing with our present enemies and I don't have the money or resources to deal with our past ones, however important they were."

This time it was Walter's turn to look at me without saying anything. He didn't have to. I could read the disappointment in his eyes.

"Listen, Walter. The war ended over ten years ago and many people here want to try and get over what happened then. They do not want to be reminded about Nazis and death-camps, about torture and lost families. Do you understand? Sometimes we just have to let the past remain in the past and move on. I'm aware as much as anyone else that there are some very painful wounds, but they should be allowed to close. I don't see it as my job to open them all again."

Walter's look of disappointment had changed to one of accusation.

"Listen, my diplomatic friend," I continued quietly and I hoped convincingly. "My budget is so tight that I have only one person whose job it is to collect and file any information we receive on ex-Nazis. This he catalogs and puts away for possible future reference. I'm telling you, this country, which hasn't even celebrated its barmitzvah yet is too busy building up its present and future to be able to spend time and money on its past. Especially the terrible past which included gas-chambers and extermination camps."

We both sat there silently facing each other thinking about what had happened less than twenty years ago. I knew in my heart of hearts that the Nazis should be made to pay for their heinous crimes, their inhuman behavior, but that we, as a small and growing country simply did not have the means to try and right all of these terrible wrongs. There was so much to do today: to build, to absorb new immigrants, to house and educate them and to defend ourselves against the Arab states that threatened daily to wipe us off the face of the earth.

Within the past few years we had fought and won our long and painful War of Independence and then seven years later we had beaten the Egyptian army in the Sinai Campaign. These major hostilities had cost the country a fortune. Who had the time and the facilities to concern themselves with the Nazis, especially those who were now hiding nearly ten thousand miles away?

So despite my being impressed with what Walter Eytan had told me, I could not put the capture of Adolf Eichmann at the top of my list of priorities. However, perhaps in order to keep my conscience clear, I promised him that I would seriously consider sending somebody to Germany to speak to Dr. Fritz Bauer. Looking back, I believed I agreed to do this despite all the reasons I had told the diplomat why I could not order an operation to catch Eichmann. I was fully aware of what this Nazi monster had done and also because of the reasons that stemmed from my own past.

I had been born in Vitebsk, a small town in Belarus, a town that had also been the birthplace of the painter Marc Chagall. Fortunately I missed all what the Nazis had done there during the war as I had arrived in Mandatory Palestine in 1930 carrying a pistol that I had smuggled in, hidden in a loaf of bread. I had arrived in Palestine despite my parents' wishes. In order to prepare myself for my new life I had joined a Zionist collective farm near Riga believing that ultimately I was doing my best to strengthen the Jewish population here in Palestine. When I arrived, I found that the Jews here were still reeling from the news about the Hebron massacre. This was a bloody event in which the Arabs of that town had risen up and murdered and wounded tens of their Jewish neighbors.

After telling the British authorities that I was eighteen years old, (I was really seventeen), I joined a kibbutz, married Rivka and remained there for five years. However, by the mid-thirties, life on the kibbutz had begun to pall, so together with my wife and daughter I left in order to start my own fruit-packing business. I was doing well but when the war broke out, I volunteered to join the British army. At the same time I also volunteered to serve in the *Haganah*, the Jewish self-defense organization where I was involved in several clandestine operations. Our major concern during this period was that the German and Italian forces in North Africa would invade Palestine. However, fortunately, they were defeated and so our greatest fears were never realized.

I stayed in the *Haganah* until 1948 when I joined the newly-created Israeli army. One of my last missions in the *Haganah* was to infiltrate into Jordan and find out whether that country would join the other Arab countries in their planned offensive against Israel. Then after the War of Independence, I worked with the army and the secret service and in 1952, was appointed chief of the *Mossad*, one of the country's three intelligence agencies. At first we were part of the Foreign Ministry, but later we gained our own independence. From then on I would make all my reports directly to the Prime Minister who at that time was David Ben-Gurion.

It was now as the *Memuneh* - 'the appointed one,' or chief of the *Mossad*, that I had to decide what to do with the information I had received about Eichmann. I ordered the Eichmann file to be sent to me and after reading it I decided that the least I could do was to send one of my operatives, Shaul Darom, to Frankfurt to meet with Dr. Bauer. He was the ideal man for the job. His mother-tongue was German and although he had moved to Israel over twenty years ago, he had spent several years living in France. There he had been involved in smuggling Jews, mainly concentration camp survivors, to Mandatory Palestine right under the noses of the British authorities. He had been working as an artist then, and it was under this guise that he had carried out much of his important work for us.

After my meeting with Dr. Eytan, I asked Shaul Darom to come and see me in my office. As soon as he arrived, I sat him down and told him what Dr. Eytan had told me.

"So how am I to be involved in this?" he asked, looking at the Eichmann file which contained a few blurred photos of the man.

"I want you to fly to Frankfurt, meet Dr. Bauer and learn everything you can about this latest development."

"But are you sure that Dr. Bauer's information is reliable?" Darom asked. "We've heard so many different rumors about Eichmann in the past: that he's in Germany, Austria, South America, even in Kuwait. No-one - and that includes Tuvia Friedman and Simon Wiesenthal - has been able to give us any really hard, solid information. Just educated guesses."

"I know that, Shaul, and I can fully understand your feeling that I am sending you on a fool's errand, but I know that Dr. Bauer is a very reliable person. I know he wouldn't have sent me this information if he hadn't felt that it was worth something. So," I said standing up, indicating that this meeting was over. "I want you to go to Frankfurt, speak to the good doctor and report back to me personally as soon as possible. I promised I'd look into this and now we will see if this information is of any use..."

"Or not," Darom added, finishing off my sentence. He picked up the file and leaving the office, he quietly promised that he would do his best.

As I heard the door close I sat there, my head in my hands, my elbows on the desk-top wondering if anything would come out of all this. And if so, what? Would the German prosecutor point us in the right direction, and if so, what would I do then, or would we end up barking up the wrong tree once again?

As the days passed, I grew more and more impatient to hear what Shaul would tell me. He was under strict orders not to tell me anything over the phone; in fact, unless there was an emergency, he wasn't to phone me at all. I just had to get on with my work patiently and wait for the day when my agent returned to report to me here in my office.

That day came. On a cold and blustery day, when dark rainclouds were scudding over the skies from the west, making the roads glisten and dangerous, there was a quiet knock on the door and my secretary ushered Shaul into the office. Under his arm he was carrying a rain coat which partly hid a rather tattered leather briefcase. After a few minutes of small-talk about his flight and meeting a few other people in Germany, we got down to business.

I began. "So tell me, Shaul, How did it go with Dr. Bauer?"

"It went very well," Shaul smiled. "He received me very well, *gemütlich*, as they say in German and he was very pleased that you had wasted no time in dealing with this matter. He insisted on telling me that he had great faith in the source of his material and that it was very reliable."

"Very good," I said. "Did he tell you what that source was? A concentration camp survivor? A bitter ex-Nazi rival? A past mistress? Who was it? Did he give you any names?"

"Ah, that he wouldn't say. All he would say was that his source was a retired German-born half-Jew who had fled Germany shortly before the war after having spent some time in the Dachau concentration camp."

"That's it?"

"Yes, more or less. Dr. Bauer said he wouldn't reveal the name of his source for the time being especially as he'd been in contact with him only by mail. In other words, he hadn't actually met him personally. The source had sent his information to the prosecutor's office in Hesse and they had forwarded it on to him. The source said that Eichmann's name had come up in connection with a trial of another ex-Nazi when it had been reported that Eichmann had disappeared off the face of the map."

"But he, this ex-German in Buenos Aires, knows where Eichmann is?"

Darom nodded. "That's right."

"Well," I asked, feeling that we hadn't got very far. "Did Dr. Bauer give you Eichmann's address, at least?"

Darom smiled. "Yes. I learnt that piece of information by heart. Here, I'll write it down for you." And leaning over, he wrote down the address in Buenos Aires in his usual clear handwriting: 4261 Chacabuco Street, Olivos.

I immediately made another copy of this for safety's sake and put it in my shirt pocket.

"Tell me," I said, "Did you learn anything else about Eichmann? His family? Is he well? Is he working? Is he in contact with any other ex-Nazis or Nazi organizations there?"

For an answer, Darom lifted up his hand. "Whoa, boss. Wait a minute and I'll tell you everything I've learned." He took out a small blue notebook and after a minute looked up. "His wife is called Vera and she came to join him in Argentina some time after he himself had settled down there. He has four sons and some of them, three of them I think, live there with him."

"Why, where's the fourth one?"

"He's in the merchant marine and is often abroad."

"I see," I said. "And what do you know about his wife?" Past experience had taught me that often the way to get to a person was to go through their family and friends.

"Dr. Bauer told me that he had tried to locate her in Germany and that he had even sent one of his investigators to speak to her mother in a town somewhere near Heidelberg."

"And?"

"He drew a blank. The mother claimed that she had not heard from her daughter for a few years, that is, since 1953 and that her daughter had moved to America with her second husband."

"Did she say where in America?"

"No."

"Hmm," I grunted. "That doesn't sound very promising, does it?"

"No, boss, especially as Dr. Bauer's investigator didn't believe the mother's story. He thought it was all a pack of lies designed to throw anyone who asked too many questions off the scent. However, I may have some good news for you," and he bent down to pull out a file from his briefcase. He slid it over the table to me.

"This is what Dr. Bauer gave me. It's a copy of the file he has built up over the years concerning Eichmann. It may be useful to us as it contains some photos of the man and also of his family."

I opened the file and immediately pulled out the most recent photo that was on top. I inspected it carefully. It was somewhat blurred but nevertheless one could make out a thin balding man wearing glasses and an open-necked white shirt. To me he looked like a typical minor government or bank official. He looked nothing like the iconic picture of the sneering and uniformed top Nazi SS officer in his sharp black uniform who had sent millions of Jews to their deaths in the gas-chambers of Auschwitz and other Nazi infernos.

After studying and musing on the photo for a few minutes I returned it to the file and put it in my safe. Then I asked Darom whether he had asked Dr. Bauer why he wouldn't give him the name of his source.

My agent shrugged. "I don't know. He just refused to say. I asked him several times, but he told me each time that he had to protect the name of his source. All he would say in the end was that he wanted us to do everything we could to verify all the information he had given us in this file. He said that if we succeeded in proving that this man was indeed Eichmann, then he would send someone from his office to help us if necessary. He also said that we could use his office to persuade the Argentinian authorities to extradite Eichmann to West Germany but to tell you the truth, he didn't hold out too many hopes that this move would be successful. He thought that we in Israel would have to apply a lot of pressure – public opinion, he called it – to persuade the Argentinians to give him up."

I leaned back in my chair. For a moment I was aware of the hissing noises made by the traffic passing below on the wet streets. Did these drivers, I mused, at least the few who knew of the existence of my *Mossad* office here ever think about the decisions we had to make in the name of the country's security?

Even if we succeeded in locating this Nazi and proved that he was the man we wanted, how would we get hold of him? How would we bring him to Israel? Could we kidnap him and, if so, how legitimate was it for one country to kidnap a citizen from another, even if the kidnapping country could justify this act? And even if we did succeed in doing so, how would we punish him? Would it be worth all the effort? How can you punish someone who has murdered millions of people? Would it bring the six million murdered Jews back to life? No, of course not. Would it succeed in closing any open wounds or would it just keep those terrible wounds open? I had no answers, just a great black cloud of pessimism hanging over my head.

My train of troublesome thought was suddenly interrupted by a knock on the door. My secretary entered. "Sorry for disturbing you, sir, but Mr. Levi from the Finance Ministry has been waiting outside for the past ten minutes."

"Ah, yes, please show him in. Shaul was just leaving." I got up, shook my agent's hand and took out the file I had prepared for Mr. Levi.

A few days later I was having another conversation with Yoel Goren, another of my operatives. After he had sat down, run his fingers though his unruly hair, he looked at me, wondering what I had in store for him.

"Tell me, Yoel. How is your Spanish? Do you still speak it fluently"

"*Si, si,*" he smiled.

"And with a Spanish accent? I mean that you don't sound like an Israeli or any other foreigner speaking it?"

"No, sir. In fact the other day someone asked me where I came from in Spain, from Barcelona or Madrid."

"Good. Then this is what I want you to do. Drop anything else you are working on now because I am sending you to Buenos Aires. You are going to be the assistant for Menashe Talmi, an Israeli now living there and doing some research into the history of Jewish settlements in that country. Talmi is a talented fellow, speaks about ten languages, including Spanish, and is very much at home there. He and his research project are to be your cover story. Is that clear?"

"Yes, sir, but my Spanish is the Spanish of Spain, not of Argentina or of South America."

"That won't matter. You will just be Talmi's assistant, not the main person there."

72

Goren nodded and then I told him what his mission was. He was to go to Olivos, the suburb where Eichmann was reported to be living and confirm the information that I had received from Dr. Bauer. I told him that he was to check out Eichmann's house, his neighbors, the neighborhood and the immediate surroundings. I reminded him that he wasn't to breathe a word about this to anyone and that there was a need for absolute secrecy.

He nodded. From his previous experience with the *Mossad*, he knew what absolute security meant.

"Ah, and there's one more thing. I'm sending someone to work with you, a guy called Haim."

"Haim? The new guy from the kibbutz in the south? The one who's good with cars and machines?"

"That's right. Although he's not so new any more. I want to give him some more international experience, that is, experience outside Europe. At the moment he's in Berlin. He's been there for a couple of weeks, there and Vienna. I'll contact him and tell him to meet you in Buenos Aires."

"Fair enough. But how is he going to fit into my cover story? Is he going to be the assistant of an assistant?"

"What about just making him a university friend of yours who spent a long time in Germany or Austria? That should cover the fact that his Spanish which, by the way, is pretty good now, still has a Germanic or Hebrew accent to it. If anyone asks you any awkward questions, say he is equally interested in helping you with Talmi's research project. And besides, Haim's dark coloring and black moustache should help the pair of you blend in more. Does that make sense?"

He said it did and after going over a few more details I wished him good luck and showed him out of my office. Then I took my hat and coat and left for a meeting with the Prime Minister.

Chapter Six
A Meeting with the Hermann's

Nearly three weeks were to pass before Yoel Goren faced me over my ever-cluttered desk again. In the meanwhile, Haim had returned to his original assignment in Berlin.

"Welcome home," I said, standing up to greet Yoel.

"Thank you," he replied. "I'm telling you, I much prefer being here than creeping around the run-down suburb of Olivos like a stray cat."

"Why? Is it such a grim place?"

"Yes, and it's hard to think that Eichmann is really living there. Still, I'll tell you everything from the beginning. I'll give you all the facts and let you decide."

"Hmm," I said. "This doesn't sound very promising but please let me know what you found out."

He took out a file from his bag and pushed it over to me. "Before you read that, this is what I have to report. First of all, on a personal level, I got on very well with Talmi and Haim. Talmi is a very clever and dedicated researcher. He also has a rather dry sense of humor and, from the way he talked, we couldn't always tell whether he was being serious or not. Haim is also a very good guy to have watching your back. He catches on quickly and was able to blend into the background very well. His Spanish, despite his somewhat heavy accent, isn't bad and he's also a good car mechanic. The car we rented - an old Fiat - broke down twice. Once with a broken fan belt and once with a leaking radiator pipe, and Haim managed to fix the problems so we were able to complete our journeys. But now I'll tell you what we did there.

"We went to the Olivos suburb to see what it was like. It's quite a way from the center of Buenos Aires and most of the people who live there and travel into the center use the General Bartolomé Mitre railroad. Most of the population are working class; the men are mainly blue-collar workers who set out from Olivos early in the morning and return home late in the evenings. The whole place is pretty shabby and reminded me of some of the slummier areas of Tel-Aviv."

"So in other words, during the day, there aren't many men

about? Just women and children?"

"That's right. Them and the old people."

"I see. Carry on."

"Because most of the people in this suburb are of a similar standing, anyone new, especially anyone who doesn't work in one of the main work-places in the city, stands out like a sore thumb. Everyone there seems to know everyone else and what they're doing."

"Sounds like the kibbutz where I used to live."

Goren smiled and then I asked, "So, despite what you've just told me, were you able to check out this house on Chacabuco Street?"

"Yes. Talmi, Haim and I walked, or rather strolled around wearing scruffy work clothes and no-one asked us any questions. The house at 4261 looks quite run-down, just like the others, but we couldn't see whether there was more than one entrance to it."

"Why not?"

"Because there were several leafy trees near the house. They blocked our view and we couldn't approach too closely without attracting some attention. But," he added, smiling, "I did manage to take a few pictures of it and they're now in the file there," he said, and pointed to the manila file now lying on my desk.

I looked at the photographs very carefully. They were in black and white and slightly blurred. However, it was easy to make out a square house standing in its own plot of land. It was not possible to see how many doors and windows there were but, under the circumstances, it was surprising that Goren had succeeded in taking even these pictures. Leaving them on the desk, I asked whether he could tell me any more about the people he had seen in the area.

"There's a lot of Germans there," he said. "That is, we heard a lot of German being spoken on the streets and some of the houses even had swastikas painted on their outside walls. It seemed to me that for some of these people the war hadn't finished in 1945."

"And did you see anyone enter or leave 4261?"

"Not really, that is, we didn't see anyone going in or coming out because we couldn't hang about too much but we did see a woman there. She was very poorly dressed and was working in the garden. Talmi and Haim and I found it very hard to believe that this was Eichmann's wife, especially as we knew he'd been a top Nazi and had become used to the good things in life. In other words, we wanted to know if he'd really fallen so badly."

"Maybe this is all a cover-up," I suggested.

Goren shook his head. "I don't think so. This situation looked too permanent, if you get what I mean. We checked out the house several times. Sometimes I went with Haim and sometimes with Talmi. But whoever went, we all had the same impression. This was a case of real poverty."

I felt very disappointed. Although I had not been enthusiastic at first about carrying out this investigation, now that I had started, I wanted it to succeed, but where would we go from here?

There was only one thing to do. To get our investigation moving quickly, that is, before Eichmann found out we were on his trail, we had to persuade Dr. Bauer to give us the name and address of his source.

Soon after Goren had given me his report, I contacted Darom, who was still in Europe and asked him to go to Frankfurt and speak to the Public Prosecutor again. Darom was to tell him that unless he divulged details about his source, we would have no choice but to drop the whole investigation.

"Won't he see that as a threat, as blackmail?" Darom asked over the phone from Cologne.

"Possibly, but tell him that this is where we stand. He helps us, or we stop."

Darom must have succeeded. The next thing I heard was that he had met Dr. Bauer on 21 January 1958 and, this time, after hearing how our investigation had come to a dead end, Dr. Bauer had agreed to give us the necessary information.

"And not only that," Darom told me over the phone using coded words, "He's also given me a letter of introduction which he says may help us in the future. I'll have it sent to you through the diplomatic pouch."

Now that I had this latest information, I decided it would be best if I sent a German-speaking Israeli to Argentina to check up on the story that Lothar Herman had told Dr. Bauer. He would make out that he had been sent there as someone working with Dr. Bauer. I decided to use Ephraim Hofstetter. He was an investigator who had spent twenty years working with the police. He had a very solid reputation for being meticulous and I felt that if the police would 'lend' him to me, then he would be the best man for the job. Fortunately, the police did agree to 'lend' him to me saying, "In any event, we were planning to send him to South America on another case," so our plans dovetailed very well.

With this answer, Hofstetter came to my office and when he arrived, I explained where we stood vis-à-vis our investigation into the Eichmann case.

"How well are you acquainted with the Holocaust?" I asked after my secretary had brought in two cups of coffee.

He looked down for a long moment and then said quietly, "The Nazis murdered my parents and my sister. Apart from that, I suppose I know more or less what most people here know. Perhaps, because of what happened to my family, I have tried to block some of it out of my mind. This, and my work are what allow me to keep going. However, what I do know of the Eichmann case is what I learned when I was involved with the Kastner trial in 1955."

I knew exactly what he was talking about. Dr. Rudolf Kastner had been a Jewish Agency official in wartime Budapest and had been accused of being a Nazi collaborator. He was found guilty and then appealed the verdict. He was given a partial exoneration and then retired from public life.

This didn't help him, however, because in March 1957, a disgruntled witness assassinated him in Tel-Aviv.

"How is your German?"

"Perfect."

"Good, because you are going to play the part of a messenger who has been sent to Argentina by Dr. Bauer."

I gave him the German Prosecutor's letter of introduction and we spent the rest of the meeting going over various legal and technical matters. I told him that his contact man in Buenos Aires would be Ephraim Ilani.

It was a humid, sticky day when Hofstetter landed at Ezeiza airport, Buenos Aires.

There he was met by agent Ilani, who wasted no time in co-ordinating their busy schedules. The next day they took the overnight train to Coronel Suárez and, in the middle of the morning, arrived at the deserted, dilapidated and station.

"Huh! this place looks like the backdrop for a cheap cowboy movie," Ilani commented as he looked around the shabby building and platforms. "Let's see if there's anyone in the booking office here." There was, an old man who was reading a cheap magazine featuring a scantily–dressed girl on the cover. He told them there was only one train back to the city that day and that it would be leaving later that afternoon. Ilani asked him for the exact time and the two of them set off in an old Chevvy taxi for Lothar Hermann's house.

"You've lived here longer than me," Hofstetter said, stating the obvious. "How do you think we should do this? Should we both go in and talk to him or just me?"

"You go in on your own," Ilani said after a few moments. "You show him your letter and you do all the talking. Talking to two people may scare him off. While you're doing that, I'll wait outside in the taxi, a little way up. But just make sure you finish talking in time. I don't want to be stuck in this miserable hole overnight."

Hofstetter nodded in agreement. The same thought had also struck him.

After a short ride, the taxi-driver said they had arrived and Hofstetter, sweating in the heavy and humid air, got out. He made his way in the direction of Hermann's house and noticed that it looked like all the other buildings in the immediate vicinity – windblown, shabby and in need of a good coat of paint. He thought he might find a *mezuzah* on the door-jamb but there wasn't one. He looked around and knocked on the front door and waited, hoping he hadn't come all this way in vain.

The knocking sound seemed to echo causing Hofstetter to think that yes, he had wasted his time after all. He knocked again, louder this time. He put his ear again to the peeling pale-green door. No answer, no sound. He was just about to knock once again when the door opened and an old man appeared. His face was heavily lined and his hair needed cutting. It was clear that he had not shaved for several days. He was short and very thin and wore an off-white undershirt hanging over a pair of grey baggy trousers. He peered up at Hofstetter.

"*Ja*," he said slowly. "Who are you?"

"Karl Huppert," Hofstetter said, using the name that he and Harel had agreed on thousands of miles away. "Are you Lothar Hermann?"

"Maybe," the old man answered suspiciously. "Who wants to know?"

"Dr. Fritz Bauer."

"Are you from Dr. Bauer?"

"*Ja*."

"From Germany? From the Prosecutor's office?"

"*Ja*."

"Then come in. I've been hoping someone would come ever since I wrote to them." He ushered the investigator into the poorly furnished front room and indicated that 'Herr Huppert' should take a seat.

"Herr Huppert, who are you? I've never heard of you. The only person I've heard of in the prosecutor's office is called Dr. Bauer, Dr. Fritz Bauer."

"That's fine then," Hofstetter said reassuringly. "He's the man I work for. I'm one of his chief investigators. I do a lot of my work in South America and he sent me here to speak to you."

"But how do I know that you're telling me the truth? Anyone can say that they are an investigator."

"Will a letter from Dr. Bauer convince you?"

"Maybe," Hermann answered slowly after a moment. "But there's a problem. I can't read. I'm almost blind. Just wait a minute," and he got up and walked out to the kitchen at the back of the house. Hofstetter could hear a muffled conversation but apart from the words 'visitor' and 'investigator,' he could not make out any more of the conversation. A few minutes later Hermann returned with a stocky woman. Hofstetter guessed that she was about sixty years old. Like Herrmann, her hair needed cutting and she was badly dressed. There was a patch on the right sleeve of her pale yellow dress which had obviously been bought many years ago. She stood by as her husband sat down again facing Hofstetter.

"This man says he is Herr Huppert," Hermann said, looking up at his wife. "He says he's an investigator working for Dr. Bauer and that he has a letter from him. Please read it and tell me what it says."

He gave her the letter and she went to fetch her glasses. When she came back she started reading. During all this time, neither Hermann or Hofstetter said a word as the investigator looked at Hermann's wife. She read the letter slowly, her lips moving as she did so. It was clear that she didn't read much and that when she did, it was a great effort.

At last she spoke up. "*Ja,*" she said in a gravelly voice. "It is from Dr. Bauer. He is the prosecutor in Germany, the one you told me about."

Hofstetter breathed a silent sigh of belief. Now he could begin.

"My dear," Hermann said. "Please go and bring us some tea, er… and some cakes as well. I'm sure our visitor would be glad of something to eat."

While she was busy in the small kitchen, Hermann began to

relax and told his guest how he had suffered before the war and that now, the only thing he wanted was to have revenge on the Nazis who had taken away his life, as he put it. "They wrecked my life and made me go blind," he said, "just because I was involved with the Socialists. Since then I have hardly worked and I live like this. Tell me, is this the way to live for a man who once had a good education?"

Hofstetter nodded, but then realized that Hermann could probably not see him in the gloomy room. Hermann continued. "Please remember, Herr Huppert, I am half-Jewish but my wife is a Christian. We live a secular life and that is how we brought up our daughter, Sylvia."

Hofstetter was pleased to note that the facts that his host was volunteering tallied with those he had read in the file Harel had given him in Tel Aviv.

Hermann stopped talking and reached behind him for his white stick. He lifted it over his head and sat there holding it between his legs. It was as though it was giving him some sort of protection.

"So that's why you wrote to Dr. Bauer? To get revenge?"

"*Ja*. Just that. Not or money, Just revenge. I don't want or need any money from the Germans. It's dirty. *Es stinkt*." He spat. "All I want to know is that what I've told Dr. Bauer and what I'm going to tell you will bring justice to Adolf Eichmann, *y'mach sh'mo*," he added, using the Jewish curse, "to that monster who has got away with murder up to now."

"*Ja*, literally," his wife added, coming into the room holding a cheap plastic tray bearing three glasses of tea and a small plate of home-made cakes.

For the next twenty minutes, the three of them sat around the low table as Hermann explained that his daughter, Sylvia, had become friendly with a certain Niklaus Klement – "She called him Nick" - and how after hearing how he had proudly described what his father had done during the war and what his attitude to Jews had been and still was – "We should have gassed them all,

81

man, woman and child" – that Hermann had began to carry out his own private investigation into the young man's father.

Hermann then told Hofstetter about his correspondence with the prosecutor's department in Hesse and how he had ended by being put in contact with Dr. Bauer because he knew that the Argentinian authorities would do nothing about Eichmann.

"They're rotten, corrupt, through and through. And besides, there are too many ex-Nazis in high places here. I was also scared that if any of them saw what I had written, they'd hush it up or come and beat me up."

"Or even both of us," his wife added.

"But tell me, Lothar," Hofstetter asked quietly. "How could you prove your theory and follow up on your hunches when, how shall I phrase it? Your eyesight isn't too good."

"Huh," Hermann shrugged. "That wasn't too much of a problem. I went to Olivos with Sylvia. She acted as my eyes. She's a bright girl and plans to go to the university soon. She was able to confirm everything that I told her to look for. Then when I felt I had enough material, I sent it to Frankfurt. It was that simple."

Hofstetter leaned back in his chair and thought about what he had just heard. It seemed unbelievable but it was true. This half-blind old man and his teenage daughter had apparently cracked a case that the *Mossad* and various other interested parties had been working on for years. It seemed that they had found out where this elusive top ex-Nazi had been hiding out without using any clever tricks or advanced technology. Hofstetter was just about to ask another question when the front door opened and a teenage girl entered the room. Taking no notice of the visitor, she immediately walked over to her mother and father and gave them each a quick affectionate hug.

Then turning to face Hofstetter, she smiled and held out her hand to him. The investigator took it and looking up into her face, was impressed by her bright eyes, genuine smile and the intelligent expression on her face.

"Hello, mom, dad. Who is …?"

"Sylvia, meet Herr Huppert from Frankfurt. He's come here to ask us some questions about your Nick and his family," Lothar said. "Please tell him what you know."

From the kitchen, Sylvia brought in the one remaining chair in the house and sat down to face Hofstetter. She confirmed much of what he had read in the file or what the Hermanns had just told him and she added a few points of her own. She described the inside of the Klements' house and how secretive Nick had been at times when talking about various aspects of his father. She said that he had boasted of his past but was more reticent when it came to talking about the present. "It was as if he were trying to hide things," she said.

She repeated the story about how Nick had called his father 'uncle' and Hofstetter then asked her if she thought the man and woman were really Nick's parents?

"Yes, I'm pretty sure they were," Sylvia said, running her fingers through her hair. "They all spoke and acted as if they were. Of course," she added, "they may have all been putting on a show, like behaving nicely in front of the visitor, me, but somehow, I don't think so. It all seemed so natural."

"That's possible," Hofstetter said after a minute. "But we must be very careful. We must not jump to conclusions. We must have more proof of what you say and saw. What I would really like is this: do you have any recent photos of any of them, especially of the father. Do you have any?"

"No. And come to think of it," Sylvia said. "I don't remember seeing any photos in the house at all. Either on the walls or on the shelves. None."

"And I don't suppose you have any documents or other pieces of paper with the father's name on them, do you?"

"No, of course not." She shrugged and smiled. "That's not something that a girl looks for when she goes to her boyfriend's house, *is* it?"

"No, I guess not," Hofstetter admitted. It had been a long shot but it hadn't paid off. He took a cake and then turned to face Lothar.

"We have to be very careful here because at the stage we have to have more real proof that the man you say is Eichmann is Eichmann. We need recent photos of the man and other documentary evidence. We need papers like copies of his driving license if he has one, social security papers and any other official piece of paper such as documents with his name and address on them. These could include papers from the municipality: bills for water, electricity and gas. Do you follow what I'm saying?"

Hermann scratched his head, thinking. "I'll see what I can do. Through my legal practice, I have a few friends and contacts in Buenos Aires and Olivos; people who work in the mayor's office and with the local authorities."

Hofstetter smiled encouragingly and then stood up. There was nothing more to add. It was time to leave. He didn't want to miss the train back to the city.

Suddenly Hermann's wife, who had been sitting quietly behind her husband throughout the conversation stood up. She put down the shirt she had been patching and said, "Herr Huppert, you do realize of course that if we, that is, my husband and Sylvia and I, have to travel to Buenos Aires it's going to cost us quite a lot of money, especially if we have to stay in a hotel for a night or two. As you can see," she added, sweeping her arm around the small room, "we're not very well off. I'm not complaining, but I'm not sure we'll be able to afford the train fares and the hotels in the city."

"You don't have any family in Buenos Aires?"

"No, nobody."

Hofstetter nodded. "Well, in that case, I'll see that you will be reimbursed for all of your expenses. So please keep all your tickets and receipts. Will that be all right?"

She nodded and picked up the shirt again.

"Good," Hofstetter said. "Now there are two more things to do before I leave. First of all, I will give you a new address for your correspondence. Please do not write to Frankfurt any more, but to this address in the Bronx, New York. The man's name is A.S. Richter. Here, let me write it down. He works with me and he knows what's going on." Hofstetter tore a page off a small pad he had in his pocket, scribbled down Richter's address on it and gave it to Lothar. He knew he wouldn't be able to read it, but he didn't want the man to feel he had been bypassed.

"And now, here is the second thing. I will give you this American one-dollar bill but I'll tear it in half first. I will keep one half and give you the other. If anyone comes to see you and claims they represent me, you may believe them only if they can show you this half." He gave half the bill to Lothar and put the other half back in his wallet.

Hermann smiled at the simplicity of this way of checking someone's identity. The investigator had answered the question that had just come into his mind: How would he know whether any other investigator who appeared saying that he was working with Hofstetter was genuine or not?

Hofstetter turned to leave, and then turned around again. "Mr. Hermann, do you have any visiting cards?"

"*Ja*. How many do you want? "

"Give me half a dozen," Hofstetter said. "That should do for now."

Hermann asked his wife to bring some of his visiting cards from the old writing desk that stood under the window. She carefully counted out six and handed them over to the investigator. He gave them back to her. "Now sign your name on the back of them and give them to me."

She did so.

Hofstetter put them in his wallet and explained what they were for. "When I write to you, I'll attach one of them to each letter. In that way you'll know that it is really from me or someone who is working for me. Is that clear?"

Lothar nodded enthusiastically and smiled again at the simplicity of the idea.

"So now I must leave and I thank you for everything you have done. It is very important and I hope I will be in touch with you soon, that is, either me personally, or someone from my office. And please remember, you are not to tell anyone about this meeting. Not a word. If a nosy neighbor asks who the man was who came to see you today, say he was from the insurance company or from the municipality. Is that clear?"

They all nodded and after a round of handshakes, Hofstetter stepped out of the poorly lit room into the glare of the Argentinian sunshine. As he walked in the direction of the station, he was feeling good. He felt that something was moving at last and he would be able to send a positive report back to Harel.

A few minutes into his walk, a dusty taxi honked and drew up alongside him. Hofstetter saw Ilani sitting in the back. He got in and they drove off immediately to the station. Despite their fears of having missed the train, it drew into the station ten minutes later. They were lucky. They had the whole compartment to themselves and so Hofstetter was able to report immediately to Ilani what had happened.

"I believe they are very serious and dedicated, especially the father and the daughter," Hofstetter added after he had given a blow-by-blow account to the *Mossad* agent. "But we must move quickly because Sylvia is planning to move to the States soon to get a university degree there. I'm not quite sure how keen the mother will be to continue this investigation once her daughter leaves. Also, there's a question of money."

"Why? Are they in this for the money?" Ilani asked. "I thought it was all about revenge."

"You are right. They're not in it for the money but, to put it mildly, they're not very well off and the mother insisted that if they have to travel to Buenos Aires, we'll have to reimburse them. I said that that would be no problem and that seemed to placate her. And there's one more thing." Hofstetter took out his wallet and handed the half-dollar note and the visiting cards over to Ilani. He explained what he had done and, like Hermann, Ilani smiled at the simplicity of it all. Although it was an old trick, it was still foolproof.

Hofstetter smiled and settled down in his seat to sleep for the rest of the journey. It had been a long day and he wondered if he had accomplished anything worthwhile. Would the Hermanns follow up on what they said? How easy would it be for the half-blind old man and his daughter to find out any more information? Would Eichmann still prove to be a slippery fish or would Harel and his *Mossad* network be able to haul him in?

Chapter Seven
Enter Ricardo Clement

While a blustery wind was blowing outside my office window in mid-March 1958, Hofstetter came to report on his journey to Argentina. After summing up all the main facts and his impressions, he said that while he believed that much of what Sylvia had told him was true, he couldn't say the same about her father.

"Because of his blindness?" I asked.

"No, Isser. I think it's because he believes what he wants to believe."

"You mean he's making up a lot of this?" I said pointing to the pale blue file that Hofstetter had laid on my desk.

"No, it's not like that. He's a very serious man, but it's just that he's not always very selective with his information. He may be right, of course, but I certainly think that we'll have to check out very carefully what he's told us. I also think, that after seeing what he's done so far, and seeing the poor financial straits they're living in, we should send them anything we owe them immediately."

I noted this down and, shortly afterward, our meeting came to an end.

Almost two months were to pass before we heard from Hermann again. After confirming that he had received the money we had sent him, he had written that he had visited the lands registry office in La Plata in the province of Buenos Aires. This is what he wrote:

"I discovered that in August 1947 an Austrian called Francisco Schmidt had bought a plot of land at 4261 Chacabuco Street. He built a house consisting of two units on it at the beginning of 1948 and, according to the local electric company, electricity was supplied to the Dagoto and Klement or Klements

families. In 1955, Schmidt sold some of this plot. This part included the area that had not been built on, but the house was still registered in his name."

I was pleased to read this part of Hermann's letter because it seemed to be based on facts and documents. I was more skeptical of the next part, which appeared to be based more on impressions and hearsay.

I am sure that Francisco Schmidt is the man we want, and the personal description of Adolf Eichmann we got from Frankfurt fits him. From what I was able to find out from people who saw Francisco Schmidt when he bought the land, his appearance matches the description of Adolf Eichmann exactly. Rumor has it that that Schmidt was landed from a German submarine on the shore of Argentina in 1945. The same sources report that he claims his face was injured in an accident. These facts and data provide grounds for presuming with certainty that Francisco Schmidt (who is Eichmann) had his face changed completely by plastic surgery.

At the end of the letter Hermann added that he had found out that Eichmann had arrived in Argentina in 1945 and had immediately moved to the interior of the country but that he, Hermann, did not know where. To find out, he had written, we would have to cover all his expenses as the country is huge and that he would have to take his daughter or his wife with him to act as "his eyes."

When I read this I thought he was exaggerating so I took an atlas but then I saw that, in terms of distances, he was right. The part of the letter that I definitely did not like appeared at the end.

If you, or the authorities, want the material necessary for advancing the matter, you will have to let me hold all the strings…As soon as you reply and carry out my request, you will hear from me again.

To me, this sounded like a form of blackmail. I decided to share my thoughts with Haim and Zvi Aharoni, one of our best operatives who was also a fluent German speaker.

Haim had been working with us for several years and with his knowledge of languages had carried out some very useful work in Europe. He had also uncovered a couple of Arab plots and had exposed several apparently innocent Germans as ex-Nazis. With his kibbutz background and his knowledge of machinery it had been no problem to provide him with a convincing cover story. This was that he was the buyer of agricultural equipment for his kibbutz, which he often referred to abroad as "my farm."

When Haim and Aharoni had sat down in my office, I gave them copies of Hermann's letter to read and then a few minutes later I got down to business. "Let me ask you a few questions about Hermann and this letter. These are the questions I have been thinking about," and I started counting off my questions on my fingertips. "Why does he need to check up on Eichmann's past and what was Eichmann doing in 1945? Does Hermann really need to travel hundreds or maybe thousands of miles all over the country to check all this out? How will this information help us? Why does he need to do this if he already believes that the father of his daughter's boyfriend really is our man? And finally, gentlemen, why does he insist as he phrases it, that he hold all the strings?"

"Maybe he's worried that we'll take all the glory if we catch him," Haim suggested.

"That's true enough," I agreed, "or it may be that he's so full of revenge, that his emotions are clouding his judgment. In any event, this is what I've decided. I want to send you two to Argentina to see what you can make out of all of this house number 4261 business. So far I've had to rely on Hermann and Hofstetter. Now I want to learn what's happening from my own people."

They got up to leave and then I said, "Wait a minute. There's something I want to add. It's this. There's often more than one way to crack a nut."

"Meaning?"

"Meaning, Haim, that if we don't succeed in tracking Eichmann down through the information that Hermann has sent us, then maybe we'll be able to do it via his wife who, I believe, is called Vera. And if we can't find out anything through her, then maybe we'll strike lucky though other members of his or her family."

"Why do you think that?" Aharoni asked.

"Because I think it's very strange that after the war, he - with or without his wife - disappeared or escaped from Germany or Austria or maybe Hungary and no-one seems to know where they are today."

Haim nodded. "Right. And that's not taking into account that some people have said that he is or was in Kuwait."

"Exactly. So if our man is in Argentina, as Hermann insists on telling us, is his wife, Vera, there, too? Or has he divorced her and is now living with another woman? And if Vera is still around, where is she? In Argentina, Austria or Germany? If she isn't living with him, does she still write to him? And finally, gentlemen, why are both of their families so careful not to divulge any information about them? In other words, you two have a lot of work to be getting on with."

A few months later, Haim, after yet another trip to Europe reported to me that Eichmann had been seen in Austria, in Bad Aussee, a small town south-east of Salzburg. He had followed up this lead but he had come to a dead end.

At the same time I received a message from Dr. Bauer that Eichmann was indeed in Argentina but that it would take him some time to be able to send me any proof. When I asked him for the source of this information, if it was Hermann or not, he clammed up as before and said he would tell me that also – but in due course.

Then on 11 October 1959 my secretary told me that Haim was in the office and wished to see me urgently. Before I asked him to sit down, he thrust two newspapers at me. "Have you seen these?" he asked. "Look at the front pages. Eichmann is in Kuwait and is working for an oil company there!"

I read the reports as he started pacing up and down in front of my desk. "Sit down or go and get yourself a cup of coffee," I said. He sat down and I read the reports. These had been attributed to a Dr. Erwin Schüle, one of the heads of the West German Bureau for the Investigation of Nazi Crimes.

I told Haim that he should look into this report and, as soon as possible, let me know what he discovered. Personally I had doubts about this report, but, as they say, I could not afford to leave any stone unturned.

Haim's investigation proved to be a definite waste of time and effort. Why wasted? Some time later Dr. Schüle published the information that Eichmann had been reported to have been in Kuwait in the past but was no longer there.

Apart from the waste of time, I was not pleased about this kind of reporting. Because of its international and sensational nature, I was sure that wherever Eichmann was hiding out, he would read these reports or hear about them either directly, or through any of his ex-Nazi cronies. This meant that he knew that he was still on the Israeli and West German "wanted" lists.

It was while this 'Kuwait' incident was blowing over that Dr. Bauer came to see me in Israel. After wheezing for a few minutes, the heavy-set man pushed his graying hair back over his head and sat down facing me. We exchanged some small talk and professional 'gossip' about who had been promoted; who had retired, who had become in charge of this or that department, and then he told me why he had come to see me.

"Herr Harel," he began in his heavy German-accented English, "I have come all this way because I have some new and very important news for you. First of all, forget about all this Kuwait business."

"I have."

"*Sehr gut*, very good. Now listen to this. I have a new source who informs me that Eichmann hid out in a German monastery after the war. From there he paid a visit to his wife in Austria in 1950 and by then he had a new name and identity. Ricardo Klement. That's the name he used then and we are sure that this is the name he is using now."

"Ricardo Klement? That's a familiar name," I said, offering him a cup of coffee.

"Good," he smiled. "But there is more. Do not think I have come here and wasted the taxpayers' money just to tell you that. We have discovered that this Ricardo Klement then sailed to Argentina using an International Red Cross passport with his new name on it. Then using the same passport again, he managed to fiddle the system and obtain an Argentinian identity card also under the name of Ricardo Klement."

"And you have proof of this?'

"I believe so. In 1952 we found the name and a matching address listed in the Buenos Aires phone book."

I sat there taking all this in and then asked, "And what did he do for money? Work? Borrow from his ex-Nazi pals, or had he smuggled in a fortune with him – money stolen during the war?"

"Your first guess was the correct one; he worked. According to my sources, at first he ran a laundry but then he or it went bankrupt."

"Where? In Buenos Aires?"

"*Ja*, in Olivos, in Buenos Aires."

"Ah," I said. "That's not the first time that this place has come up in connection with Eichmann. And do you have any more recent information about him, such as what happened after that?"

"*Ja, ja*. After that he worked for a banking company called Fuldner y Compañía in Buenos Aires. Here is the address," and he took a folded piece of paper from his inside jacket pocket. I looked at it but it meant nothing to me except that it was written in Spanish.

"And what did Ricardo Klement do there? Was he a clerk, a manager, what?"

"No, none of these things," the German prosecutor said. "This bank wasn't just an ordinary bank like you find on your regular high street. It was a bank that worked directly with industry. As far as we've been able to discover, it was headed by another German immigrant who had set up a subsidiary company called CAPRI."

"Capri, as in Italy?"

"*Ja, ja*, but this company had nothing to do with Italy or tourism. It was interested in exploiting waterpower to make electricity. H.E.P. Hydro-electric power."

"Like in Norway."

"That's correct. So it seems that our Ricardo Klement worked there for a while and, in fact, my source told me that when he made enquiries there last year they said he was still working there."

"In Buenos Aires?"

"No, near a city called Tucumán. This is a city in the province of the same name. It is in the north of Argentina. It's about seven hundred miles north of Buenos Aires, fairly near the border with Chile, Bolivia and Paraguay."

I leaned back and digested this new information. On the one hand it confirmed that Eichmann was still in Argentina but, on the other, he was nowhere near where we thought he may have been. I also thought about tracking him there, near Tucumán. Tracking someone in an isolated place might make it easier to find him in the beginning but keeping an eye on him afterward might prove to be more difficult. It would be easier to trail someone in a crowded city such as Buenos Aires once we had got him in our sights.

Then I leaned forward again. "Dr. Bauer, can you tell me this time who gave you this information?"

He shook his head emphatically. "No, Herr Harel. I promised this person I would never divulge his name."

I was silent for a minute. I hated answers like this. It wasn't as if I were going to broadcast his answer to the world. All I could do was believe him and hope that as an experienced prosecutor he was correct in judging his source's reliability.

"Then, Dr. Bauer, I have one more question for you about your source. Is there any connection, however great or small, between your source and the Hermanns?"

"No," he said. "Absolutely none."

"I'm pleased you told me that. Because that means we have a new and unconnected source to work on."

Dr. Bauer sat there impassively as I continued.

"And I'll tell you something else. It also means that your new source has confirmed two other important facts we already know. One, Eichmann seems to be living in Argentina and not in Kuwait or anywhere else. Two, he also seems to be using the name Ricardo Klement. Hermann also gave me that name in connection with the man who is or was living in 4261 Chacabuco Street. That surely cannot be pure coincidence."

Dr. Bauer nodded. He too had come to the same conclusion. We then talked for a few more minutes about various topics of mutual interest and then he rose to leave.

"I have a meeting with your Ministry of Justice in Jerusalem this afternoon so I will leave you now," he said. "Please make sure you keep me informed about what happens about this case. As you will understand, as a Jew, as a German and also as a prosecutor I am very interested in whatever progress you make. *Ja?*"

He then made a quick bow from the waist and left. After he had closed the door I sat back in my chair and thought how I could take this case from here. It's true that I hadn't been interested in taking it on at the beginning. In fact, I had not wanted to take it on at all. But now that I had received this new information and invested quite some time and effort in it, I found myself becoming quite involved in its progress. Should I send some other people to Argentina? Should I concentrate on locating Eichmann or his wife or perhaps both? Was there any point in contacting any of my people in Austria and Germany? All of these questions would have to be thoroughly investigated and, needless to say, with absolute discretion.

That evening I decided that the only way to cut this Gordian knot, that is to find out whether Ricardo Klement was really Eichmann and, if so, was he still living in Olivos was to send Haim and Aharoni to Buenos Aires. Both of them spoke German, Haim also knew Spanish and Aharoni had his own personal reasons to see that Eichmann was brought to justice. Like Haim, he too had lived in pre-war Germany, but he had left much later, soon after the infamous November *Kristallnacht*. He had arrived in Palestine with his mother and younger brother but the rest of his family had been later wiped out during the Holocaust.

However, I had to wait for two frustrating months because before Aharoni could set out on this new mission he had to clear up a few outstanding matters in Europe. During this time I continued trying to persuade Dr. Bauer to divulge the name or names of his source but he was adamant and kept politely refusing me.

I decided therefore to exploit these two months in another way. I contacted E., one of our top agents in Europe, and asked him to use his language skills and his wits to find out as much as he could about Vera Eichmann. Was she still married to him and, if so, E. was to find out as much information as he could about her, especially where she was living.

E. had arrived in Israel in 1949 from Romania where he had become disenchanted with the political system. I asked him to find out whether the records we had on Vera Liebl belonged to who we thought was Eichmann's wife, and what had happened to her after the war. Somehow, she and her children, like Eichmann, had vanished off the face of the map after the war. Was this a coincidence or not? We knew her father was still running an electrical equipment business in Linz, Austria, and we hoped that if he was still around, it might help us trace his daughter as well as his son-in-law.

For weeks, Haim, E. and a couple of other agents in Europe

poked and probed to learn all about Vera Eichmann's family and connections, but to no avail. It was as though all of them had been sworn to secrecy. All we unearthed during this period were two important facts. The first was that after living in an isolated village somewhere in southern Europe in 1950, Vera Eichmann and her three sons had suddenly disappeared, leaving no trail behind them. The second was that none of the West German consulates in Europe would divulge the names on the passports that they had issued to Vera Eichmann and her family.

Time passed. By now it was February 1960. The war had finished fifteen years earlier and although I was using some of my best agents in Europe, I still had no absolute proof where Eichmann, and maybe his family, were living and what he was doing. And this was assuming that he was still alive. If he was, then he would be fifty-four years old. As I said, it was all very frustrating. I would just have to control my impatience and hope that Haim and Aharoni, once they arrived in Argentina, would find out what we all wanted to know.

Chapter Eight
Still on the Trail

After bidding my wife and children goodbye, "as I have to go abroad for work," I left Ein Hamidbar early one morning. I met Aharoni at Lod airport, Tel Aviv, and from there we flew to Buenos Aires using different routes. I arrived at Ezeiza airport, Buenos Aires, via London and New York. Aharoni flew in via Rome and Recife, Brazil. Due to careful planning Aharoni arrived just two hours after me. We met in an airport café where we met Yosef, an Israeli driver, who took us to the embassy to meet the staff.

Early the next day we met four others who, unlike us, lived in Buenos Aires. They knew their way around and of course spoke Spanish fluently with the local accent and expressions. These four included a lawyer called Lubinsky, an engineering student and a young couple. We called these four and other locals who would help us later, *sayanim*, assistants. They were all volunteers, were happy to help us without payment and would help us by providing services such as medical aid, safe houses and transport. We had a bank of people like this in most of the big cities around the world and past experience had taught us that their help was indispensable to the success of an operation. In this particular case, it was important that one of these *sayanim* was a woman. A young couple trailing a subject or checking out a building would attract far less suspicion than a single man or a pair of men carrying out the same task. We did not tell our assistants why we needed their specific help, just that we were keeping our eyes open on a few local anti-Semites. It was enough for them to know that, in their own way, they were doing something important by helping the State of Israel.

That same day, Aharoni and I rented a nondescript-looking car and, with a detailed map of Buenos Aires, started driving around the city. The aim was to become familiar with the main roads and where the different suburbs were and where they were in relation to each other. We had learned that it was one thing to try and 'learn a city' from a map, but it was another to actually travel around the same city in a car. After driving around for most of the day we met Lubinsky at a pre-arranged time in a café near the Parque 3 de Febrero, a park celebrating the 1813 Battle of Lorenzo. We asked whether he could draw on his legal background and connections and find out who was living at 4261 Chacabuco Street.

"We want to know who exactly is living there now and also if a woman called Vera Liebl arrived in Argentina in 1952 or 1953, together with three children."

"Is that all you want from me?" asked Lubinsky.

"Not quite. We also need a Buenos Aires telephone book for 1952."

Lubinsky shrugged. Apparently we hadn't asked him to provide anything particularly difficult to obtain. The next day he was back with everything we had asked for.

"How did it go?" I asked.

"Easy," he grinned. "I went to a private investigator my office uses and told him I'd been asked to check out an inheritance and all sorts of details about the potential heirs. I told him that this was very hush-hush," he added, putting his finger to his lips, "as it involved a lot of money as well as some very rich people who were spread out all over the world, including here in Argentina."

He then put the 1952 phone book on the table and told us what we wanted to know about Vera Liebl.

Aharoni smiled and said, "Seeing that you have been so successful with that task, I'm going to give you another. See if you can find out about this guy, Ricardo Klement, and his work record. Where he is working now and where he has worked in the past. Again, remember, you are not to breathe a word to anyone, not even your boss about this. If anyone asks you any questions, just tell them it's a routine matter passed on to your office by a government ministry."

"That shouldn't be a problem," Lubinsky smiled. "I'll tell my contact that my clients may wish to get in touch about some new projects, something vague like that."

I said that I thought that that was a good idea and we parted company.

The next day we decided to check out the information that Lubinsky had given us and to see at first-hand what 4261 Chacabuco Street really looked like. So far we had only heard about this place. We had never seen it for ourselves. We took Roberto, our student *sayan*, with us to help us with the local geography thinking that his Spanish might also come in useful.

It did not take long to find the house especially after we had asked a couple of local people for instructions.

"Did you notice that those two men we just spoke to had strong German accents?" I asked.

Aharoni nodded and pointed at three buildings on his left. "And look over there. It's just like we were told. There are three houses with swastikas painted on them."

We drove past 4261 but not too slowly as we didn't want to draw any attention to ourselves.

Then we pulled in by the side of the road a few hundred yards past the house.

"Listen, Roberto," Aharoni said. "Take this blank postcard, write 'Regards from George' on it in Spanish and sign it 'Dagosto.' All right?"

"*Si*," and Roberto wrote down what Aharoni had just told him. "And what about the address?" he added.

"Write 4263 Chacabuco Street."

"Fine, and then what do I do?"

"Go to 4261 and ask where 4263 is. While you're there asking, hopefully you'll have time to look around and see what's there. Is that clear?"

Roberto smiled. It was clear he liked the simple deviousness of this trick. He got out of the car and we waited for his return. While he was away, I asked Aharoni why he had chosen the name 'Dagosto.' To me, it didn't sound like a Spanish name.

"It isn't. But it's close enough to 'Dagoto,' the name that the electricity company recorded as the residents of that building. That and Klement."

We had to wait for over an hour for Roberto to return. And until he did, Aharoni and I were both very nervous.

"How did it go?" I asked as he clambered into the back of the car.

"It was just as you said - well, more or less. I was about to go up to 4261 when I saw a young girl nearby. She was very pretty, long black hair and nice eyes and…"

"Yes, Roberto. But what did she say?"

"She said that as far as she knew, nobody called Dagosto lived at 4261 or anywhere near there. And then when she had left I went to have a closer look at 4261. Nobody was around so I knocked on the door and looked through the windows. The house was empty, there was no furniture in it, but I did see two painters who were busy in one of the rooms at the back. I also noticed that both of the apartments on that plot of land were empty."

"This isn't good news, "Aharoni said.

"Why not?"

"Because it's going to be hard chasing up the Klement family. There's no-one there to ask unless maybe we ask the painters who is employing them. By the way, Roberto, did you think of speaking to the painters?"

"Yes," he smiled. "That's why I took such a long time in coming back. I asked them if they knew where a Nick Klement lived as I had to deliver this postcard personally to him."

"And they told you?"

"No, not exactly, Haim. One of them told me that the Klements had moved out about two weeks earlier and were now living in the suburb of San Fernando. He was very helpful. When I said I must speak to Nick personally, he took time off from his painting and took me to where Nick worked in a nearby auto-repair shop. When we got there the painter pointed out Nick's red moped and then Dito, which is the nickname for Nick's brother, Dieter, came out to speak to the painter."

"But wasn't that dangerous for you?" I asked. "I mean you might have blown your cover story, or at least made him suspicious."

"No," Roberto smiled. "I bluffed it out with him. I told him that I had a present for Nick from a friend and that when I'd gone to their house at 4261, I was told that they had moved."

"He didn't ask to see the present or ask who the friend was?"

"No, because his boss was shouting at him to get back to work and to stop wasting time. He said the workshop was a place of work and not a social club."

"But did you get the new address at least in San Fernando?" Aharoni asked.

"No. He sort of clammed up when I asked him. All he would say was it was a place called Don Torcuato and that the streets there didn't have any names. I thought this was a bit strange but I didn't say anything and I left quickly after that, and here I am."

We drove Roberto back to the center of town and dropped him off near a bus-stop. We told him he had done a good job and that we would be in touch with him in the near future.

That night Aharoni and I compared notes.

"First of all, we know that Eichmann has three sons; one is called Niklaus and one is called Dieter, so that part of the story checks out. We also know that there's not a big difference in their ages so that's another useful fact to go on."

"That's true, Haim, but it also seems to me that this family is hiding something. I mean, if someone came up to you and said that they wanted to deliver a present to your brother, wouldn't you give them your address and not just something vague?"

I agreed and then suggested, "What about getting Lubinsky to see if he can help us again? He was very quick in getting the answers to our first questions. Maybe he'll be just as lucky solving another problem or two."

"I don't think so, Haim. First of all, I don't like over-using our *sayanim*. And second, it might look a bit suspicious if we turn up again with the same people, don't you think?"

I wasn't convinced and said that detective agencies had to be persistent. It was part and parcel of their work.

"Maybe, but I still don't like it. Let's see if we can come up with another idea. If not, we'll use Lubinsky and his connections again."

"So how about the following idea?" I said. "Roberto told us that Nick had a red moped which, it seems, Dito also uses. So what do you think about following him home one day? It shouldn't be too hard, especially as it's probably a distinctive looking machine."

"Right, and now we know what his license number is."

I took our map of Buenos Aires and spread it out on the coffee table. "Here is Don Torcuato," I said, "and here is San Fernando. There's only about three miles separating them. So we can cover the area on our own if you don't want to use Lubinsky again."

Aharoni seemed pleased with that idea and so we took a break, made some coffee and turned on the television to watch the news. Just as the anchorman was interviewing a local trade union boss about a strike, Aharoni suddenly stopped drinking his coffee and looked straight at me.

"Haim, I've just had an idea. Listen. March the third is in a few days, right? And March the third is Nick's birthday."

"Yes. So what?"

"So what? Couldn't he receive a present on his birthday?"

"And?" I wanted to know where this was going.

"So if we make out we are friends who are looking for him at his new address to give him a present, no-one will be suspicious if we ask a few questions. Do you follow? Doesn't such an action look and sound quite normal?"

"Go on," I said. From the way he was talking I knew that he had already worked out many if not all of the details. I was right.

"We buy an impressive - looking present, have it wrapped up nicely and stick a gift card in with it. We'll write something on it, such as, 'To my friend, Nick, with best wishes on your birthday.'"

"And who is going to deliver this present paid for by the Israeli taxpayers to an ex-Nazi's son?"

"One of our *sayanim*."

"How?"

"I'll tell you." And after Aharoni had filled in all the details and answered all my questions, I thought that his plan stood a good chance of succeeding.

The next day we contacted another of our *sayanim*, a young man we hadn't used until now. We knew from previous reports that he was reliable and that we should call him Juan. We told him we didn't want to know his real name and he accepted this without question. All we told him of our mission was that he was helping the State of Israel to find out where a certain anti-Semite lived.

"But make sure you deliver this to Nick Klement personally. We must have his exact address. Is that clear?"

"*Si*," he said, looking serious.

We left the gift card unsigned but addressed it to Nick Klement, 4261 Chacabuco Street.

"So this is what you have to do," Aharoni explained. "Drive to 4261 and ask everyone where Nick Klement has moved to. Since you look and sound like a local, no-one will give you a second thought. Just say you've been asked to deliver this present for his birthday. If anyone asks you anything else, just be vague. Don't add any more details. That's most important. And don't say who gave it to you. Just say Juan or Franco or some other common name. Is that clear?"

"*Si, Si*. But what if someone asks me what's in the packet?"

"You don't know. Juan or Franco just asked you to deliver it – and that's it. You don't know anything else. Just play dumb, OK?"

Nodding his curly head again, he left, leaving us to wonder whether it had been a good idea to ask a local *sayan*, not schooled in our kind of work, to help us discover such an important piece of information.

As we sat there in the hotel room, alternately playing cards and watching the television news, we kept asking each other questions.

"What if Nick presses him about who gave him the present?" I asked, and then another thought came to me.

"What if Nick's father is at home and starts asking all sorts of questions? Won't that tip him off, especially as he's just moved to wherever he is now?"

"Yes, I've thought about that, Haim, but I doubt if the father, and let us hope it is Eichmann, will believe his son when he says he has no idea who sent it. He'll probably think that his son just wants to keep this particular affair secret."

"Hmm," I shrugged. "Let's hope that the ways of love have never changed. I mean children keeping their love affairs secret from their parents."

That evening we went to a café to meet our *sayan*. He was not smiling as he had been in the morning.

"What happened?" I asked after we had received our coffees. "You don't look very happy. Didn't it work out as planned?"

"Yes and no," he said. "But I think more yes than no."

"What do you mean?" Aharoni asked, looking somewhat concerned.

"I'll tell you and then you can see if I'm right," and he began his report of the day's events. "I went to the house as you told me to, to 4261 Chacabuco Street. I found that it was all open, all the doors and the windows. There were some painters inside and then I saw a woman, a housewife, outside who looked local, that is, she wasn't well-dressed and she was carrying a shopping bag with some groceries in it. I asked her if a Mr. Klement lived in 4261 and she asked me whether I meant the German guy who had three sons. I said I wasn't sure about how many children he had but that I had to deliver a parcel to him. She said that I was out of luck because Mr. Klement had moved away about two weeks earlier. 'Ask one of the painters,' she said. They may know. I went back to the house and asked the painters."

"What did they say?" Aharoni asked, hoping to hear something positive.

"He said that they'd moved to San Fernando but that one or two of the sons was working nearby in an auto-repair shop."

Aharoni and I smiled at each other. At least this story confirmed what we had already heard before.

"The painter told me the repair shop was on Parana Street and I thanked him and set off to go there. There were two or three mechanics there and one of them pointed to a small moped-motor-cycle and said it belonged to the Klement kid. When no-one was looking, I looked at it carefully and noted that it was a ..." and here he took out a crumpled piece of paper from his wallet. "It was a Motonetta Siambretta 150 Sports. Then a young man came into the garage and he looked like he also worked there. He was wearing a greasy T-shirt and jeans and was carrying a large wrench. From what I saw and heard, I guessed he was German, or at least more European than Argentinian. He was just about to check the front tire of one of the cars there when one of the other mechanics pointed me out and said I wanted to talk to his father.

"What did he say? Did he look like he'd trust you?"

"No, not really. He just said that he had moved recently and that he could take the packet himself. I must admit that I wasn't quite sure what to do because I kept thinking of your instructions about delivering it to the right person and finding out the correct address at the same time."

"So what did you do?"

Juan turned to face me. "I decided to play dumb," he answered half-smiling. "I said I'd been told to deliver it personally and asked the Klement boy if he could give me his address."

"And did he?" Aharoni and I asked in unison.

"Well, sort of. He said that the street he now lived on didn't have a name and that the houses didn't have any numbers on them. People just knew which was their own house."

106

"That's impossible," I said. "It doesn't make sense. Every city or suburb has street names and house numbers. Even the slummiest ones, even if you can't always see them."

"I know," Roberto said. "That's what I thought. But then he said it was a new house in a new area. He said that if I gave him the packet, he'd promise to make sure it was delivered to the right person. I still wasn't sure what to do, but then he said that if I needed to contact him again in the future, I could always find him here in the garage. So seeing that he didn't seem suspicious about me or the packet, I gave it to him." He shrugged. "That's it, and that's why I said it was a yes and no story."

Aharoni told Juan that he had done a good job and that he would contact him within the next twenty-four hours. As before, he gave the *sayan* the usual warning about not telling anyone what he had been doing and after shaking the hands of everyone present, Juan left.

"Listen, Haim," Aharoni said. "This is what we're going to do. We'll go back to the garage with another *sayan* to check up on what Juan has told us."

"Why? Don't you believe him?"

"I do, but we can't afford to make any mistakes here. We must be absolutely sure that Klement is Eichmann."

"I agree," I said. "But won't we be arousing their suspicions if we suddenly turn up there?"

"Yes, there is a chance of that but the reason I want to go back now is not to give Eichmann time to learn that someone has been asking about him. All we need now is for him to go into hiding. We both know that there are a lot of ex-Nazis out there who'll help him if necessary."

That afternoon we returned to the garage, but this time we took a different *sayan* with us. He was called Lorenzo and we asked him to dress like a businessman, complete with a suit and tie. We pulled in a couple of hundred yards away from the garage entrance but didn't go inside. We just sat in the car waiting for the Klement boy to come out. We must have waited for over an hour but Dito did not come out.

"Lorenzo," Aharoni said at last. "Get out and walk past the garage. See if you can see a red moped in there with this number on the back license plate."

Ten minutes later Lorenzo was back. "No," he said. "I didn't see it there."

We drove off feeling very disappointed - like hunters who felt that somehow their prey had eluded them. Had Dito become suspicious? We couldn't know but it was clear that we needed a new strategy.

"You know what we'll do," Aharoni said a few minutes later. "We'll send Lorenzo to 4261 and see if he can confirm Juan's story and maybe, since he looks official, he may be able to learn Eichmann's new address."

We drove Lorenzo over to a spot about ten minutes' walk away from Chacabuco Street and arranged where we would be when he finished his mission.

This part worked out as planned. We picked him up half an hour later at a small kiosk and as we drove back to town, he told us the following:

"I went to 4261 as you told me and I saw the painters there. I told them that I was an insurance agent and that I had come to see Mr. Klement. At first they wouldn't say very much. But when I told them it was very urgent for me to see him as it was a question of several hundred dollars, they said he had moved three weeks ago. I said I had to have his new address and they told me that they didn't have it but that I'd find him in the San Fernando area. I may be imagining it but the painter who spoke to me looked as though he'd been told to keep his mouth shut and that he'd already said too much. He kept looking around all the time as if though were expecting someone to come in."

"And that's it?" I asked.

"Yes, more or less. He said Mr. Klement had three sons but he wouldn't say anything more. The only other thing he said was that if I wanted to get in contact with the father, then I should speak to the son who worked in a garage on Parana Street."

Feeling subdued and depressed, we drove back to the center of town. After telling Lorenzo not to breathe a word about the afternoon's activities, we let him off and returned to our hotel. There, after a quick meal in the dining room, we went up to our room to analyze our situation. We weren't making much progress and were feeling very frustrated. It was more than annoying to know that our man was somewhere in San Fernando but that we didn't know exactly where. We couldn't go there and start asking questions as we were sure that if he heard about this, he would disappear and we would have to start all over again.

"Now let's see what we have," Aharoni said. "The painter told Juan and Lorenzo that Eichmann has a small son, about six years old. That means that he is probably living with a woman who may or not be Vera."

"True, and there's another thing that doesn't add up," I said. "Some people have told us he has moved to San Fernando and other people have said he moved to Don Torcuato. We know they are fairly close to each other, like the Neve Sha'anan and Florentine areas in Tel Aviv."

Pushing the coffee cups aside, I pulled out our map of Buenos Aires and laid it out flat on the table.

"Look," I said, using my finger to point out San Fernando and Don Torcuato. "Here they are. There are only a couple of kilometers between the two. It's as though someone's trying to pull the wool over our eyes."

Aharoni nodded. He had no other possible answer to this mystery.

"Remember," I added. "Eichmann was one of the most important Nazis. It's possible that there's a whole network out there whose job is to keep him and his hiding place a secret and that's why we keep hearing so many conflicting stories."

Aharoni nodded again. "True - we've been told that he's here, or still in Germany or Austria, or even in Kuwait – in fact, anywhere. Even Wiesenthal or Friedman haven't come up with any solid evidence. And they started looking for him much earlier than we did." He paused and continued. "We should do what I suggested earlier. Follow young Dito on his moped and see where that leads us. What do you think?"

I thought this was a good idea and we sat down to work out the necessary logistics. That evening Aharoni went to our embassy in town and sent the following coded message to Harel: *The driver is red*. This meant that we were on Eichmann's trail, but were still not completely sure whether our suspect was the man we wanted.

Now all we had to do – the only thing that we could do was to follow the man who we thought was Dito and hope that he would lead us to his father, Adolf Eichmann.

110

Chapter Nine
Finding Eichmann's House

Aharoni and I had to contain our impatience for two days because it was a weekend and young Klement wouldn't be at his workplace.

7 March found Aharoni, Roberto and me sitting in a different, but equally nondescript looking car waiting at the junction of Sarmienta Street and Avenida Santa Fé. For some reason, Dito did not appear or, if he did, we missed him. And so after waiting for three long hours, we returned to our hotel, feeling extremely frustrated.

The next day we had better luck. Fortunately for us it was raining, so the sight of a couple of men standing in a doorway sheltering from the rain looked quite normal. In addition, the heavy rainfall also meant that there were few people outside. Luckily for us as the rain began to ease off toward the early evening, a moped suddenly shot out of the yard of the repair shop and headed off in the direction of San Fernando. Roberto, who we were using again, and I rushed back to the car where Aharoni had already switched on the engine and we set off in careful pursuit of the red moped, rear license-plate no. 84099. It was now rush hour and we were facing the problem that is an integral part of all pursuits: to be as close to the subject as possible without losing him, yet not being too close so that the subject realizes that you are after him.

For ten minutes we kept a fair distance between the moped and ourselves when suddenly he turned off into a small side-street – Haedo Beccar Street - near the San Isidore railroad station.

"Does this lead anywhere?" I turned round to ask Roberto.

"*Si*, to San Fernando. But look, he's just pulled into the side and he's rushed into that building."

111

We stopped immediately hoping that three men sitting in an old car in a side-street would not arouse any suspicions. However, we didn't have long to worry. A few minutes later Dito came running out of the building and without looking around, jumped back on the moped and set off again with us continuing our careful pursuit. Allowing the distance between us to grow, we were relieved that the unexpected stop and waiting in the side-street had not made him suspicious.

A few minutes later we found ourselves in the main square of San Fernando and, among the cars, trucks and buses wheeling around the central traffic island, we lost sight of the moped.

"There he is," Roberto shouted from the back seat. "There, behind that yellow bus."

"No, you're wrong," I said. "That moped's got a different license plate."

"Ah, but there he is," Aharoni said quietly, pointing to the right. "We're all right now." But he had spoken too soon because just then he had to brake as a funeral procession suddenly crossed our path.

"Come on, come on," I willed the line of black cars to move, but of course my muttered wishes didn't help. By the time the last big black American car had driven away we knew that our chances of picking up Dito again were down to zero. Nevertheless we set off again in the vain hope that we might catch up with him again.

"Can't you go faster?" Roberto called out from the back.

"Sure I can," Aharoni answered him. "But all I need is to pick up a ticket for speeding. So Roberto, keep your eyes open and leave the driving to me."

After ten minutes of fruitlessly searching and scanning the road we were forced to admit that to continue with our chase today was pointless. We had lost Dito and had no idea where he might be.

"Well," I said reluctantly "I think it would be best if we were to go back to the hotel and try again tomorrow." Aharoni agreed and we turned around and set off back toward the center of San

Fernando.

A few minutes later, the Fiat's engine started making some weird noises and I noticed a few wisps of smoke curling up from under the hood. Aharoni had also noticed this and we pulled in to the side of the road.

"I wonder what's happening. Seems like something's burning under there. Maybe a short circuit in the electrics."

Aharoni stopped the car and we got out as quickly as possible. We were scared it would suddenly burst into flames as the smoke was now becoming thicker and smelling of burning plastic.

I told the other two to stand back and then pulled up the hood and looked underneath. "Yes," I called out to them. "There's been a short circuit and half the wires have burnt out. This car's not going anywhere. We'll have to call the car-hire company and tell them."

Half an hour later, a tow truck turned up and I asked the burly driver if it had been a short circuit that had made us stop.

"Yes," he said, wiping a greasy, blackened hand across his forehead. "Something caused a short between the distributor and those wires there," and he pointed to the charred remains of what had once been part of the Fiat's electrical circuit.

"So, you won't be able to fix it, even enough to get us home?"

"No, *señor*, no way. I don't carry distributors like that and anyway all those wires need replacing. The best that I can do is to tow the car and drive you back to the company's offices."

And that is what he did. He hitched our useless Fiat to his tow-truck and with Aharoni sitting with the driver and Roberto and I in the Fiat, we began our return journey.

"Well," I said later that evening as Aharoni and I were sitting in our hotel room, watching but not concentrating on a television news program, "Let's look on the bright side. Luckily the car broke down near the center of town and we weren't close behind Dito at the time. Because, if that had happened, he might have looked back to see what was going on behind him."

However, this really was not much compensation for a day that had started out with the high hopes of finally being able to discover where Eichmann really lived.

"You know what we should do," Aharoni said, stuffing a small cake into his mouth. "We should split our forces and have more than one car following Dito the next time we go after him. That way, if someone gets in trouble or loses him, then the chances are that the second car will be lucky."

"So we'll have to call up some more *sayanim*."

"Right. I'll tell them we're after some important anti-Semite…"

"Which is true…"

"And that we need their help. I'm sure they'll be happy to help us and they can use their own cars."

The next day we phoned several *sayanim* who said they were willing to help but then the rainy weather made us put all our plans on hold.

Three days were to pass before we could resume our activities. On the fourth day Aharoni, Roberto and I set off again. After Dito had left the repair shop on his red moped, we followed him for several kilometers until we reached Route 202 without any problems.

"Why are you hanging back?" Robert called out from the back seat. "We're going to lose him."

"We've got a problem," Aharoni said. "There's hardly any traffic now so we can't close up on him. He'll know we're following him."

I nodded in agreement and was just wondering what to do when we saw that Dito had stopped at a small roadside kiosk.

"Keep driving past," I said. "Let's make sure that he is our man."

We drove past, and saw that it was Dito's moped. "But the driver doesn't look like Dito," Roberto said. "I'm quite sure of that."

"Maybe a couple of guys share that moped," I suggested as we continued down Route 202 before turning round to head back to

114

town.

That night, feeling very frustrated, we agreed that we had no choice but to try again. "But this time we'll use a different car," Aharoni said.

"Third time lucky," I said hoping that this would be the case. But it wasn't.

As the evening darkened, we followed Dito and all seemed to be going well when he stopped outside a house in San Fernando and went inside. We parked some distance away from the house and were able to keep an eye on it. After ten minutes, Aharoni sent Roberto to walk past the house to see if he could spot Dito inside.

Fifteen minutes later he was back. "No, I don't think he is in there," he reported. "I sneaked up as close as I could to the window and was ready to say if someone had asked me what I was doing that I was looking for a piece of paper with an address on it that the wind had blown out of my hand. I looked through the curtains in the only room that had lights on and Dito wasn't there. I'm quite sure of this, unless he has changed so much since I saw him last in the repair-shop."

Aharoni was furious and crashed the fist of one hand into the open palm of the other. "This is ridiculous," he said, trying to control his frustration. "How many times do we have to try and find out who he really is and where he lives? We know what he looks like. We know what his moped looks like. We follow him as carefully as we can and he disappears into the thin air. There must be another way of doing this."

Aharoni's temper was infectious and we all felt the same. We sat there for a few minutes in the dark wondering how to save the situation.

"I know what we'll do," Aharoni said at last, turning round to face Roberto. "Tomorrow, you will go back to the repair-shop or 4261 and tell Dito, wherever you find him, that your friend is very angry. Tell him that your friend says that he never delivered the present, which was very expensive, and now he wants the money back. Tell Dito that he must give you the address so you can speak to Mr. Klement about all this. Is that clear? Do you think you can do this?"

Roberto said that this shouldn't be a problem, and after working out a few more details as we drove back to our hotel, we dropped Roberto off and hoped for better luck the next day.

Twenty-four hours later, after spending the day in our room, cooling our heels by watching television, reading and playing chess, we heard the triple knock on the door that we had told Roberto to use. Making sure that no-one had followed him to our room, we let him in and sat down immediately to hear his report. From his face it looked as though his mission had not gone well but we had to contain our impatience and listen to what he had to say.

He took out a cigarette, lit it and began. "It was like this," he said slowly. "I went back to 4261 as you told me to see if Dito was there and if not, if one of the painters there maybe could help me. I told one of them that the present had never been delivered and that I needed Mr. Klement's new address."

"And?" I couldn't help asking.

"I must have looked so sad that the carpenter there took some pity on me and he said that if I wanted to find Mr. Klement, I should go to the bus station in San Fernando and take the bus, the 203, to Avellaneda Street. I'd find a small kiosk on the corner and I should ask there for the house where the German family lived. He said that it should be easy to find the house since it was not far from the kiosk and that it was a half-finished building with a flat roof."

Aharoni smiled for the first time that day. "Well done, Roberto. Now it looks as though we have the correct address, or at least we know where we are looking for. So, did you do that? Go to Avellaneda Street?"

Roberto shook his head. "No, I went back to Dito's repair-shop and I told him the story about the present not being delivered and he started shouting at me. He said of course it hadn't been delivered. There is no such person as Nick Klement.

116

His name is Nick Eichmann."

Aharoni and I felt elated. We felt at last that we were making progress but we could hardly tell that to Roberto. He got up to leave and Aharoni patted him on the shoulder. "Thank you very much," he said. "Take this money for your expenses. You've done pretty well and have helped us quite a bit, but you must never tell anyone what you have been doing for us. Is that clear?"

Roberto smiled and after a round of handshakes, he left the room.

As soon as the door closed I said to Aharoni, "You were somewhat cool with the thanks. It looks as if he has actually found our man this time, well, at least his address."

"I know, but I didn't want him to feel that he had done something so important that might cause him to boast about it. But anyway, enough of that. Let's look at a map and see where this Avellaneda Street and the kiosk are. We should go and check them out tomorrow."

The next day, following Roberto's directions, we drove down Route 202, taking the route the 203 bus used until we reached the junction with Avellaneda Street.

"Look, there's the kiosk," I said pointing to the right, and we continued looking for the half-finished building that Roberto had described.

Suddenly, Aharoni slowed down. "There it is. On the other side of the street. Half-built with a flat roof and just one story high."

"Huh," I grunted as Aharoni picked up speed after passing the house. "If Roberto and the painter are right about the address, then it looks a pretty miserable place for an ex-top Nazi to be living in, doesn't it?"

"You're right. That house looks more like a small prison block. Did you notice the barred windows and the wall surrounding it? Like he doesn't want visitors or people looking in."

"And there are no other buildings near it, apart from that small cottage to our left, for at least two hundred yards. And there's another thing I noticed," I continued. "I was looking out for power and phone lines and I couldn't see any. It all looks very primitive to me, as though the whole thing is temporary. I hope it isn't, not after all the hassle we've gone through finding it."

"Right, and we're still not sure that Eichmann lives there, either," Aharoni agreed. "Come, let's turn around higher up the street and drive past once more. See if you can shoot a decent picture while we do so, but we're going to do this just the once. All we need is for some sharp-eyed local to spot us."

A few minutes later, driving at a normal speed we passed the house again and both of us noticed a poorly dressed woman working in the garden.

"How old do you think she is?" Aharoni asked.

"About fifty. And that little boy holding the basket looked about six, I would say. About the same age as my cousin's kid in Jerusalem."

As we drove back to the hotel, I saw that Aharoni was smiling. "I believe we're on the right track this time. And if it isn't Eichmann there in that house, let's hope he'll be back from Tucumán or wherever in a few days."

"Why then?"

"Because, Haim, I was checking over some details about the man's life and next week is his silver wedding anniversary."

"So what?"

"So what? Which dutiful husband is going to stay away from home on such a day?"

I hoped Aharoni's hunch was correct as now it seemed that at last, we were finally making some progress.

That night Aharoni went back to the Israeli embassy and sent the following message in code to Tel Aviv:

Danny, the driver's third son is definitely identified: Lives here under his real name of birth. Lives with his mother. Also the new address of the family has been discovered. It is being

118

claimed that the mother has remarried and that the stepfather, named Klement, is in Tucumán almost 1,600 kilometers from Buenos Aires.

Chapter Ten
Real Progress at Last

Now that we felt we were on the right track, we decided to take a risk and drive past the house again and take some more pictures. The ones I had taken had not come out well. They were too blurred to be of any use.

"We'll take the briefcase camera," Aharoni said the following morning. "The one with the built-in Leica."

"The one where you press the button at the bottom?"

"Right. So this is what we're going to do. We'll drive up to the house as close as we can without looking suspicious, park the car and lift up the hood as if we're having trouble with the motor. While you are repairing the non-existent problem, I'll be busy taking some shots of the house."

"Good idea," I said. "There's no tricks like the old ones. And by the way, if you're lucky, you might be able to get a shot or two of the woman and her kid as well. Or maybe of Dito if he's there."

That afternoon we carried out our plan; there were no problems. We parked the car fairly near the house and then I bent down under the hood with a screwdriver in my hand. Luckily no-one came along to volunteer their help while Aharoni was operating our special briefcase camera. The Leica had been built into an ordinary looking briefcase that any government clerk would carry; it had been designed by the service's technical staff in Tel-Aviv. Now Aharoni was using it to take pictures of what we hoped was Eichmann's house and its surroundings.

"Did you get any pictures of the woman?" I asked as we drove away a few minutes later.

Aharoni shook his head. "No, she wasn't there or at least she wasn't outside."

That was our first step in confirming our hopes that this isolated prison-like building was indeed the house where Eichmann was living. Up to now we had never seen the house close-up but now we had   photographic evidence.

The next step took place the following day. Using the services of Michael, another *sayan*, a local architect, we went to the administration offices of the San Fernando area to check out details of the plot of land on which the Eichmann house stood. Would Michael discover any relevant details about its owner? Under which name had Eichmann registered himself and the plot of land?

Eichmann? Klement? Another name that we hadn't come across so far? Maybe even Liebl, his wife's maiden name?

When the bald-headed clerk in the office asked us why we needed this information, Michael had an answer ready for him.

"My associates," he explained, pointing to where we were sitting at the back of the spacious office, "are interested in buying a plot of land like this in the San Fernando area with the idea of setting up a small factory there. This plot," he said, pointing to where Eichmann's house stood on the map, "is among others where we would like to build our factory. We are interested in learning about the sizes of the plots of land there and where they are situated exactly. Maybe the owner of this plot would be willing to sell it for a tidy sum." Michael smiled at the clerk and continued. "After all, we wouldn't want our factory to be too near any other buildings and disturb the neighbors, would we?

"And by the way, could you give me some information about the railroad line in the area, and maybe a map of its route? This would be very important for us, you understand, as a means of bringing in raw materials and also for distributing the finished goods."

"Why? What sort of factory are you planning to build?" the clerk asked. "Not one that makes a noise and causes pollution? Remember, this is going to be mainly a residential area together with some light industry. At least, that's what we aim to build when this whole project is finished."

"Oh, just a sewing factory, children's clothes and the like."

"I see. That sounds pretty clean. I'm sure you'll have no problems in obtaining building permits for that. And now, what else do you want to know?"

Michael asked him a few architectural and technical questions and also went into details about zoning rights and planning where the water and electricity lines would be. "And of course," he added, "once we get this factory in full production, it will be good for San Fernando. It will provide many jobs for the local women while the men will be able to work in the technical and maintenance departments."

The clerk promised to help us. We should return tomorrow when he hoped he would have the necessary information. Michael shook his hand warmly and we left the office to check out the "Eichmann house", the building we now believed it to be. As we drove off Aharoni said that he hoped our photos would be better this time.

"Michael," Aharoni added. "Use the same cover story about setting up a factory when we go to the house next door to the one we're really interested in."

Michael nodded and soon the three of us were walking up to a run-down looking cottage that was two hundred yards away from our real target. Just as we were about to enter the front garden a woman came out. She had a rag in her hand and looked like she had been cleaning something inside the cottage. She looked at us suspiciously and Michael tried to disarm her with his bright smile. He asked whether she knew the name of this street as he and the two gentlemen with him were looking for Liberation Street.

"No," she replied, pointing to the area around us. "None of the streets around here has a name."

"Ah, that's a problem," Michael said, looking somewhat crestfallen. "Because the two gentlemen here want to buy up some of the plots of land around here to set up a sewing factory."

"Hmm, well if that's the case," the woman said, a smile beginning to form on her dark face, "I'll be very happy to sell you my plot and move away from here. How much are you paying? I could do with some money to start again. And besides…"

But she wasn't allowed to continue for just then a slim dark-haired woman walked up to us.

"Who are you and what do you want?" she demanded. "We don't like strangers around here."

"Don't worry, *señora*," Michael smiled again. "We have no intentions of making any problems. In fact, the opposite is true. We just want to know a few things about the land here."

"Why? Who are you?" the woman asked, stepping forward. "Are you from the government?"

"No, no, *señora*. We are private investors. Businessmen. We want to see if this area near the railroad and Route 202 is suitable for setting up a sewing factory." She did not look convinced.

"I don't believe you. You are government snoops checking up on us poor people. You want to know what we are building here. You want more taxes. I've seen people like you here before. If you are who you say you are, what is the name of your company?"

As Michael gave her a suitable name I nudged Aharoni and whispered that we should make some excuse and leave as quickly as possible.

"No, stall her for a bit," Aharoni whispered back. "I'd like to take a couple of more photos of the house and the area. Tell Michael to keep talking a little longer while I'm busy."

"Ah, wait a minute," the first woman said. "If you want to build a factory here, what are you going to do about water and electricity? If you look, you'll see that there are no power lines here. We don't have any electricity and neither do they," she added, pointing to Eichmann's house.

"Don't worry about that, *señora*," Michael smiled again. "Our company will have that all arranged for you. Electricity and water and yes, a better sewage system and…"

"Yes, but," she began, but then I interrupted. "I think, gentlemen, we've seen enough for now. I think we need to have a look again at our map. It's in the car, so goodbye and thank you ladies," and we left to return to the car. We drove for a mile and then stopped.

"I just hope they don't put two and two together," I said. "Because that's all we need. She obviously knows something about her neighbors and if I'm not mistaken, I could hear a trace of German in her Spanish."

We returned to the center of Buenos Aires and dropped Michael off near his office and told him – as we had with the other *sayanim* - not to say a word about what he'd been doing. He promised to keep his lips sealed and would contact us as soon as he had some more information from the land registrar's office.

As we continued on to our hotel Aharoni told me that he believed the second woman we had met was Eichmann's daughter-in-law, Margarita, but he wasn't sure.

Two days later Michael called us and we met him at a café near the Israeli embassy.

"This is what I've discovered," he began. "I think I've found out what you want. I spoke to a contact at the GEOFINK building company and they say that the first plot we saw, the one with the unfinished house on it, is on plot number fourteen and is registered in the name of Veronika Liebl de Fichmann. Does that help you?"

"Yes, Michael, that has really helped us," Aharoni said shaking his hand. "But now we have to leave because we have an important meeting to attend. So just remember, none of this ever happened. All right?"

The *sayan* smiled once again and we split up. "Who is our meeting with now?" I asked.

"Nobody," Aharoni said. "I didn't want Michael, however helpful he was, to be with us any longer. He might start to ask questions. Come on, let's get back to our hotel."

There, over coffee and pastries we went over what we had learned and what we would do with this new information.

"First of all," Aharoni said, "This Veronika name must be Eichmann's wife, Vera. It's too much of a co-incidence for it to be otherwise."

"Right, and the Fichmann name must either be a genuine mistake or Eichmann deliberately misspelt to throw anyone off the scent."

Aharoni nodded in agreement. "Now I feel we're really making progress, I want to go back tomorrow with another car, a black Chevy or Ford should be good as they are very popular here, and take some more pictures of the house and also of the Vera lady."

"Is it worth the risk?"

"Yes, Haim, it is. Before we go any further with this, we must make absolutely sure that we have the right people. We can't afford otherwise. Enough missions in the past have gone wrong because the agents thought they'd found the right targets and then the whole lot blew up when it was discovered that they hadn't. And besides, I want to see whether Eichmann has returned from Tucumán for his anniversary. What is it, Haim? You don't look very happy."

"I'm not. This is a small neighborhood and I'm sure everyone knows each other. I think that if two or three strange men keep turning up asking questions about all sorts of things, we're are going to have problems. I think what we need is a woman to come with us when we go back there. It will look far less suspicious."

"Good idea. Let's see if we can 'borrow' a secretary from the embassy," Aharoni said. "And if not, we'll see if one of the local *sayaniot* can help us. We don't have to tell her much. We'll just use the usual story about checking up on some local anti-Semite in the area."

"Is that safe?"

"Sure. Especially if we take one of the secretaries from the embassy. A couple of them know I work for the *Mossad*, but that's it. They don't know what I do and they also know not to ask questions. Come on, we'll go to the embassy tomorrow and see if they can help us."

The next day we drove to the embassy and everything went according to plan. After a brief meeting with the ambassador, we borrowed one of the secretaries (whose name I am still not allowed to divulge) and then set off for what we hoped was Eichmann's house. As we were driving there, Aharoni told me that the apparently nameless street where we were going actually did have a name.

He said that Michael's contact at GEOFINK had found out that it was called Calle Garibaldi - Garibaldi Street. He said that it linked Don Torcuato y San Miguel with Pedro Leon Gallo.

"Do you think we'll be able to get any more shots of the house?" I asked.

Aharoni shrugged. "I don't know. But if not, we might see more of the house and the area around it. Anyway, we're in the area now so keep your eyes open and…"

"Look, Zvi, over there!" I interrupted him. "That man in the garden holding those sheets. The balding one with the light shirt and the glasses. That's him! I'm sure of it!"

"You're right, Haim. That's him. At last."

"*Sof, sof*," I said in Hebrew. "At long last."

"Get your camera, Haim, and see if you can get a picture."

"Too late. He's just gone inside."

And there he was. A balding, bland looking man who had just taken in the family's washing, the chief architect and executor of the Sho'ah, the Holocaust, history's most inhuman effort to wipe its fellow man off the map on the greatest scale ever. As I sat there I could not believe that this boring, average-looking man with his receding hairline and large glasses – a man who looked like thousands of petty clerks the world over – had been directly responsible for the deaths of six million of my fellow Jews. But not only that. He had also caused the deaths of millions of other men, women and children throughout Europe. From the steppes of Russia in the east to the Franco-Spanish border in the west, this man had broken up families, murdered and mutilated millions and millions of people. He had done this for no reason other than they were Jews, gypsies, homosexuals, cripples and anyone in fact who didn't believe in his warped Nazi ideology. It was too much to take in in one go.

Without thinking I let out a cry of anguish.

"What's up?" asked the secretary, looking up from the magazine she had been reading.

"Nothing," I said, realizing what thoughts had just passed through my mind. "I was thinking of something that happened recently, that's all."

"That's right," Aharoni said. "I don't think there's any point in hanging about around here any longer today. Come on, let's go back to town."

I didn't argue. Suddenly, despite my joy in having tracked down our man at last, I felt empty. All I wanted to do was to get away from this place, this building which now housed one of the most despicable men who had ever been born.

That night Aharoni sent the following message in code to Tel Aviv:

A man has been observed at Vera Eichmann's house; he definitely resembles Eichmann. I had assumed he would come today because their silver wedding falls next Monday. On my part therefore there is no further doubt that Klement is Eichmann. Any further observation or investigation could endanger the success of the forthcoming main operation. I assume he will return to his work in Tucuman on Monday. I will also go to Tucuman although it will not be easy to locate him there. I recommend that I return to Tel Aviv immediately in order to assist in the planning of the main operation. I again recommend termination of all investigation activities in Europe.

That night as we sat down in our hotel, Aharoni told me that he wanted one of our sharper pictures to be sent to Tel Aviv. "I'm convinced that he is our man but we have to persuade Isser of this as well."

"That's true, but we can't keep driving around San Fernando in different cars all the time. One day someone's bound to notice us and tell Eichmann."

Aharoni scratched his head and I knew he was thinking of a new strategy. "You're right, Haim. You've just said the key phrase. Different cars. Next time we won't use a car, we'll use a small truck instead."

"A truck? Won't that attract even more attention?"

"No, my friend. Not if it's used only once."

"So what are you planning to do with it? Deliver some furniture to his house by mistake? And while you are arguing there, I'll take some pictures?"

"Good idea, but no, Haim. We'll use it like bird-watchers or wild-life photographers: they use a camouflaged hide to take their pictures of birds and other animals. I'll hide in the back and take my pictures from there."

"But someone will see you."

"Not if the back of the truck is completely closed and I shoot through a small hole in the back flap."

"Zvi, that is brilliant," I said and clapped him on the back. "But I do have one small question. Where are you going to get a truck from? The rental company?"

"No, from one of our *sayanim*. When we were at the embassy one of the secretaries gave me the name and address of a person in the community who has a small removal business. He has a three-ton truck with a tarpaulin which covers the rear half. The embassy uses it occasionally. We'll drive it over there and use a telephoto lens so we don't have to park too close. What do you think?"

I told him I thought this was a good idea and the next day we picked up the truck and drove it over to San Fernando and parked it near the kiosk. I slumped down in the driver's seat with a cap pulled down over my face while Aharoni lay in the back with his camera and a selection of lenses.

He was able to take his time and point his camera at Eichmann's house without attracting any attention at all. We stayed there for half an hour. During that time, Aharoni was able to take shots of the house as well as of Eichmann himself. At first he was wearing a suit but then he went into the house and emerged five minutes later wearing a loose-fitting shirt and pants. While Eichmann was outside in the garden, Aharoni managed to take some shots of him playing with his youngest son while talking to Dieter at the same time. After about ten minutes of this, they all went back into the house and Eichmann closed the heavy door behind them.

"I think that's about it for the day," I called back to Aharoni. "It doesn't look like they'll be coming out any more today."

"Good," Aharoni said, climbing back into the cab. "I was beginning to get cramps in my legs lying down back there. But I think I took some good shots, especially of Eichmann. I took a series of him standing by the fence while he was facing me. I got some full-frame shots of his face and the upper half of his body. I took a couple of close-ups of Dieter and the little boy but I concentrated mainly on Eichmann. But come on, let's get out of here. I've had enough of this place."

On the drive back, Aharoni added more details. "If I wasn't sure in the past, now I'm absolutely sure that he is our man. As soon as I saw him in that dark suit standing in a certain way, it didn't need much imagination to compare him to the pictures we've got of him in our files in his black SS uniform – all trim, official and efficient."

"Yes, I also thought the same," I said. "It was weird to see him like that. No longer the petty clerk, but the murderous Nazi that he was," and I shivered at the thought. But now, we must send these pictures to Tel-Aviv as quickly as possible."

"Right, that is why our next stop will be at that photography shop we've used before in town. If anyone asks any questions, which I doubt, we'll say that they're pictures of my cousin and his family in Sao Paulo. Let's hope this batch of photos has come out all right."

But we had no need to worry. Our German camera had lived up to its reputation and a few days later Aharoni sent a detailed coded report to Harel in Tel-Aviv. This report included the following points:

Vera Eichmann lives with Dieter and her youngest son, a son of about five in a free-standing house 30 kms. south of the center of Buenos Aires. It has heavy shutters, barred windows and a heavy front door. The family moved into this house last month from Chacabuco Street in Olivos.

We learned that the tenant who moved in was a German named Ricardo Klement. His son's name is Dieter Eichmann (not Klement) and works in an auto-repair shop in San Fernando. His father works in the Tucuman area.

The house is registered in Vera's maiden name (Liebl). Although the area of the house is part of San Fernando, no local taxes are collected, there are no public services and during the rainy season the area is flooded.

A man closely resembling Eichmann was observed near the house (Vera's). He looks much like the photos we have of Eichmann in our files. The name Ricardo Klement does not appear in police files in the greater Buenos Aires area. If Klement had emigrated to Argentina legally, he would have to be registered. His name does not appear in the local voters' register either.

Conclusion: *Klement must be Eichmann and he entered the country illegally.*

I think we must begin the next phase of this operation. I have no doubt that we have seen Eichmann, and the bread vendor confirms that Vera is married to this man. We observed that the man played with the little boy in the garden and then went into the house to change his clothes. If he is married to Vera but not called Eichmann, why is the house not registered to him under his real name? Why doesn't Vera carry his name?

A final identification can be made only when the team is ready to go into action. Any steps to confirm identification that are too obvious may cause him to disappear. He is quite careless about his personal security. The whole family (except him) is called Eichmann and Dieter revealed his new address to a total stranger (one of us). They made no effort to cover their move from Chacabuco Street.

They do not appear to fear any danger at the moment. We should move now as waiting might mean our chances of success will decline.

We should catch him in San Fernando and not in Tucuman which is 28 hours away by train. We must prepare everything here and then lie low until he returns from another visit to Tucuman. We are awaiting instructions.

The next day I wasn't feeling well. It was probably due to something that I had eaten. I was feeling weak and suffering from stomach cramps. I decided to rest in the hotel and if it didn't pass in a day, I would contact the embassy for a doctor.

It was at this time that Aharoni decided that he needed to get as close as he could to Eichmann's house as possible. He would do this at night but the problem was how to do so without looking suspicious.

"You can't leave the car unattended there and I'm not in a state to come with you."

Aharoni thought for a moment and then snapped his fingers. "I know what I'll do. I'll ask the embassy to 'lend' us two people – a man and a woman – and they will be the courting couple in the car while I am busy checking out Eichmann's house and garden."

This sounded quite feasible and after a call to the embassy, Aharoni's plan was put into action. He left that evening and I did not see him again until early the following morning when he woke me up as he came into the room. He looked dirty and disheveled and there were streaks of oil on his face and shirt.

"What happened?" I asked. "Did you have an accident?"

"Yes and no," he replied, walking over to the basin to wash his hands and face. "Give me a few minutes and I'll tell you what happened."

Five minutes later, with a clean face a clean shirt and a mug of coffee, Aharoni told me of his nocturnal adventures.

"I picked up the embassy people as arranged without any problem and we drove to the house. As I got out I told them to stay in the car and not to open the windows to anyone except me. All we needed was for some nosy local person to ask questions and hear their foreign accents. So far so good. I walked over to the house and saw that there were no lights on. I assumed that because they didn't have any electricity they had all probably gone to bed. Since I couldn't peep inside there was no point in hanging about so I went back to the car, which was actually a Jeep with a covered roof."

"Right. Then what happened?"

"Then, as I walked back to where the Jeep should have been parked, I saw that it wasn't there. I looked around and then saw it a little way off lying in a ditch by the side of the road. It was empty. The embassy people weren't in it. Then I heard some strange noises, like twigs snapping, like an animal moving about in the roadside undergrowth and then I saw the young couple lying down on the ground nearby."

"Dead? Wounded?"

"No, Haim, hiding."

"Hiding from what? What had happened?"

"Avi had decided that while I was away snooping around he would turn the Jeep around so we'd be ready for a quick getaway if necessary. In order not to attract any attention, he did this without turning on his headlights and that's when the trouble started. While he was turning the Jeep around, his rear wheels went over the side of the ditch by the side of the road."

"Were they hurt?"

"No, not really. She had a bump on her forehead. That was all. They got out and saw that the Jeep was OK and then decided to hide a little way off from it. The problem now was how to get the Jeep out of the ditch without attracting too much attention."

"So how did you do that? Call for a tow-truck?"

"No, there was nowhere to call from. We stopped a local bus and went to the center of San Fernando. From there I phoned Vardi, a local Jewish banker who has worked with us before. I told him I needed a tow-truck immediately and that he wasn't to say anything about any of this to anyone but that we'd meet him at the San Fernando bus station. He said that he would do his best and see us in half an hour. He was as good as his word. He turned up forty minutes later driving his big Chevy followed by a tow-truck. We then drove back to where we'd left the Jeep and there we had another surprise."

"It wasn't there. Someone had stolen it."

"Not quite, Haim but someone had stolen one of its wheels."

"So you had to use the spare, right?"

"Right. And that was a bit of a problem as well, as we had to work in the dark. Also, some of the locals came out to see what was going on."

"Including Eichmann?"

"No, not him, and none of his family either. Anyway, we got the Jeep out of the ditch and saw that the motor hadn't been affected by any of this. It started immediately and we drove off to the nearest filling station and replaced the oil which had leaked out. I then took Avi and his 'girl-friend' back to the embassy and came back here, all dirty and greasy. And now, if you don't mind," Aharoni yawned, "I've got to catch up on a few hours of well-earned sleep. But tell me, how are you feeling now?"

I said I was feeling better but another day's rest wouldn't be a bad idea.

During the following week we drove past the house in different vehicles driven by different *sayanim*. We took some more pictures of the area and then at the end of March we flew the seven hundred miles to Tucumán. We took Roberto with us as we needed a Spanish speaker with a local accent with us. Aharoni pretended he was a German lawyer, a cover story for his German-accented Spanish. We wanted to check up on the Eichmann/Klement connection with the local CAPRI company. CAPRI's official name was *CAPRI, Proyectos y Traliz Ind.* (Company for Real Estate Projects).

During the next three days we heard that he had worked there but had left seven years earlier in 1953 to start a laundry business in Buenos Aires.

Thinking that we had learned all that we could in Tucumán and had merely confirmed something we had already heard, we flew back to Buenos Aires.

Back at the embassy we found a cable waiting for us from Tel-Aviv. It told us to return home immediately in order to submit a complete report and to prepare a detailed plan for the final operation. We booked a flight home on the next available 'plane, an Aerolineas Argentinas flight to Tel-Aviv via Paris. Before leaving, we contacted all our *sayanim*, thanked them for their help and then returned our last rented car at the airport before the long transtlantic flight home. Imagine our surprise when on boarding the second leg from Paris to Tel-Aviv who should we see on board but the *Memuneh*, Isser Harel, himself.

Obviously we could not talk about what we had been doing on the plane. All he did was raise his head from behind the *International Herald Tribune* and ask, "Are you absolutely sure he is our man?" For an answer, Aharoni showed him one of our best shots of Eichmann in the yard of his house in Garibaldi Street. Isser rewarded us with one of his rare smiles and gave us a thumbs-up and settled down again behind his newspaper as we moved further down the aisle to find our own seats.

Now I knew we were well on the way to catching this mass murderer and that our operation had taken an upward turn, I allowed myself to relax and settled down to read the latest edition of *Paris-Match*.

We landed at Lod airport five hours later. It was a good

feeling to be home, to speak Hebrew openly and to know that the next day I'd be able to take a few days' leave and see my wife and family. Buenos Aires and Eichmann and all he stood for were thousands of miles away and all our rides up and down Garibaldi Street could remain in the background at least for a week or two.

Harel however, wasted no time. That evening we had our first debriefing in his Tel Aviv office.

"I know you told me on the plane that you were absolutely sure that you had identified this man in Buenos Aires as Eichmann," he began, "but apart from the photo you showed me, have you any other proof?"

"Yes," I said. "On 21 March when we were staking out his house, we saw him get off the bus at his usual bus-stop. He was carrying a large bunch of flowers all nicely wrapped up, with colored ribbons and pretty paper. Then when he reached his house, the front door was opened by his wife who this time was wearing a smart frock, as opposed to her usual drab clothing. She looked very pleased to see him and the flowers and hugged him. We also saw one or two of his children in the doorway as well."

"So what does that mean?" Harel asked.

"It means, Isser," I said proudly, "that we have nailed him. March 21st. was Eichmann's silver wedding anniversary. It's too much of a co-incidence for this man at number fourteen Garibaldi Street not to be Eichmann, considering all the other information we have collected about him and his house and his past career. Yes, sir. This time, and after all these years, I think we've got him," I couldn't help keeping the victorious tone out of my voice, and as I was saying this, I noticed that Aharoni and Harel were also smiling.

135

Chapter Eleven
Adolf Eichmann: The Facts

If I thought I could now enjoy a long home-leave, I was wrong. Two weeks later, on 24 April 1960, to be exact, I was back in Buenos Aires with Aharoni. Isser Harel had given us some new instructions and, before leaving Tel-Aviv, he had called both of us together with several others of the 'Operation Eichmann' team to a special meeting at his headquarters.

As we were sitting down in a semicircle facing a white screen and blackboard, Harel entered the large room accompanied by a bushy-haired man carrying a stack of books and two rolled up maps. Harel called us to order and introduced David J. to us.

"As most of you know," Harel began, tapping his pen on the table in front of him for attention, "David works in our research department and I've asked him to come here today and give us a talk about Eichmann's personal history and background. The idea is that he gives us all the information: who Eichmann was and what caused him to become the monster he turned out to be. If you have any questions, please save them for the end of the talk, and keep them short and to the point. Thank you. David, the floor is yours."

Harel stood aside and David took his place.

Unused to talking to over twenty people at once, David coughed nervously, looked around, waited for a moment and then began.

"Adolf Eichmann was born in Solingen, an industrial town in western Germany on 19 March 1906. His family was Protestant, of good middle-class German stock. His father was called Adolf Karl Eichmann and his mother's name was Maria. Her maiden name was Schefferling. Like most women then, she did not go out to work and seems to have been a typical German *hausfrau*. She died when she was only thirty-two years old. This is probably not surprising as life in Germany had become very hard due to the postwar austerity measures, and besides, she had been more or less continuously pregnant for nine years.

Adolf was the oldest son and soon after his birth three more boys were born: Emil, Helmuth and Otto. There was also a sister called Irmgard.

"During the war, that is, the First World War, Eichmann's father served in the Austro- Hungarian army and when it ended in 1918, the family moved to Linz, Austria. For him this meant being promoted from being a pre-war book-keeper to becoming a commercial manager for the Linz Tramway and Electricity Company. At first he moved to Linz on his own and a year later - when he felt more fully established - he called for the rest of the family to join him there.

"They lived in the center of Linz and soon after his wife died, the father married again. His second wife was also called Maria. Unlike his first wife, the second Maria came from a prosperous family, had good connections with Viennese society and some of her family were married to well-off Viennese Jews. As far as we know, the family seemed to have lived a normal life-style although there may have been some problems for the Eichmann family as they were Protestants and Linz was a mainly Catholic town."

David looked around the room. "So that's his background so far. Are there any questions?"

There were none so he continued.

"Eichmann's life as a young man was quite typical for the time. School, the local church club and the YMCA. Like many good middle-class children he learned to play a musical instrument and he became quite a good violinist. Later he joined the *Wandervogel*, a sort of Boy Scouts group that went in for hiking and camping. So far, so good. But what wasn't good was his progress in school.

Unlike his brothers and his sister, he wasn't a good student so his father took him out of school and sent him to a vocational college instead." Here David looked at his notes and carefully read out the name of Eichmann's college, the *Höhere Bundeslehranstalt für Elektrotechnik, Maschinenenbau und*

Hochbau. "He wasn't a very good student there either and after only four terms he left without acquiring any qualifications and began working in his father's business instead.

"This however, was not a good idea. His father's business, the second one that he had tried, was not successful. Then his father invested the family's savings in the construction of a mill in the Innviertel area in Austria; this also failed miserably. These failures however, did not seem to have dampened the father's desire to make money as he then invested in a light engineering company in Salzburg, Austria. This also failed as Eichmann's father's new business partner was a con man who, when the company went bankrupt, went and hanged himself.

"From then on Eichmann senior worked for a firm which was linked to the electrical company he had first worked for when he'd arrived in Linz after the First World War. His job was connected to the production and selling of electrical goods. This was satisfactory for a while but then, in the late 'twenties, this firm also faced difficulties and so Eichmann's father became a salesman again, selling parts for batteries and radios."

"And all this happened while the Depression was hitting Germany?" I asked. "No wonder young Eichmann grew up with such a negative view of life."

"No, Haim, surprisingly that was not the situation. Linz managed to survive better than many other cities in Austria and Eichmann's father was able to find work for his oldest son. He found him a job with the Untersberg Mining Company and when he quit there for some reason I haven't been able to discover, Eichmann spent the next two and a half years working as a sales clerk for the Oberösterreichische Elektrobau Company. Then in the spring of 1933 he changed jobs to become the district agent for the Vacuum Oil Company, a subsidiary of the American company, Standard Oil.

"His job there included arranging fuel deliveries for the company's customers as well as looking for suitable sites for building gas stations."

"In other words," Aharoni remarked bitterly, "he gained a lot of experience by traveling around, experience which would help him later with the setting up and running the concentration camps."

David nodded and then someone asked, "And when did he first become involved with the Nazi party?"

"I was just coming to that," David said, looking at his notes. "While he was working for the Vacuum Oil Company, he became a member of the youth section of Hermann Hiltl's right-wing war veterans' movement – the *Jungfrontkämpfer-vereinigung*."

"But he hadn't taken part in the war. He was only a small boy then."

"I know that, Reuven," David replied, "but, at that time, many right-wing people joined such movements. They, and the growing number of left-wing and Communist movements were a useful release for all of their political aspirations. Then in 1933 Eichmann moved back to Germany and two years later married Veronica Liebl, a woman Aharoni and Haim have been calling Vera. They had four sons altogether: Klaus, Horst, and Dieter who were born in Europe, and Ricardo who was born in Argentina and who is now about five years-old."

"David," someone called out, "you still haven't told us when he joined the Nazi party."

David coughed apologetically, looked down at his notes and continued. "The answer to your question is that he joined the Nazi party on 1 April 1932. He was supported or sponsored by his friend Ernst Kaltenbrunner, and his membership number was 889,895. He first joined the Austrian branch of the party, the *NSDAP*, and he also became a member of the *Schutzstaffel* or the SS. His membership number for that was 45,326. At first he was accepted as a provisional candidate but by November 1932 he had become a fully-fledged member, that is, he was now an *SS-Mann*. We also know that during this time he began to read the Nazi newspapers, especially the *Völkische Beobachter* which carried regular reports about the street fighting between the main Nazi groups, the SS and the SA against the Communist ones."

"And when did he start playing a leading role in SS affairs?" I asked.

"That was in 1933 when he returned to Germany from Austria," David answered. "He became a *Scharführer* – a squad leader and joined the admin staff at Dachau. This was the first concentration camp; it had been set up in 1933."

"Of course he must have been in his element there; a party hack with the power of life or death over his prisoners," Aharoni commented.

"No, Zvi, you're wrong," David said. "Apparently he was bored by the military training he had to undergo and from then on, over the next few years, he began to get himself promoted within the Nazi organization. This included working at Elder von Mildenstein's 'Jewish Section' II/112 at its headquarters in Berlin. It seemed that Mildenstein, a top Nazi who had worked for Heydrich, another top Nazi, recognized Eichmann's organizational abilities and told him to learn what he could about Jews and Zionism. This was perhaps Eichmann's biggest break within the party, because from then on, he became known as the expert on the 'Jewish Question.' At that time, Eichmann tried to learn Hebrew and Yiddish so that he could become even more efficient and by 1937 he was commissioned as an *Untersturmführer*."

"A second lieutenant," Aharoni whispered to Reuven.

David overheard him. "That's right, Zvi. And then in 1937 Eichmann, together with Herbert Hagen, his superior officer, sailed to Palestine. Eichmann's cover story was that he was a journalist and Hagen's was that he was a student. They arrived in Haifa at the beginning of October but the British wouldn't let them stay for more than twenty-four hours as they were very busy trying to contain various Arab uprisings and they didn't have the time for these two Germans. While they were in Palestine, Eichmann and Hagen toured Haifa and visited the German Protestant Templar colony. The next day they sailed to

Alexandria, planning to obtain visas there and then re-enter Palestine from the south.

"They stayed in Alexandria for a short while time and then continued on to Cairo. The British there refused to give them visas, probably because of the increase in rioting in Palestine and, in the end, Eichmann and Hagen had no choice but to return to Germany."

"David, do you mean to say," I asked, "that all the stories I've heard about Eichmann coming to Palestine are exaggerated and that he spent only one day here?"

"Yes, Haim, but Eichmann exploited this trip to the full. When he returned to Germany he made sure that everyone knew that he was the expert on Jewish affairs and Zionism. This he reinforced when on 1 November 1937, a few days after his return, he gave a talk to the *Judentagung*, a conference about Jews. He claimed that the Jews were a powerful and dangerous racist enemy who were waging war on the German people. He said that they should be removed from German society as quickly as possible and he even put forward the idea that the Germans should work with the Zionists in order to ship the Jews off to Palestine.

"He must have been good at his job because soon after the *Anschluss*, when the Nazis took over Austria in March 1938, Eichmann was promoted to *Obersturmführer* – first lieutenant. By now he was known as the acknowledged expert on the Jews. As head of the office for Jewish emigration, he began to oversee the setting up of concentration camps and ghettos as well as organizing the plundering of Jewish property and wealth."

"In other words, he was organizing the first stages of the 'Final Solution.'"

"That's right," David confirmed Yigal's comment. "But that particular phrase did not come into use until later."

At this point, David stopped talking and pointed to a large wall-map of Europe during the Second World War and showed how the *Wehrmacht*, the German army, had successfully invaded Poland, France, Belgium, Norway and Denmark.

"After these successes," David continued, "Eichmann's promotion through the ranks was very fast, especially if you take into account that he was not a combat officer fighting on the front lines. "

"Yes," I whispered to Aharoni. "He was just a *jobnik*," - the derogatory Israeli term for a desk officer.

"A short time later, when the war broke out in September 1939, Eichmann was promoted to *Haupsturmführer*, captain, and then a year later he was promoted to *Sturmbannführer*, major, and less than one year later he was made an *Obersturmbannführer*, a lieutenant-colonel. By now he was at the heart of things and was based at the *RSHA*, the *Reichssicherheitshauptamt*, the Reich Main Security Office. Within this organization he was given the responsibility of running the sub-department, the *RSHA Referat* IV B4, which dealt specifically with the evacuation and deportation of Jews, as well as Jewish affairs in general. His boss was *Brigadeführer* Heinrich Müller, the head of the Gestapo.

"Eichmann continued with his evil work and in June 1941 Hitler invaded Russia. It was during this period of heightened activity that another top Nazi, Reinhard Heydrich, told Eichmann that Hitler's plans called for the murder of all the Jews in Nazi-controlled Europe."

"Are you referring to the Final Solution and the Wannsee Conference?"

"Yes, Haim. I am. Heydrich ordered Eichmann to attend this meeting of the fifteen top-level Nazis at Wannsee, a Berlin suburb. The aim of this meeting was that Heydrich, appointed as the chief organizer of the 'Final Solution to the Jewish Question,' was to co-ordinate the activities to be carried out by the various Nazi organizations. He wanted to ensure that they worked in conjunction with the *RSHA*, the highest authority for this dirty work, when it came to dealing with the Jewish Question.

"It was during this meeting that Heydrich approved of two important plans. The first was a general plan how to improve and speed up the deportation of Jews in the future. The second called for the specific deportation of all the Jews in Nazi-controlled Europe and North Africa to the German-occupied areas in Eastern Europe. In addition, the Jews were to be worked to death in slave-camps and working on road-building and similar projects.

"This meeting lasted for about ninety minutes during which Heydrich spoke for nearly an hour. At the beginning he put forward his ideas and said that he had been appointed, presumably by Hitler himself, to be the chief organizer of the Final Solution. He outlined the numbers of the different minority populations such as the Jews and the Gypsies and here he was helped by Eichmann who had presented him with a report on the current situation. Heydrich then stated quite specifically that those Jews who did not die as a result of slave-labor would be killed. They also discussed the situations in which Jews had intermarried as well as talking about the question of those who were half-Jewish and whether certain Jews would be exempted from deportation.

"As part of the Wannsee Conference, Eichmann presented two lists which divided the Jewish population of Europe into two: List A and List B. List A included countries that had already been occupied by the Nazis, such as Germany itself, Austria, the Baltic republics, Norway, Denmark, Belgium and Holland while List B included neutral countries or countries that had friendly relations with Nazi Germany. These included: Bulgaria, Rumania, Serbia, Hungary and some others. The total number of Jews to be annihilated totaled eleven million."

David stopped for a minute for us to take in the enormity of the plans for mass murder, the genocide that the Nazis had planned. I sat there thinking that if the Nazis had won the war they would have slaughtered almost double the number of Jews they had murdered, to say nothing of the millions of the non-Jews destined to be exterminated or killed in battle. I shivered at the thought and then noticed that other people were sitting in the room with their eyes closed or clenching their fists while thinking about the dry facts that David had just given us. How could such terrible actions have been allowed to happen? Couldn't anyone have done anything to stop them?

On a practical level, I realized that it was useless to think such thoughts because these acts of organized mass murder had already taken place. But I am sure that, like everyone else in the room, I was thinking of the cold-blooded enormity of this act of genocide and how it had been carried out in such an organized and industrially efficient manner.

I was quite aware that in the past, various nations and religious groups had risen up, revolted and massacred those whose views, religious or otherwise were quite different from their own.

Protestants had killed Catholics; Catholics had massacred Protestants; the English had killed thousands of Irish and the Russian peasants had wiped out thousands of Napoleon's soldiers in 1812. But all these actions, even if they had been ordered by their nations' authorities, had taken place over relatively short periods of time. Nobody involved had compiled lists, organized transport for deportations or concentration camps. These acts of mass killing had often been spontaneous reactions or short-lived outbreaks of government-inspired violence. The numbers of the victims were generally reckoned in hundreds or thousands, not in millions, or even tens of millions as the Nazis had planned.

Had Queen Elizabeth I's Protestant advisors sat in a committee to organize the efficient death of England's Catholic population? No, they had thought of how to rid the country of the individual Catholic leaders. Had Catherine de Medici taken time off to arrange an organized massacre of the French Protestant Huguenots on Saint Bartholomew's Day in 1572? No, and besides this, however terrible this killing spree was, it had lasted for only a day or two. It had not gone on for over ten years.

No, here at Wannsee, a group of nominally cultured and educated people had sat around a conference table in a comfortable Berlin villa and calmly organized the cold-blooded deaths of millions of Jews for no reason other than that they were Jews. At the center of this sat Adolf Eichmann, writing out his notes and putting forward his suggestions on how this 'mission' could be carried out in a quicker and more efficient manner.

Thinking these thoughts made me even more determined that if he were to be captured and brought to Israel to face his accusers, then I wanted to be one of the team who would bring this about.

David tapped on the table as a sign that he wished to continue. "One of the major decisions made at Wannsee was that Eichmann was appointed to be the Transportation Administrator for the Final Solution. This meant that he was now responsible for co-ordinating all the trains which would carry the Jews from wherever they were caught to the death-camps which were mainly situated in Eastern Europe. These camps included Chelmno, Treblinka, Sobibor and of course, Auschwitz-Birkenau. There were also some in Germany, itself, such as Dachau, Buchenwald and the mainly women's camp at Ravensbrück.

"From this point on, Eichmann worked as the extremely capable and more or less faceless chief bureaucrat whose only concern was to make sure that the Nazi extermination centers were fed with a steady supply of Jews and others for the ovens or for the battalions of slave laborers. Nothing, absolutely nothing was to be allowed to stand in his way of fulfilling his quotas. Even towards the end of 1944, when *Reichsführer* Heinrich Himmler, who could see that Germany had lost the war, ordered Eichmann to put a stop to his activities, Eichmann refused and continued with his plans to wipe out the whole of Hungary's Jewish population of over seven hundred thousand souls.

"It was also about this time that Eichmann said, "I will laugh when I leap into the grave because I have the feeling that I have killed five million Jews. That gives me great satisfaction and gratification." It was also during this period when the whole Nazi leadership could see that the war was lost did Eichmann call a halt to his organized extermination plans and to start thinking seriously about making his escape from Nazi Germany. In this, of course, he was not alone, but we are concentrating today on Eichmann and not the others, several of whom were condemned to death or to long terms of imprisonment at Nuremberg between 1945 and 1946."

David put aside the notes he had been using and finished the glass of water on the table in front of him. The room was silent as we all tried to take in what he had just told us. Even before David's lecture, all of us in that room had known something about the evil that was synonymous with Eichmann. But now that David had filled in many of the details and given us the dry statistics, we were all the more convinced that although the planned capture and trial of Adolf Eichmann was not directly linked with our own country's national security, we had a moral duty in bringing this man to justice.

That evening I went to the *Mossad* library and began to read and reread several of the files we had on Eichmann. Reading them reinforced the hope that I would be one of the team who would be sent to Buenos Aires to capture this inhuman architect of death.

Chapter Twelve
Return to Buenos Aires

My hopes were realized. Two weeks later, on 24 April, I flew back to Buenos Aires. I was part of the advanced guard that included Zvi Aharoni, Zvi Malkin, Menashe Tavor, Yacov Gat and four others whose names I am still not allowed to divulge. For the record, I will call them A, Sh, Y and A number two.

However, before we flew into the Argentinian capital, via different routes and using fake passports, we had a very important meeting with Isser Harel in his Tel Aviv office. There he outlined the three main challenges that would face us.

"The first two points are these," our short, balding director pointed out, "The first is that you will be operating in a foreign country well over eight thousand miles away from home, and the second is that Argentina is not on especially good terms with Israel. You should also remember that its former president, Juan Perón, who ran the show for nine years until he was deposed five years ago, allowed many ex-Nazis to find shelter there. Some of these have become quite influential.

"Perhaps it is no coincidence but in January this year several Jewish clubs and synagogues were attacked and so were several important members of the Jewish community there.

"In addition," the *Memuneh* continued, "you will be operating while using false passports, papers and identities. This, of course, is nothing new to you, but if you are caught, you will be on your own, that is, it will be very difficult for me or anyone else to save you or help you out of any tight spots. This does not mean that we will abandon you, but it does mean that rescuing you may take a long time. In addition, you must be very cautious in how you use the services of the local Jewish community. I know that Zvi and Haim used several *sayanim* to help them but this sort of thing must be done very carefully. We cannot have the community there suffering a backlash from what we are planning to do. They've suffered from enough anti-Semitic actions

147

recently. We don't have to supply the local ex-Nazis with any more excuses.

"And of course, you must take into account who you are dealing with. Eichmann has spent the last fifteen years on the run and looking over his shoulders all the time. By now, living like this must be second nature to him. He must be a very suspicious man. He probably trusts very few people and by living in his isolated house, it may make it even more difficult for us to catch him. As Zvi and Haim have noted, the area where he lives, San Fernando, seems to be a closed community and any strangers there will be noticed immediately. However, and this I must add," and Harel smiled one of his rare smiles, "his isolated house might mean, *dafke*, that it might make it easier for us to catch him. Who knows? Time will tell. All we know is this: he is living under a false name; he has made sure that he has hardly had his picture taken since the war and that he's benefited from the various rumors that have circulated saying that he is dead or living in Austria or Germany."

"Or Kuwait," someone added.

"Right," Harel repeated. "Or Kuwait. Then we have another problem or two. First of all we'll have to keep him hidden in a safe house and then we'll somehow have to smuggle him out of Argentina, but don't not worry about that. I'm working on it now."

"Maybe we could roll him up in a carpet and send him here as freight," someone behind me whispered.

Harel heard him and actually smiled again. "That trick may well have worked for Cleopatra," he said, "but I doubt if we'll be able to do the same. Anyway, let's first make sure we catch him and then we'll deal with the problem of bringing him back here.

"So now that I've made you aware of what you're letting yourselves in for, I'll continue this meeting and discuss the various details which will be very relevant to the success of this mission.

"But before I do so, I want to thank you all for volunteering to take part in this mission. I must admit that I was not too enthusiastic at first about using our limited resources to capture this man and hopefully bringing him back here. I believe that our security services should deal with the country's present enemies, not our past ones. However, in this case, an exception has had to be made and now I fully agree with it. In addition to all this, I must also tell you that the Prime Minister supports us completely and has told me not to worry about how much this operation will cost.

"The last thing I want to say before we break up into groups to go over certain points is that your contact at the Israeli embassy in Buenos Aires will be Efraim Ilani. Among his jobs, he will be responsible for sending and receiving cables from there. Rafi Eitan will be leading the operation on the ground there and his number two man will be Avraham Shalom."

There had been rumors that these two would be leading the operation and when I heard Harel say so, I was very pleased. Both men had been with the service for many years and had accumulated much experience on the way.

Rafi Eitan was short and stocky. He was also very short-sighted and wore thick lenses in his glasses. However, despite not looking like the popular image of a leader of men, he was highly respected in the service and was known as an efficient organizer. Thirty-four years old, he had been a member of the *Palmach*, the elite unit of the *Haganah*, the country's first army. During this period he had acquired the nickname, 'Rafi the Stinker' because in one of his actions during the War of Independence he had had to climb through a sewer in order to blow up a British radar installation on Mount Carmel. His bravery ensured he was promoted rapidly and now it seemed it was quite natural that he would be called on to lead this complicated operation.

His number two man, Avraham Shalom, was equally talented. Like Eitan, he had also served in the *Palmach* and had been rapidly promoted through the ranks of the security services. Born in Vienna in 1928, he had arrived in Mandatory Palestine just before the war and had spent his first years on a kibbutz. During the War of Independence he had fought as a regular soldier and was later recruited by Eitan to be a scout for the army. After the war he became a truck driver in Tel Aviv.

Then one day he met Eitan who promptly recruited him again - this time to work for the *Shin Bet* security service. Then Harel had sent him to Paris to be one of his key men in Europe and now after several years, he was to be sent to Argentina to be part of 'Operation Eichmann.'

So now here we were back in Buenos Aires, about to put into place a daring plan in territory thousands of miles away from home, in a country that was new for most of the team. I must admit that I gave this a lot of thought as I sat in the plane during the long, boring flight over the South Atlantic from Europe to Buenos Aires. I could not help smiling to myself thinking of the irony of the situation. Here I was, using a German passport as part of my cover disguising myself as a respectable German businessman coming to Argentina instead of being the Israeli I really was, working for the *Mossad*. A couple of the others who had flown in were also posing as German businessmen. Only Efraim Ilani, the only genuine diplomat among us, was now returning to Buenos Aires after having attended several of Harel's preparatory meetings.

After collecting my baggage and passing through Customs and the usual security arrangements common to all international airports, I made my way over to the hotel I would be using. It was, of course, a different hotel from the one that Aharoni and I had been using two weeks earlier. We had all been assigned a new list of hotels, together with another list in case of difficulties. In the same way, each of us had received lists of various restaurants, cafes, parks and street corners where we could meet as if by chance in order to co-ordinate our future activities.

The first thing I did after checking in at my hotel was to draw the thick curtains and have a good sleep. Jet lag had started working on me and I knew that from the next day I would have to be fully alert and on my toes for any surprises that might come along. Mistakes caused by fatigue would not be tolerated.

The next day, 25 April, dawned bright and clear. I left the hotel after a quick breakfast and with my list of contacts in my pocket I met Aharoni and Sh. as arranged at a café on the Avenue Belgrano. From there we set out, three German businessmen and hired a car, a dark blue, medium-sized Ford that would blend in with our image and the local scenery.

"Now it's time to meet Avraham," I said. "He should be waiting for us at a café on Corrientes Street. Let's hope he's there."

He was. Sitting there at a corner table in the back facing the door, Eitan's deputy was half hidden behind a copy of the *Argentinisches Tageblatt*. When I asked him whether he could read it, his eyes twinkled. "Of course I can. Am I not a German businessman from Cologne?" Then he asked if we had eaten breakfast, and on learning we had, said, "Let's go. I want to see where Eichmann and his family are living."

"What, Just like that?" I asked.

"Sure, why not? But before that, I want to sit down, study a map of Buenos Aires and work out some details so that we'll all be fully co-ordinated. Haim, Zvi, you've been here before, where should we meet now? I suggest an open park where we'll look like a group of friends gathering for a chat."

I suggested a small nearby park off the Avenida Santa Fé. Aharoni and I had used it at the beginning of the month when we had met up with one of our *sayanim*.

We left the café and set off in our newly-rented car for the park. We spent some time there revising various details and then split up into two pairs for a late lunch. Later we returned to the park for another hour before driving off in the direction of Garibaldi Street.

The sun was beginning to set as we approached the kiosk; we began driving up the street toward Eichmann's house. Suddenly Aharoni hissed between clenched teeth, "There he is! There, to the left."

"Don't stop," Shalom ordered said. "Keep driving past the house and stop further up over there by those trees."

Aharoni did and then, getting out, he got out and opened the hood as if we were having engine trouble.

"You two," Shalom said to Sh. and me. "Lie down in the back as low as possible. We don't want anyone passing to see four men here."

"Can you see what he's doing?" Shalom asked Aharoni crouched over under the raised engine hood.

"Yes, he's outside, talking to a woman."

"Are they the same man and woman you saw two weeks ago?"

Under the cover of the hood, Aharoni adjusted his binoculars. "Yes, they look exactly the same."

"Good, then let's get out of here," and Aharoni and Shalom got back in the car and we set off back in the direction of the center of the city.

As we were driving back, Shalom remarked several times on the poverty of the area and how miserable Eichmann's house looked. "This man was one of the most important Nazis in Europe," he kept repeating. "And look at him now. What a hole of a place to be living in. It looks just like one of those jails you see in cheap cowboy movies. And that woman. She looks so poor and that dress - it looked pretty shabby. Oh, how have the mighty fallen," he said cynically.

"Yeah," I added. "And let's hope he falls into our hands, and soon."

"Amen," Aharoni said, "and now let me drop everyone off at their hotels."

"No, Zvi," said Shalom. "Let me off near the embassy first. I have to meet Ilani and send a message to Tel-Aviv."

That night, as the rest of us were in our hotels, Shalom, together with Ilani sent the agreed code-word, 'Carrot' to Harel. Shalom, after speaking to Eitan had confirmed that our operation was on. Shalom had seen Eichmann himself.

The next day Shalom arranged to met Aharoni and me in a park near the zoo to plan the next stages of our plan.

152

"This is what I want," Shalom said, munching on an apple. "I want to know Eichmann's daily timetable and I want as many details as possible. When he leaves for work in the morning; when he returns and how he goes to work and back. Does he go by bus or train? Does he go on his own or with someone else? Does anyone pick him up in a car and, if so, when and where? Does he go out at night to a club or anywhere else? And if so, where? I also want to know what time he goes to bed. What time do the lights go out in that miserable house of his? Is all that clear?"

"Getting that information is going to take some time," I said.

"I know that Haim but if we've waited fifteen years to catch this man, a few more days aren't going to hurt. We can't leave anything to chance. We'll probably have only one opportunity to grab him and we can't afford to make any mistakes. One wrong move and we'll lose him for another fifteen years. Just remember that."

We all sat there quietly for a minute thinking of what we had to do. Shalom was right. No mistakes would be tolerated. We had to get it right first time.

"So this is what we're going to do," Shalom continued. "I want you, using different people and cars each time, to take turns in building up a profile of this man. Grabbing him near his home in the evening seems to me to be the best idea, but all options at this stage are open. The house is isolated and I noticed that the street…"

"Garibaldi Street."

"Yes, Garibaldi Street seems poorly lit and that should also work in our favor."

We all agreed. It looked as though a night time snatch would be the best, but it was still too early to arrange the final details.

From then on, for the next few evenings, using the nearby overgrown railway embankment as a 'hide,' we took it in turns to keep an eye on Eichmann – when and how he returned from work and if he did so alone or accompanied by a workmate or not. We checked whether his wife came to meet him at the bus stop. By the end of the week we came to the conclusion that she did not. We were pleased to tell Shalom that as a dutiful German *hausfrau* she was probably at home, looking after their small son and preparing the evening meal.

We recorded that he would return home each evening on bus number 203 from his job at the local Mercedes-Benz plant at 19.40 hours. From the bus-stop near the kiosk he would walk along the deserted street, carrying a small flashlight which he would switch on if he felt the need. "This man is so methodical," I said. "He's a joy to follow."

"Of course he's methodical," Aharoni replied. "He's a German-born bureaucrat, isn't he?"

"Well, let's hope he stays that way."

Our 'spying' activities were disturbed on only one occasion. One evening as Aharoni and I lay there hidden among the high grasses and low bushes, a group of what we presumed were railroad workers began walking towards us along the railroad line. Fortunately they were laughing and talking so loudly that we were able to scuttle away and disappear in the dark surroundings before they could see us.

Over the next few days the remaining members of the task-force arrived in Buenos Aires.

Like us they arrived via different routes from various European and American airports. Some declared themselves to be tourists while others claimed they had come to Argentina for business purposes. This last group included Eitan and Harel. That Harel was also there was quite unusual. The *Memuneh* usually remained behind in Tel-Aviv during an operation, but it was clear that this time he saw this one to be of prime importance. He wanted to be on the scene if anything untoward happened.

A couple of the team were not too happy about having 'the boss' around, but I was pleased. It meant that if necessary we would have the best back-up possible if anything went wrong.

That night, Harel called us together and we learned how we were going to smuggle Eichmann out of Argentina. Although in theory we had three options: by air, by land or by sea, it was obvious that once we had caught him, we would fly him out of the country. To smuggle Eichmann over the border to another country, say Uruguay, Brazil or Chile and use one of their ports would be too risky, especially as there were no Israeli ships due to sail from them in the near future. Besides, smuggling him out of the country overland or by sea would take too long and therefore leave more possibilities for us to be stopped and searched by the various South American authorities.

"As you may have guessed," Harel began, "assuming that we succeed in catching him, we'll be flying Eichmann home. Before I left Tel-Aviv, I had several top-level meetings both with the Prime Minister and Yehuda Shimoni, the deputy director of El Al. As a result, they are now as fully involved in this business as we are."

"Hmm," I murmured. "That wouldn't be the first time our own airline has been involved in irregular activities."

"That's right, Haim," Harel said. "El Al has been used to fly in arms and refugees in the past and this time it's going to be used to fly this evil man back home to face his accusers. But, gentlemen, back to business." He rubbed his hands together and continued. It was clear that despite his previous opposition to this operation, he was now enjoying working on it and being out 'in the field' with his team.

"First of all, we are very lucky. It just so happens that soon, Argentina will be celebrating its 150th anniversary of gaining independence from the Spanish. As a result, official delegations from all over the world have been invited to attend these celebrations. This includes Israel, and this means that…"

"Our delegation will fly in on El Al and Eichmann will fly home with them," Shalom said, finishing off Harel's sentence.

"Exactly. Avraham has got it right. The Prime Minister and Golda Meir are sending Abba Eban, our current Minister of Education and past ambassador to the States with a delegation here by El AL and we will fly Eichmann back with them on their return trip home. Here I must add, Eban knows nothing about his special passenger for the return trip and I'm leaving that to the Prime Minister or the Foreign Minister to tell him. I'm not sure that he will be very pleased but, thank goodness, that is not our business. Our business is to catch Eichmann and look after him until we get him onto the plane."

"That may be easier said than done," I said.

"That's true. Therefore, we will have to take into account lots of small details to make sure that this operation goes as smoothly as possible.

"First of all," he began, counting off the various points on his fingers, "we must always remember we are operating in a foreign country far away from home and where we have rarely operated before. We will need to fly him back by the shortest and quickest route possible, which will not be easy considering that the flight will be over ten thousand miles long. Naturally we will have to stop once or twice en route for refueling and this itself leaves us open to all sorts of problems. We'll be using one of El Al's newest Bristol Britannias on a route that no El Al pilot has ever flown before. Although this plane, also known as the 'Whispering Giant' can carry one hundred and forty passengers, we will not be returning with anything like that number."

"That's good," Sh. said. "It will be lighter and therefore should be able to fly faster, especially as we'll have a tail wind behind us to help us along."

"Right," Harel continued. "Now, according to the top brass at El Al and their chief pilot, Zvi Tohar, they've used this plane before to fly from New York to Tel-Aviv non-stop, a flight of over 5,700 miles without any problems. So although this is good news for us, it's not quite good enough, because as I said, we will have to stop somewhere for refueling."

"That'll be somewhere in West Africa," I guessed. "Senegal, Liberia or Sierra Leone."

"Probably," Harel acknowledged, "but so far we haven't got to that stage of the planning.

"Besides, that aspect, for obvious reasons, we will leave to

Captain Tohar and El Al. They've had more experience than we have at this sort of flight. All I know is that Aerolineas Argentinas flies to Europe, and I presume other airlines usually stop to refuel at Recife in Brazil and West Africa and Rome. Therefore, I have asked the captain to look into this aspect of the flight very carefully and report back to me as soon as possible."

Captain Zvi Tohar was the ideal man to have on our side for this operation. Born in pre-war Germany, he had witnessed his father being beaten up and humiliated by the Nazis. Later he had fled to Britain and joined the RAF as a pilot. He then came to Israel and became one of the country's first pilots and had flown many dangerous missions during the War of Independence.

Later we heard that once he learned that he was to captain this special flight, he had put forward his own suggestions on how to improve our plans. These included the filing of false flight plans in order to foil anyone who might become too interested in our flight home. He also said that, due to the length of the Tel-Aviv – Buenos Aires return trip he would need two full crews. While this meant that another dozen people would be involved, Tohar said that he could guarantee that anyone in the know would keep their lips sealed. "After all," he explained. "None of my men will want to lose their job because they can't keep their mouths shut, do they?"

"In addition," Harel said, "there are many other problems to be dealt with, and the most important one is secrecy. Complete and utter secrecy. Naturally we will have to deal with the El Al crew as well as with all the various maintenance people and technicians and they're not used to working like we do. This means that they'll be working in the dark and not know what is really going on. Captain Tohar has assured me that he will choose the best passenger and technical crews he can. All that they'll be told until we are on the way home is that they will be part of El Al's special flight to Buenos Aires as part of their independence celebrations."

"Yeah, a very special flight," someone behind me muttered.

Harel ignored this and continued. "This flight will leave Tel-Aviv on 11 May and is due to arrive here the following day. If we're lucky, we'll all be out of here two days later. As I said, El Al will worry about flight-planning, food, clearances for taking off and landing as well as other aspects such as dealing with the airport here. These will include parking in an isolated spot and security. In other words, gentlemen, nothing must be allowed to interfere with our exit plans once we get started. Nothing. We and a limited number of the El Al people must be in control of everything, absolutely everything. Nothing can be left to chance."

"True," Aharoni said. "Including the weather."

A half-smile crossed the Memuneh's face. "Yes, that too. We'll also have to take that into account. Even though I am not a religious Jew, I believe that the good Lord will bless this operation and not allow the weather to spoil it."

"Amen," a couple of people added.

While Harel and the top brass at El Al were dealing with their own specific problems of flying Eichmann home, the rest of us were equally busy with our own problems. These included finding safe houses and renting and changing cars without arousing any suspicions.

At this point we had one safe house which we code-named *Ma'oz* – fortress. Any other safe houses – 'bolt holes,' I called them - had to be large enough so that several cars parked near them would not look out of place. In addition, these houses had to be fairly isolated, have a fenced or walled off perimeter and it would be best if they had a closed garage directly attached to the house itself. This was important because it meant that once we had Eichmann in our hands we would be able to move him from the car into the house without anyone seeing this from the road outside.

Of course, the safe houses had to be near the main roads and fairly close to the airport. It was obvious that the shorter the journey with our 'special passenger' to the airport would be preferable when the right time came. We could not risk the 'stop and search' tactics and the numerous road barriers that the

Buenos Aires police were in favor of using.

Finally, we had two more conditions for any safe house that we rented. They had to come without any staff, such as caretakers and gardeners; and they had to include a room which would serve as our prisoner's cell until we could fly him out of the country.

After two days of non-stop searching by the whole team, we found two more houses that suited our purposes. They were both owned by local Jews but of course we could not tell them why we wanted to rent their property for just a short while.

We named the first one, *Tira*, 'palace,' a large two-story building eighteen miles south-west of Buenos Aires in Florencio Varela and the second one, *Doron*, which is Hebrew for 'gift.' It was a large rambling structure two hours drive away from Garibaldi Street. We decided we would use *Doron* in emergencies only as the house came with a gardener whom we were not able to fire for the duration.

"So let's give him a few days' paid holiday," I suggested, "and maybe increase his regular pay while we are here. That should keep him out of the way."

Later, we also rented three other safe houses code-named *Ramim*, 'Heights,' *Kohelet*, 'Ecclesiastes' and *Moledet*, 'homeland.' These too would be used only for emergencies, that is, if we had to stay in Buenos Aires for much longer than we had originally anticipated.

As well as looking for suitable safe houses, we were also looking into the problem of renting reliable vehicles. We could not afford to be caught out now with a car which wouldn't start at a critical moment. Apart from being able to count on the reliability of the vehicles, we had to rent cars that were popular and would blend into the scenery. Some of the old 'bangers' we had rented earlier had been an insult to the motor industry but they had been cheap – but now we had a more or less unlimited budget. These ancient bone-shakers had included a Jeep with an unreliable reverse gear, a Fiat with a faulty electrical system and a Ford with a leaking radiator. All three of them had had several hundred thousand kilometers 'on the clock.'

However, as with the safe houses, luck was on our side. On the same day during the first week we managed to find a large black Buick and an equally large Chevrolet. In Israel such cars would have stood out but here in Buenos Aires they looked quite normal. Of course we did not wash their bodywork but one of my jobs as the team's mechanic was to make sure that they were reliable and ran smoothly.

By now we were feeling good. Our plans seemed to be progressing well and we were moving ahead on schedule. We had less than one week to make our snatch and now that we had sorted out the basic problems of safe houses, vehicles and airplanes, we could concentrate on what we had been sent here to do – to grab Adolf Eichmann and bring him back with us to Tel-Aviv.

Chapter Thirteen
Tightening the Screws

Our plan to capture Eichmann was basically very simple. On the evening of 11 May, our team in two rented cars, a Buick and a Chevrolet, would be parked somewhere on *Calle Garibaldi*, Garibaldi Street. They would be standing between the bus stop where Eichmann would get off his bus on his way home from work and his house at Number 14. Two of the men in the first car, a black Buick, would be standing by it with its upraised hood pretending to fix the engine. As soon as Eichmann passed them, they would seize him, bundle him into the back of the car and drive off to one of our safe houses. As you may have noted, we had used the trick of using the upraised hood before, but we felt that it would still be safe to use it again to explain why an unfamiliar car was parked in the neighborhood. It was also the first time we had used the Buick to drive near Eichmann's house. The team in the second car, a dark-colored Chevrolet, would be there as a back-up, for extra security and protection. If necessary, it would tail the first car and prevent anyone from getting too close to it.

Each car would carry four men. The team's doctor, Dr. Elian, would be in the second car, his job being to sedate Eichmann if he became too violent or hysterical.

The Chevrolet would be parked on Route 202, about thirty yards before the junction to Garibaldi Street. We would use its headlights to blind Eichmann or any passing car if they threatened to cause any problems during the abduction.

While we were going over all the details and discussing what could go wrong with our plan I asked Harel and Eitan what we should do if Eichmann did not 'play his part' as planned, that is, get off the 203 bus at 19.40 and then walk along the darkened street to his house.

Harel nodded. "Haim, I'm sure that he'll do what we're expecting him to do. We're dealing with a man who has been

161

used to giving and receiving orders all his life. We've noticed that he is a predictable creature of habit. I am absolutely sure he will 'play his part,' as you phrase it, to the full. To do otherwise would be against his nature."

"And besides, he's a *yekke*," Shalom added, describing Eichmann with the somewhat disparaging Yiddish term for the precise, meticulous German stereotype.

"Let's hope you're right," I replied and then turned to listen to Harel filling in more details about our future plan.

"We do have an alternative plan to Plan A, the plan that I've just described to you," Harel said and turned to a large diagram of the area he had pinned onto a board. "The major difference is where our cars are to be parked during the snatch. As I said, in Plan A, one car would be parked between the bus-stop and Eichmann's house, and the second car would be parked about thirty yards away on Route 202 near the corner of Garibaldi Street. In Plan B, the first car would be standing on Garibaldi Street facing Route 202 and the second car would be waiting on Route 202 itself. Both cars would be parked in such a way so that each team could keep an eye on each other. Plan B also calls for the driver in the car on Route 202 to flash his lights to warn the team in the 'snatch car' that Eichmann has got off the bus and is on his way. Then the snatch team would start driving slowly toward Eichmann and grab him at the junction of Route 202 and Garibaldi Street. As with Plan A, the driver of the back-up car would use his flashlights to blind any motorist who happened to be coming along just then."

While we began to discuss the pros and cons of each plan, Harel, standing there like a teacher, called for our attention to discuss our escape routes.

"After consulting the maps carefully and having driven around the area personally with Zvi and Haim, I can see that we have three different possible escape routes." He turned back to the board behind him and flipped over the map showing Eichmann's house over to reveal a Buenos Aires road- map. "The first escape route is to drive along Route 202 via San Fernando and Vincente

Lopez and then continue back to Buenos Aires and the Doron safe house. The second route would be to drive toward central Buenos Aires, use the *Tira* safe-house and go there via the 202 and Route 197. The third possibility would also use *Tira*, but to get there via Route 202 and the Bancalari railroad station," he said, using a ruler to point out on the map exactly what he meant.

"Are there any questions?" he asked after we had studied the map.

"Yes," I said. "What happens if for some reason the police suddenly show up? What do we do then?"

Harel thought for a minute and then stood up to answer me. "If that happens and you run into any kind of trouble with the police, you are not to let Eichmann out of your hands. Not at any price. One of the team, the one who is sitting nearest to him in the back of the car, will handcuff himself to him and throw away the key. If the police start asking questions, say you are Jewish volunteers who have discovered where Eichmann has been hiding all these years. You must not agree to let him go. Is that clear? Under no circumstances is he to be released. You must demand to see the highest level police officer possible and make sure that Eichmann will be locked up while an investigation is being carried out. And by the way, if anything goes wrong at the moment of capture itself, you are to use the *Ramim* safe house and not *Tira* or *Doron*. It will be easier to get there than the others and, if necessary, we will be able to move him to one of the other safe houses later. Is that clear?"

I noticed that as Harel was describing the possibility of failure, everybody was nodding somberly. It was a terrible thought, that after Eichmann's hiding for fifteen years and after all our efforts, something - anything - could happen and this evil man could slip away once again. We could not allow ourselves to fail. It simply did not bear thinking about. All our work would have been in vain. No way.

In this serious mood we moved on to discuss other possible scenarios. What should we do if we became involved in a car-chase with the police? Naturally we would try and escape, but if we failed?

Harel talked about extreme actions such as ramming police cars if necessary but whatever happened those of us not arrested as a result of police 'interference,' were to make their escape and leave Argentina as laid out in our special contingency plans. Although it was against the tradition of the Israeli army and secret services, no-one was to stay behind to rescue their fellow team-mates.

Such help would come later, Harel stressed. The assistance would come probably through the local Israeli embassy or our own Foreign Ministry in Jerusalem.

Aharoni raised his hand to attract Harel's attention. "What should we do if despite all the efforts made by Haim and me a couple of weeks ago, we find out that the man we thought was Eichmann is not really him? In other words, Ricardo Klement really is Ricardo Klement, an ex-German living here in Buenos Aires?"

Harel answered immediately. "I've thought of that but I hope - especially after studying the evidence that you and Haim have shown me - that it won't come to that. However, if it does, then Zvi Malkin and Moshe Tavor are to drive him north, several hundred miles out of Buenos Aires and leave him there."

"What? Just like that?"

"No, not exactly. They will leave him with enough money in his pocket to get home. Also, they are to make sure they can't be identified, so be sure Eichmann is blindfolded as much as possible. And of course, none of you in any circumstances are to call each other by your real names."

"And after he's dropped off?"

"Zvi and Moshe will cross the border with Brazil and get home from there. From the airports at Sao Paulo or Rio de Janeiro or, if necessary, even Recife, which is much further north. But," Harel added, "let's hope and pray it won't come to that."

"Amen," Aharoni said fervently.

Harel raised his hand. "Any more questions?"

"Yes," I asked. "What if - and I hope this won't happen - but what if Eichmann somehow escapes during the snatch and manages to get to his house and barricades himself inside? Do we leave him there? Or do we try and get him out later? Should we break in and grab him there and then?"

Harel had an answer for that one, too. "You will break into the house and grab him there and then drive him to the safe house as planned. I doubt whether he'll give us another opportunity to come back and grab him later. I know that if I were in his shoes, I certainly wouldn't stay in that house waiting to be grabbed again." He looked at us and asked if there were any more questions.

"Yes, I have one more question," I said, thinking of my wife and children and guessing that the others were thinking along the same lines. "What if we are caught and arrested by the police or by any other Argentinian authority – how long do you think we'll be sent to jail for, that is, for breaking the law?"

Harel's answer was immediate. "Ten years. I've already checked that point out with our legal department."

You could hear the others echo "ten years" while thinking about their families back home in Israel. It was certainly a heavy price to pay for trying to capture one of the chief Nazi mass murderers.

"And who will look after our families if that happens?" I asked.

"I will – together with the *Mossad*. That is part of our responsibility to you," Harel answered without any hesitation. "But let us hope that this scenario won't ever happen. We've trained enough for this operation and you all know what to do, so there is no reason why it should fail. But just remember, if you do have to get out of Argentina in a hurry, use the trains and not airports. The police will be sure to have them covered first - and more thoroughly. Are there any more questions?"

There weren't any. We were all silent and thinking about the forthcoming 'snatch' operation.

"In that case, I have one more piece of information for you. I was informed earlier today that we're going to have to change some of our dates and timing. After we get hold of Eichmann, we are going to have to keep him in the safe house until the twentieth of May."

"Not the twelfth?"

"No, Shalom. Until the twentieth. I've just received a message from El Al. The special flight that was supposed to have left here on the twelfth has been delayed to take off on the twentieth instead."

"Why?"

"Because the delegation coming with Abba Aban is to stay here for eight to ten days and not just one or two days as originally planned. El Al, for obvious reasons, doesn't want to leave one of its best planes hanging around here for a week doing nothing during the tourist season. The message said," and here Harel took out a folded piece of paper out of his pocket bearing the El Al logo. "It says that our return flight will leave Tel-Aviv on 18 May at 13.00, fly to Rome for refueling and then continue on to Buenos Aires. It should arrive here, Buenos Aires, on the following day, the nineteenth, at 14.00 hours local time."

"So, excuse me chief, but why didn't you tell us that earlier?" someone asked.

For once the *Memuneh* looked slightly apologetic. "I did try to get some changes made in the meanwhile, but I wasn't able to do so. There is a limit to what we can ask El Al to do for us, and asking them to leave one of their prize Bristol Britannias here on the tarmac for a week was just too much. Besides, leaving a plane like that sitting around doing nothing for a week would certainly have aroused some suspicion. Airlines run on quick turnarounds and I'm sure you'll agree that a plane this size cannot be hidden very easily and especially since this is the first time we, that is, El Al will have flown here."

He paused for a minute to let us take in this latest piece of information and then he continued.

"So, knowing that, this is what we're going to do. We'll carry on as planned, that is, we will check out of the hotels we're using as originally planned and then move into the safe houses for the rest of our stay here."

"And the rented cars? Aren't we going to return them on time?" I asked.

"No, Haim, we're not. I've already made arrangements with the rental companies to delay their return and everyone has been very well paid for this. Don't worry. Money talks. No-one has asked any awkward questions. Remember, such things do happen in the world of business. We're not the only ones who change their plans. It happens every day."

There was a certain truth in what he said and no-one made any further comments other than that we would have to keep Eichmann under wraps for a whole week instead of for a day or two. As we were about to get up, Harel tapped the table again and asked us to remain seated.

"There is something else that I must tell you. Judith Nessayahu will be arriving tomorrow. She's to play the role of Ya'acov's wife in one of the safe houses. This way," Harel smiled briefly, "we'll look more respectable, at least to any outside observer or nosy neighbor."

"And the other safe houses?" someone asked.

"Unfortunately we don't have enough women to go round, so Judith will be staying in the safe-house where we'll be holding Eichmann."

I was pleased when I heard this. For Judith to play the role of another man's wife was somewhat strange. We knew that although she had been working for the *Mossad* for several years, she was an observant Jew. However, this had not prevented her from serving in the army during the War of Independence or, later, from working undercover in Morocco and other places. There she had helped to arrange the illegal transport arrangements for spiriting groups of Jews out of these countries to Israel.

Despite her religious background, she had dressed up as a Gentile on occasion, her female presence adding an air of respectable normality to more than one of our past activities. Working on 'Operation Eichmann' must have been especially satisfying for her. Somehow she had managed to escape the Holocaust in her native Holland and had succeeded in making her way to Palestine. Later she learned that the Nazis had murdered most of her family.

Just as I was thinking these thoughts, I heard Harel say that if no-one had anything to add we should return to our hotels and safe-houses. "Remember," he added. "Those of you I have told, will meet up tomorrow at the café at the top of the list. Now start leaving here in pairs and make sure you leave five minutes between each pair. So good night gentlemen and as the old saying goes, 'Good hunting.'"

As Harel turned to study the large-scale map of San Fernando and Route 202 behind him, we broke up into small groups to discuss tomorrow's operation. Everyone was talking about its chances of success and what would happen if it failed. I found myself talking to Zvi Malkin.

Zvi - or Zvika as we usually called him - had been chosen by Harel to be the agent who would actually stop Eichmann near the bus stop and overpower him before bundling him into the waiting car. He had been chosen because he was known to be a strong and fast fighter. His speed was an essential part of his nature. Like many of us, he had managed to escape from Nazi Europe and arrive in Mandatory Palestine before the War of Independence. From the stories he had told us, he had been something of a wild teenager. With a gang of like-minded youths he used to steal from cars and shops and then exploit his intimate knowledge of the alleys and side-streets of Haifa to make his getaway.

Later he had joined the *Haganah* who had learned to use his restless energy and unconventional knowledge and skills. They taught him to use explosives, make bombs, set up booby- traps and clear mines. After an exciting number of activities during the

War of Independence he had joined the secret service.

But it was not only his natural patriotism and restlessness that motivated Zvika to take part in this operation. Much of his desire to capture Eichmann and bring him back to Israel stemmed from what he had learned from his mother. Before he left Poland, she had told him that his married sister, Fruma, had wanted to leave the country with the rest of the family but that her husband had not agreed with her. He had convinced her that the violent Nazi anti-Semitism was merely a passing phase and that life would settle down again in the near future. But it was not to be, and Fruma and her family were caught by the Nazis. From letters later Zvika's mother had received after the war, he learned that Fruma and her family had been murdered near Lublin, eighty miles south-east of Warsaw.

Zvika was an ideal man to be on our team. He was brilliant at disguises and at following people and had the ability to blend into any situation where he found himself. By borrowing a hat, a suit or thick glasses, he could easily transform himself into a completely different character. He was also a very talented artist. He wasted no opportunity to draw and even while sitting in a café, he would find the time to paint and sketch pictures of the local population. Later, he would paint an impressive, sad portrait of his sister, Fruma, as well as making sketches of Eichmann, our prisoner in the safe-house.

But for tomorrow, he was going to use his hands. Not for art, but for snatching Eichmann from a dark, quiet street as the first stage of his journey to Israel and justice. Actually, to say that he was going to use his hands isn't strictly true. Zvika had bought a pair of leather gloves especially for this purpose. As he told me, he didn't want to soil himself by touching this arch-murderer with his bare hands.

It was interesting how the different members of the team were reacting and thinking about their own roles in catching our victim. Like me, Zvika had learned all he could about Eichmann: what he had done during the war as well as being responsible for the death of his sister and her family. He was out for revenge. Some of the team wanted to talk about Eichmann and his past while others preferred to keep their thoughts to themselves.

Harel expressed his feelings by stressing the historical importance of our operation and told us that we had been chosen by destiny to make sure that one of the most evil men who had ever lived would be made to stand trial at last. "This will be," he said, "the first time that the Jews will judge their murderers; and the whole world will hear about it. You must not fail. Everything will depend on you."

That night, lying on my bed in *Tira*, thinking about Harel's words, I wondered what could go wrong. Would a nosy neighbor suddenly appear and interfere with our plans? What if Eichmann managed to shout for help and one or more of his sons rushed out to help him? What if, for some reason, he didn't show up at all? What would happen if we were stopped at one of Buenos Aires' innumerable police blockades or that we had an accident? And then the one nagging question that none of us could answer until we had him in our hands: Was the man really Eichmann himself?

But at the moment there was nothing else we could do. We had refined our plans as much as possible. We had taken them apart to find the weak points and had tried to plan for any emergency. Although some of us may have looked as calm as the Sea of Galilee on a windless day, we were all as tense and taut as the proverbial bowstring. By this time tomorrow we would know whether we had succeeded or not.

While I was trying to keep calm, Zvika Malkin had been walking around, practicing sudden half-nelson neck-grabs on his team-mates. Shalom Danny, our special forger, was also feeling nervous, hoping that all the counterfeit documents he had produced would stand up to police and airport security scrutiny. As far as I could see, he had no reason to be concerned. This quiet and somewhat withdrawn professional had to be one of the best forgers ever. He could be asked to create a visa, a driving-license or a date-stamped passport and then produce a faultless document within hours. He always traveled with the tools of his trade, together with a few half-completed sketches, brushes and tubes of paint. These were his cover. If he were stopped, he could always claim that he was an artist.

Like several of the team, this gaunt, sad-looking man had survived the Holocaust but his father had been murdered at Bergen-Belsen. Using his skills, Danny had forged passes that had enabled him and his immediate family to survive by hiding out somewhere in Austria. Then when he had the opportunity he made his way to Palestine. After the War of Independence he studied art in Paris and from there, had helped the *Mossad* by forging documents and passports which enabled thousands of Moroccan Jews to escape persecution and make their way to the newly founded State of Israel.

That night he had showed me the false Israeli passport and flight crew identification card he had prepared for Eichmann. They were made out to Ze'ev Zichroni, an El Al flight navigator. They showed a photograph of a balding clerk-like face next to the details, which regularly appeared on such documents: name, profession, height, and color of eyes and hair. Danny had done this cleverly by working in some genuine details together with Eichmann's new cover. This 'Ze'ev Zichroni' – a typical Israeli name – was born in Austria on 12 December 1906, but his Israeli address was given as 83 Yahalom Street, Ramat Gan, an ordinary Tel-Aviv suburb.

In the same way, Danny had also prepared similar documents for other members of the team. For the purposes of airport security and the flight back home, Harel was to become Haim Ben-Dror, an El Al flight engineer born in Afula and our doctor, Yona Elian, was now an ex-French citizen, Joseph Aronovitz who, like Eichmann, would also be listed as an El Al flight navigator.

It was this scrupulous attention to every detail, both by Danny and the rest of the team that would contribute to the success of our operation – or not. Would it be enough? I thought as I drifted off into a restless sleep. Only time would tell. Tomorrow we would know.

Chapter Fourteen
Final Preparations

11 May 1960. After an unsettling and dream-filled night – somewhat like Richard III's night before the fateful Battle of Bosworth - I woke up and got out of bed. Pulling the heavy curtains aside, I noticed that the clouds were dark and threatening. Huh! Wintertime in the southern hemisphere, I thought as I imagined people at home who would be sunbathing on the Tel-Aviv beaches while I was hoping to catch Eichmann. I looked out beyond the walled perimeter of the safe house and saw a young couple, hand in hand was walking past, all bundled up in heavy coats, the man carrying a rolled-up black umbrella.

Would the rain help us or not? On the one hand, it would mean that there would be fewer people and cars about but, on the other hand, it might mean that Eichmann would change his daily routine, which would then spoil our plans. I shrugged. There was nothing that I could do about the weather other than hope it would be in our favor.

Shaving quickly and getting dressed in darker clothes than I normally wore, I went downstairs to have breakfast.

"Come on, lazybones, we've a job to do today," Aharoni winked at me. "There's eggs and salad ready and Judith has made a pot of coffee. Is that all right?"

I said it was and sat down to join the others. A few minutes later Judith brought over a tray bearing six steaming mugs of coffee. I noticed she had put a small vase of flowers on the table and two larger ones on the window-sill. If anyone had decided to look over the outside wall of the safe- house, all that they would have seen was a large middle class house, complete with half-open curtains and vases of flowers. It was nice to have a woman's touch about the place. It added a feeling of homeliness to our rather masculine world and the bachelor-type existence we had been living since the beginning of the operation here.

After breakfast, Harel, who had arrived in the meanwhile from one of the other safe houses, handed out new identity documents and driving licenses. We studied them carefully and then put on the clothes which we would wear that night including wigs and glasses as well as fake beards and moustaches. These would have to match the photos staring out at us from Danny's brilliantly executed passports and other documents.

As part of his own preparations, Harel gave each one of us an itinerary of the various cafés he would be using as temporary 'offices' in Buenos Aires for the next few days. This list contained the names and addresses of the cafés and the specific times of when and where he could be contacted.

The fact that the *Memuneh* was actually 'on site' was very rare. It meant that 'Operation Eichmann' must have been very important for him, both personally and professionally.

Before leaving to return a couple of our rented cars, I went upstairs with Aharoni and Moshe Tabor to make a final check on the special room where we would be holding Eichmann from the time we grabbed him until we were ready to take him to the airport for the flight home. This room had been carefully prepared by Tabor. No doubt, as with many of us on the team, it had given him special satisfaction in doing so especially as he knew that the Nazis had murdered many of his family in Lithuania during the war. Tabor could best be described as a 'gentle giant'. However, over the years I had known him to be less than gentle when it came to overcoming some of the 'opposition' we had had to deal with.

He had arrived in Palestine in 1924 when he was seven years old and had later joined the British Army's Jewish Brigade. Toward the end of the war, when he had learned what the Nazis had done to his family, he had joined one of the unofficial *Nokdim* Revenge Squads operating mainly in Austria and Germany. Like the squad of which I was a member, his squad had also tracked down many SS men and quietly killed them, disposing of their bodies in lakes or abandoned buildings. As far as Tabor and his fellow Jewish soldiers were concerned, it was important to rid the world of these Nazis as quickly as possible before some sort of order descended on Europe once again.

In the period preceding 'Operation Eichmann,' Tabor and Malkin had taken part in various operations tracking down German scientists who were trying to help the Egyptians develop their anti-Israel missile technology.

As I went upstairs with Tabor and entered the small 'cell' he had constructed for Eichmann, I noticed a special glint in his eye.

"Just imagine, Haim, Adolf Eichmann, *yemach sh'mo*, being held here as a prisoner, here in this room that I have specially built for him. True," he added, his eyes now misting over, "it won't help bring my family back, but it will help me to know that I did something to bring him to face his accusers."

We looked around the small ten-by-twelve foot room, which Tabor had designed. It looked like a normal part of the house, just in case anyone not on our team did come into the safe house.

"You know, it gave me such pleasure in planning all the details and then carrying them out," he said. "Do you see those thick blankets covering the windows and nailed to the walls? They'll stop him looking out and also muffle any screams, although I think I heard Harel say that he'll be gagged or maybe sedated most of the time that he'll held here."

"Moshe," I asked. "What's that bell for? Room service?"

"Sure, Haim," he smiled sarcastically. "That's for you to bring him his morning coffee and croissants. No, my friend," he added, but not smiling this time. "That is a special emergency bell. It'll be rung from downstairs or from the front gate to tell anyone guarding him here that the police or whoever have come to search the house."

"Well, let's hope it won't ever be rung," I said fervently. "That's all we need, police interference."

Tabor nodded in agreement and checked out the storage space in the little room and showed me that the bed was attached to the floor.

"And of course," I said, "we must remember never to leave anything here that he could use to escape or cry for help or..."

"Or even try and kill himself," Tabor added. "That would be just too much. Having made all this effort and then to let him escape punishment would simply be not fair."

"That's sure some understatement," I said. "But come now, I don't really think we're likely to let anything like that happen. So let's get on and finish our other preparations."

We left the room after a last look to ensure that we had left nothing behind and that everything was ready for our 'guest.' Tabor slid a panel across the door so that if anyone did come into the house, all that they would see was a cream colored wall covered with four cheap typically Argentinian views of the rolling Pampas plains on that side of the room.

Leaving Tabor with Danny, I went out into the closed-off courtyard with Aharoni to check on the tires of the Buick. I had had a feeling that one of the rear tires had a slow puncture in it. I had to make sure the car was ready for this operation. It was not.

"We've got a flat battery," I said, trying to start the engine. "Switch on the lights."

I did, and they glowed for a few seconds before going out completely.

"Wait a minute. I'll check the battery contacts and try again. Maybe last night's dampness caused a bad contact."

I undid the terminals, dried all the wires and then tightened up the small bolts again. "Try again," I told Aharoni.

He did but all we heard was a faint click from the starter motor. He got out of the car and shrugged his shoulders. "We'll have to take out the dead battery and see if we can buy a new one. We don't have any choice."

We took one of the other cars and twenty minutes later we stopped at a small garage leading to Route 202 where we bought a new battery. As I drove the Chevy back to *Tira*, Aharoni said he thought we had paid too much, but all I could do was shrug my shoulders. What else could we have done?

"Let's hope that's the only problem we have today," Aharoni

said as we drove through the gates of the Tira safe-house. "Now let's go and find the others."

We found them downstairs. Two of them were playing gin-rummy, Danny was trying to solve a crossword puzzle and Tabor was scribbling some numbers on a diagram on a piece of squared paper. "It's a math problem I'm trying to work out, but I'm stuck. See if you can help me."

Leaving Aharoni to help him, I went back outside to check up on the license plates. Up to now, we had been driving around using the regular Argentinian black and orange ones but now we had pale blue ones ready - the ones that the diplomatic corps used. Past experience had taught us that by using such plates, the local police were less likely to stop and search our cars.

"Have you got the car licenses in your pockets that match the new plates?" I asked Aharoni who had come out of the house to ask me about the Buick's tires.

"Yes," he said pulling out the long yellow document headed *Municipalidad de la Ciudad de Buenos Aires Dirección de Rentas*. This was followed by details of the rental company, its address as well as the make and license number of the car.

"Good. I'll go and check that the bolts holding the number plates on are well oiled so we can make a quick change." I did so and then said to Aharoni, "You know what else we can do? We can do the trick we used to do on the kibbutz when we wanted to drive the cars and tractors when we were under age. Smear some oil on the number plates and then throw some dust and road dirt on them. They'll be hard to read but 'naturally' dirty."

Aharoni grinned. He hadn't heard of this trick before. "Good idea. We'll see about it later."

By now it was nearly lunch time and some of us had to have a final meeting with Harel and Eitan. Since we did not want too many cars to be seen entering and leaving the courtyard of the safe house, we met in a cheap restaurant in a side street not far from the center of Buenos Aires arriving there in ones and twos. There, among the grilled steaks and empanadas so beloved by the

Argentinians, we went over our final plans once again and then discussed some of the technical details.

We decided that it might be a good idea if we had a siesta, a short rest, in the afternoon so that we would be fully ready for action that evening.

"Haim, Haim, wake up!" I felt a persistent tapping on my shoulder. "Time to get ready."

I was instantly awake and went to splash some cold water on my face. Like the others, I put on my disguise and went down to the courtyard to make sure that both of the cars were running well. The Buick would be the car for the snatch and the Chevrolet would be the back-up vehicle. Aharoni got into the driver's seat of the Buick, Eitan sat next to him and Malkin and Tabor sat in the back. As I walked over to the Chevrolet I could hear some strange persistent muttering coming from the back seat of the Buick. I smiled to myself. It was Malkin endlessly repeating the Spanish phrase he would use to ask Eichmann for help as he walked past the Buick with its upraised hood.

I got into the Chevrolet's driving seat and Shalom sat next to me. The doctor with his medical bag containing injections and sedatives sat in the back next to Yaacov Gat.

That morning, Doctor Elian had told me that he hoped he wouldn't have to sedate Eichmann after we caught him.

"Why not?" I asked. "Surely that will make our job easier?"

"Not necessarily, Haim. We don't know which drugs, if any, he's taking and what his general state of health is. If he's been taking a certain medication or had an alcoholic drink a short time beforehand, the sedatives could endanger his life."

Huh, I thought. To kill him unintentionally before we could bring him home to face his judges. That's all we needed. I was brought out of these pessimistic thoughts by Aharoni calling out my name.

"Haim, are you ready?"

I gave him a thumbs-up which he returned and we pointed the

two cars at the courtyard's double gates. Yaacov Gat was standing there to open them and we slowly pulled out. Stopping just long enough for him to close them and climb into the back of my car, we set off.

This was it. Now we would see if all our plans and preparations had been in vain or not. 'Operation Eichmann' was now entering a critical phase. It was one thing to say, "Let's grab him and bring him back to Israel," but would we actually be able to carry this out? In an hour or two we would know whether we had succeeded, at least with the 'grab' part of our plan.

Chapter Fifteen
"Un Momentito Señor"

The moment we left *Tira* we separated and each car made its own way to a pre-arranged meeting place not far from Eichmann's house. While some of us had been busy in the safe house that morning, others had gone out to check the area to see as far as possible that there were no road-works, police checkpoints or barriers set up in this part of San Fernando. We had to make sure that nothing would interfere with our getaway plans.

It was quite dark when we pulled up at our pre-arranged meeting place, at the point where Route 202 intersects with Garibaldi Street. Malkin and Tabor got out of the Buick and raised the large hood and waited. They were both wearing wigs and Tabor was also wearing a dark overcoat. Apart from Aharoni, who was wearing a dark suit and tie in order to look respectable in case a policeman happened to appear and ask him some questions, the rest of us were wearing dark jackets and slacks.

As we sat there waiting in the dusk, with dark storm clouds swirling in over the horizon, I began wondering what Eichmann was doing now and how this evening's actions would affect his life – and ours – in the future.

From our recent observations, we hoped that Eichmann would be carrying out his normal daily routine. Two of our men had noted that, as usual, he had left for work that morning. He caught the 203 bus to the Mercedes-Benz plant where he worked as a foreman and would stay there all day until he returned home, getting off the bus at 7:40 in the evening. He would get off the bus, walk the short distance home and there spend the rest of the evening with his wife, Vera, and one or more of his four sons.

This was his daily routine, a routine we had noted that he had not deviated from during all the time from where we had been observing him. This had been from a safe hiding place further up the road, hidden in the grassy, overgrown railroad embankment. We had also found out that   he   had   not   joined   any

180

political or social club which would cause him to be away for the evenings and that he did not go out anywhere with his wife or family. It was this dull predictable routine that we were counting on as a major factor in the success of our operation.

And now we were waiting for him. Waiting to close the trap on this unsuspecting victim.

That's right, I thought. This time it will be you, you, Adolf Eichmann, who'll be the victim and not one of the millions of innocent people you murdered in Europe twenty years ago.

Suddenly I could feel my whole body becoming even tenser and I could sense that the others in the Chevrolet were also feeling the same. The 203 bus was approaching; its headlights cutting through the inky black darkness. Automatically, we lowered ourselves in our seats and waited for Eichmann to make his appearance.

Now we could hear it approach. Its heavy tires made a crunching sound on the gravel as it slowed down and then came to a halt at the bus stop. I could feel my heart pounding as I cautiously peered out of the window and watched the passenger door open, and I waited for Eichmann to step down. But he didn't. The only person who did was a short fat woman carrying an overfull shopping bag. The driver waited for a few seconds and then, with a grinding of gears, the old bus continued on its way down Route 202.

"What's happened?" I whispered to the others. "Where is he? Has he found out somehow?"

Shalom shrugged. "Don't know. Maybe he just missed the bus. We'll simply have to wait for the next one. That's what our instructions say."

"When's it due?" asked Gat.

"In about ten minutes. So keep quiet and keep your eyes peeled."

"For what?"

"For anything."

What an anticlimax, I thought. All that planning, and for what? Had he found out somehow, and if so, how? Had we become careless over the past few days and given ourselves away? I was sure I wasn't the only one who was thinking like this. Suddenly my thoughts were distracted as I noticed a young man on a bicycle pedal over to where Malkin and Tabor were crouched over under the hood of the Buick. From the cyclist's and Malkin's gestures it appeared that the young man was offering to help the two apparently stranded motorists. I saw Malkin shake his head, look at Tabor who did the same. Then they closed the hood quietly as if they had fixed the problem. Malkin appeared to thank the young man and waved him on his way. As soon as he was out of sight, they lifted up the hood again and returned to their previous ambush positions.

"Let's hope we don't have any more Good Samaritans," a voice said from the back.

"True, but when's the next bus?" Shalom asked quietly. "It should have been here by now."

"Here it is," I said, seeing its lights approaching in the rear-view mirror from where I sat slumped down in the front seat. Like the first bus, its tires crunched on the roadside gravel as it drew up and stopped at the bus-stop. The doors opened and a man stepped down and began to walk in the direction of Eichmann's house. But it was not Eichmann. It was a tall curly-haired man carrying a carton of some sort, which made light metallic noises as it rattled with his springy step. Unknown to him, eight pairs of eyes were watching him as he walked up Garibaldi Street and straight past Eichmann's house at number fourteen.

Only then did we look at each other. Frustration, disappointment and questions were written over all our faces. What had gone wrong? It was possible that he had missed his regular bus but for a man like Eichmann who, as far as we knew, was as precise and predictable as a Swiss watch to miss two buses, that was too much. For the past week, we had observed him getting off the bus at 7.40 exactly every evening - and now

182

this. It just did not make any sense. What were we to do?

Suddenly I felt a light tapping sound on the passenger side front door and Eitan squeezed in. "What's up? I asked. "Has something gone wrong?"

Eitan shrugged his shoulders. "I don't know what's happened," was all he could say.

"Are we going to pack it in for tonight?" Gat asked. "How long can we wait here without someone becoming suspicious?"

"I know, I know," Eitan replied in a flat voice. "But I've just spoken to the others and we'll wait for the next bus. Let's hope we'll be lucky this time." He shrugged his shoulders again and looked at us though his thick glasses. "Maybe there is no explanation. Maybe he just left work late. Maybe there was a problem there. Who knows?"

Trying to smile encouragingly, he slipped out of the car and crouching down, he ran back to the Buick. Just as we saw him climb in from the side not facing the street, we saw the lights of a car approach us from the distance. Its headlights were cutting through the dark, lighting up the embankment we had been using as our observation spot.

"I wonder who that is?" I whispered and then realized it was pointless to whisper as whoever it was could not have heard me anyway. However, it didn't matter as we saw from its headlights that the driver had turned off in the direction of San Fernando leaving us tensed up and waiting in the dark again.

"How long are we going to wait for?" asked Gat, popping a piece of gum into his mouth.

"Don't know," Shalom replied. "Eitan didn't say. We'll just have to take our lead from him and... Look! There's another bus coming. Everyone get down."

Again we all slid down low in our seats and watched intently as the third 203 bus drew up at the rusting bus-stop. We all heard the now familiar crunching sound of the bus's wide tires on the roadside gravel.

"Look!" I hissed. "There are two people getting off. A fat lady and there's a man behind her."

"Is it Eichmann?" Gat whispered.

"Yes, I think so."

"Are you sure?"

"Yes, pretty sure." And as I said this, the passenger doors closed and the bus pulled out into the road and started moving off down Route 202, leaving the area quiet and dark.

"That's him," I said. "I'm sure of it now."

"How do you know?"

"From the way he looks, balding and glasses; and from the way he walks, bent forward as if he's in a hurry to get home."

Carefully wiping away some of the condensation that had steamed up the inside of the windshield, I stared out to where Eichmann was drawing close to the front of the Buick. I saw Malkin suddenly step out from where he had been hidden by the car's large hood and face Eichmann. I would have done anything to have been there at that moment and this is how Malkin described the snatch to us later that evening.

"There he is," Moshe whispered to me. "He's coming. Are you ready?"

I nodded and stretched up from where I had been crouched over under the hood ready to spring onto him.

"Look!" Moshe whispered to me. "He's slipped his right hand into his pocket. Maybe he's got a gun there. Be careful!"

"This threw my plans for a moment. I had planned to grab him in a certain way so that I could pin his arms behind his back while I covered his mouth. All I needed was for him to cry out for help not far from his house. Now I had to make sure he wouldn't reach for the gun in his pocket.

"He was now only a few yards away. I could even hear his footsteps in the dark. I could hear them coming toward me, every one shortening the distance between us. My heart was pounding. This was it! I stepped out straight in front of him from the car. He slowed down, cocking his head to one side.

"*Un momentito, señor,*" I said quietly.

"Our eyes came together and suddenly I saw realization and panic spread over his face. He sprang back turning to run but I reached out and grabbed him. I pinned his right hand to his body – the hand I thought that was holding the gun. He pulled back trying to wriggle out of my bear-hug and then he suddenly tripped on a rock half-hidden in the mud. We both fell rolling onto the ground by the side of the road. He was on top of me but, try as he might, he could not escape because of the way I was holding him. I could feel his terrified breath on my face and I immediately clapped my hand over his mouth to stop him from calling out. Then I rolled over on top of him. The second I let go of his mouth he tried to shout something but then, at that point, you, Zvi, started revving the engine to drown out his shouts. I'm telling you, the noises he made sounded like the desperate cries of a cornered animal.

"Where's Moshe? I thought. It seemed as if minutes had passed and no-one was helping me. I was wrong. Only seconds had passed since I had stopped Eichmann and now Moshe with his powerful bear-hug was helping me subdue him before dragging him out of the ditch into which we had rolled. Eichmann kept struggling and tried to stand up. But that was useless on his part. Between my knowledge of the martial arts and Moshe's grip he didn't stand a chance. Suddenly Moshe kicked Eichmann's feet away from under him and he fell completely, like a sack of potatoes. All the fight had gone out of him. He stopped trying to scream and I eased my gloved hand off of his mouth. I stuffed a rag into it and Moshe and I threw him into the back of the car. I immediately covered him over with a blanket and Eitan covered his eyes with some blacked out goggles. We didn't want him to recognize any of us or the route we were taking back to the safe house.

"Then when we thought he would remain still, he started wriggling from side to side under the thick blanket.

"*Ein Laut und Sie sind tot* – One more shout out of you and you are dead," I said remembering my German. He stopped moving completely as if I had hit him hard. Suddenly in the darkness of the car I felt more wriggling under the blanket.

"What's happening?" I asked.

"Don't worry, Zvi. It's only me," Eitan grinned and pulled out a cylindrical object out from under the blanket. "There's your gun," he said and handed me Eichmann's flashlight. "I bet he's wishing he'd used it tonight, but now we've got him it doesn't matter, does it?"

Suddenly, Eichmann started wriggling again, but not as violently as before. Zvi, who was now in the back hissed at Eichmann in German, "Lie still and nothing will happen to you. If you don't, we will shoot you. Do you understand?"

Suddenly he stopped wriggling and lay there completely still. Had we suffocated him with the gag? Eitan pulled the rag out of his mouth and all we could hear was his heavy breathing and watch his chest rise and fall under the blanket.

"Quick, let's get away from here before anyone sees us," Eitan said and we started driving up the road in the direction of San Fernando. We stopped after half a mile. Eichmann had not made a sound. Zvi bent down over Eichmann's body again and just as he was about to say something, Eichmann lifted his head and in a thick but clearly understood voice said in German, "I am resigned to my fate."

These were the best words I had heard for a long time. We had not suffocated him and we were sure now that our 'passenger' was indeed Adolf Eichmann. We had successfully carried out the first part of our operation!

Chapter Sixteen
The First Interrogation Sessions

Driving the second car, I followed the Buick for about a mile along Route 202 before we pulled into a dark side street. Our presence there was shielded by the darkness and some thick trees. We quickly switched our license plates again and now both cars were fitted with home-made but convincingly looking Argentinian diplomatic plates. We also made sure that our forged Argentinian diplomatic papers were at hand in case we were stopped.

"Isn't it ironic, Haim?" asked Gat. "We're using false Austrian papers to catch this ex-Austrian scum. Yes, I like that. By the way, what's Rafi doing with him now?"

"He's feeling under his shirt for any identifying marks, such as where he had his old SS tattoo removed."

"What? Isn't he sure even now that we've got the right man?"

"Yes, I'm sure he is," I said. "It's just that he's doing what Harel told him to do. We don't want any more mistakes like the Tubianski affair, do we?" I was referring to the War of Independence incident when Meir Tubianski, an Israeli army officer, was wrongly executed for treason.

Eitan came over to us rubbing his hands. "OK, everybody, I'm sure we've got the right man so let's get moving. We still have a lot more work to do this evening."

We got into the cars again and I began following Aharoni back to *Tira*. Ten minutes later we came to a stop. We had arrived at a railroad crossing. We were expecting this and had no alternative but to wait for the long and slow-moving goods train to pass. Later, Aharoni told me that while we were waiting, Eichmann had started wriggling about and making noises again despite his being gagged and lying under a heavy blanket. "I warned him to be still and not make another sound, otherwise I would shoot him, and after that he lapsed into silence."

What Eichmann did not know was that for this particular operation, we had been ordered not to carry any guns. If for any reason we had been stopped and been found in possession of any firearms, this would have complicated matters intensely. Harel said that we all knew enough ways to defend ourselves; and besides Malkin was an expert in the martial arts.

Eventually the railroad crossing barriers lifted and we continued on our way. Remaining close behind the Buick, I followed it until it turned off the main road again, and we changed our number plates for the second time that evening. Having waited at the railroad crossing for nearly ten minutes, someone may have become suspicious of two large American cars traveling together bearing diplomatic plates. We couldn't risk that. We set off once again and an hour after the snatch, we pulled into the courtyard of *Tira*. Aharoni drove the Buick straight into the open garage and its doors closed immediately behind him. Eichmann was hauled out of the back of the car and rushed immediately into the safe house. Now that he was inside *Tira*, away from the possibility of any prying eyes, he was now truly our prisoner. He didn't try to speak and none of us spoke to him.

Taking over from Moshe, I helped Aharoni take him upstairs to the room we had prepared for him and left him standing in the middle of the room, blindfolded, gagged and completely bewildered. This room was to be his cell for the week that followed.

He stood there completely motionless. Only his fists were opening and closing in some sort of nervous reaction. Reaction to what? He did not know. He could not know. He must have been terrified, standing there rigidly still wearing his ridiculous black-taped goggles. But what he thought was going to happen to him wasn't our problem.

Dr. Elian moved forward to carry out his first medical inspection. As he touched Eichmann's chest, the ex-Nazi flinched and instinctively jumped back. Then consulting a list of distinguishing marks that Dr. Fritz Bauer had sent Harel, Dr.

Elian methodically measured and examined Eichmann's body.

A three centimeter scar beneath the left eyebrow Two gold bridges in upper jaw
A one centimeter scar on left tenth rib Tattoo under left armpit listing blood type Height about 5 ft.10ins.
Circumference of head: 22 ins. Dark blond hair.
Blue-gray eyes
Shoe size: 8½

Without saying a word, apart from occasionally muttering "*ken*, yes" to himself, Dr.Elian completed his inspection and nodded to Eitan that Eichmann was ready for the next stage of his interrogation.

"I've checked his teeth as well, the false ones, I mean," the doctor added, "to see that he hadn't hidden any potassium cyanide capsules in them. It wouldn't be fair if he killed himself like Goering did at the Nuremberg Trials, now would it?"

Now it was Aharoni's turn to take over.

"You and you," he said, pointing to me and Gat, deliberately not using our names. "Lay him down on the bed."

Eichmann flinched again as we touched him, but allowed us to lay him down on the iron bedstead without showing any resistance. At this point he was still fully clothed, although somewhat disheveled where our doctor had pulled his shirt out of his trousers to check his body.

"*Was ist Ihr Name?* - What is your name?" Aharoni barked at him.

Eichmann was silent for a moment and then replied weakly, "*Ich bin Ricardo Klement.*" Aharoni continued in German.

"*Was ist Ihr Name?*" he repeated.

"Ricardo Klement."

Aharoni put his face next to that of Eichmann who, on feeling Aharoni's breath on his cheeks, pulled his own face away. We could see that he was petrified with fear.

"Für das dritte Mal, was ist Ihr Name? For the third time, what is your name?"

"Ricardo Klement."

Aharoni smacked one of his fists into his own open palm. The sudden sharp noise echoed around the small room. It must have terrified our blindfolded captive, but none of us was concerned by that.

"Für das vierte und letzte Mal, was ist dein Name? For the fourth and last time, what is your name?"

"K-K-Klement. R-R-Ricardo Klement."

Aharoni turned to Gat and me. "Take off his coat, jacket and shirt," he said in Hebrew. "Now we'll have some answers."

As we rolled Eichmann over to remove his clothes, we could feel him tremble uncontrollably.

I expected him to shout and scream and had a wad of cloth ready to gag him if he did. I threw the muddy clothes into the corner and Aharoni continued with his interrogation. Apart from removing his top clothes, we hadn't touched him at all.

"Now I am asking you again," Aharoni said quietly in German. "What is your name?"

"Otto Heninger," Eichmann replied quietly, using one of the false names he had once used to escape from the Allies after the war.

Aharoni decided to change tactics. Poking the scar where Eichmann's SS number had once been tattooed, Aharoni asked him sharply, "What was your SS number?"

Eichmann said nothing.

"Your number was 45526."

"Nein. Es war 45326."

"Good. Now tell me your name."

"Adolf Eichmann."

You could hear a collective sigh of relief from all of us standing by the bed. Although we knew we had caught the right man, it was a great feeling to have this confirmed. A great load had been taken off our minds. There were no more thoughts of 'What if?'

"Now stand up," Aharoni said to Eichmann, prodding him to get off the bed. He got up and stood there once again in the middle of the small room. A pathetic balding figure standing there barefoot in his grubby undershirt and mud-stained trousers.

As he was standing there, trembling and fearful, I couldn't help feeling that this miserable creature, this once evil bureaucratic butcher had once sent millions of innocent Jews and others to their deaths in his well-organized extermination camps. Was this shabby individual responsible for so much pain and murder? It was almost impossible to imagine.

Aharoni then looked at Eitan, nodded and leaving Eichmann standing there fearfully, the *Mossad* man began to ask him a list of prepared follow-up questions. These were deliberately jumbled up so as not to give him time to organize his thoughts.

"What's your date of birth?"

"19 March 1906."

"Where were you born?"

"Solingen, Germany."

"What's the name of your third son?"

"Dieter."

"When was he born?"

"29 March 1942."

"What is your shoe size?"

"Nine."

"When did you come to Argentina?"

"1950."

"What is your size in shirts?"

"Forty-four."

"Under what name were you born?"

"Adolf Eichmann."

Yes! He had admitted it again. Just as I was feeling good about this, Malkin tapped me on the shoulder. "H.," he whispered. "I've just realized that Eichmann doesn't have his glasses with him. They must have fallen off by the roadside or into the ditch when I was trying to subdue him." I shrugged.

"So what? He doesn't need them now."

"I know that but what if someone in his family finds them? That will give them a clue to what happened to him tonight. They'll probably be broken or twisted and covered with mud. I must go back and find them."

"Are you sure? And if so, how will you go? You won't be able to use the Buick or the Chevy."

"I know. I'll take the 203 bus. I know the way by now. I'll just go and check with Rafi first."

On his return he told me that he had caught the bus without any problems and had got off near where he had fought with Eichmann. Carefully searching the area in the dark so he wouldn't attract any attention, he found a few broken pieces of glass in the mud and threw them away in a wide circle. He continued looking for the frames by the roadside and in the ditch for a few more minutes but then gave up. Then he returned to *Tira* by bus without any problems. It was only much later that we found out what had happened to Eichmann's missing glasses.

As soon as Malkin had left to complete his own mission, I returned to the room in time to hear Eichmann ask for something to drink. Perhaps as we had not hit or hurt him in any way, he was trembling less and feeling a little bolder.

"Can I have some wine, please. It will help to steady my nerves."

"No, you can have some water."

He finished off the glass quickly and then started talking of his own volition. "I knew you were Israelis as soon as you told me to keep quiet in the car or you would shoot me," he said. "I recognized what you were saying was Hebrew."

"How?"

"Because before the war I had learnt some from Rabbi Leo Baeck. Remember, I was our expert on the Jews," he said with some sort of pride. "I knew you were talking Hebrew even though I couldn't understand what you were saying. Listen," he added, sounding more confident. "I can say your special prayer. *Shma Yisroel, Hashem Elokenu...*"

"Stop!" Aharoni shouted at him. "How dare you say our holy prayers! Keep your mouth shut!"

Aharoni was right. Even though most of us were not religious, hearing this evil man reciting the *Shema* was anathema. In fact, as he started to recite this prayer, I noticed that the team started closing in on him as he stood there blindfolded; they were ready to hit or throttle him. He was completely unaware of the feelings of intense loathing he had caused by displaying his very limited knowledge of Hebrew. What he had tried to do was either to show how clever he was or try to ingratiate himself with his Hebrew-speaking captors. He failed in both.

Eitan raised his hand and signaled for us to back off and calm down. It was a tense moment. Many of us had lost family and friends in the Holocaust and here was an opportunity to find some crude form of relief from the memories and the pain. A few seconds passed and we started to step backwards from the goggled and half-naked balding creature who had caused so much pain and suffering.

Aharoni, who spoke the most fluent German among us, signaled for us to leave the room. "Make yourselves something to eat," he said in Hebrew. "You deserve it after tonight's work. I'll be down soon and someone will come up and relieve me here."

We left the room and since it wasn't my turn to be on guard duty that night, that is, to remain in the small cell with Eichmann to make sure that he didn't harm himself in any way, I went to bed after eating a light supper.

The next morning I got up early, washed, shaved and had breakfast. As I was drinking my coffee, Aharoni told me that he had driven to Buenos Aires earlier that morning with Avraham Shalom to return the Buick to the rental agency. They had left the car at a pre-arranged spot and one of the team who had not taken part in last night's snatch returned it after carefully wiping off any fingerprints from the car. He told the clerk in the rental agency that as his wife had suddenly been taken sick, he would not be needing the car for a planned vacation trip.

Later they went to see Harel at one of his café 'offices' to give him a full account of what had happened the night before. As a result, Harel contacted the local *Mossad* agent who sent the message 'The typewriter is OK' to Tel-Aviv. There it was passed on to Ben-Gurion and the Foreign Minister, Golda Meir.

When Aharoni returned, I went upstairs with him to witness the next interrogation session.

The first thing we did was to open the window in order to air the stuffy room. Then Aharoni approached Eichmann and removed the black-taped goggles he had been wearing continuously since we had caught him. As soon as he felt Aharoni's hands on his shoulders he flinched but calmed down when Aharoni removed his goggles. He slowly opened his eyes, blinked a few times and then looked around the bare walls of his cell.

"Sit up straight," Aharoni ordered in German. Eichmann managed to do so, though not easily since one of his legs was shackled to the bed-frame.

"Is that really necessary?" I asked in Hebrew, pointing to the shackles.

Aharoni nodded. "Yes, and just remember who we are dealing with here and also there's still some spunk left in this scum. Remember how long it took us to get him to admit to his real name? He escaped from the Americans after the war; we're not going to let him do that again. No, H, do not be fooled at how helpless and miserable he looks now. This guy is a schemer and if he sees the faintest chance of escaping, he will try and do so. He's spent the last fifteen years being cunning. It's now second nature to him. Don't forget how he told everyone he was Dieter's and Nick's uncle. That was just a small part of it. Don't underestimate him. Just remember who he was and what he did. That's all."

Then Aharoni turned to face our prisoner and said in German, "I have a few questions to ask you and I will be very pleased if you'll answer them truthfully and with as many details as you can."

"*Jawohl, mein Herr.*"

"First of all, can you tell us where Mengele is hiding?" Harel was obviously hoping to catch two ex-Nazi birds for the price of one. He had briefed Aharoni to ask Eichmann hoping that the infamous doctor, Josef Mengele, the doctor who had conducted so many cruel experiments on his 'patients' at Auschwitz, would also be hiding nearby in Argentina, perhaps protected by the ex-Nazi community there.

"I don't know anything about him."

"Is he in Argentina?"

Eichmann shook his head. "I don't know."

"What about Martin Bormann?" Aharoni asked, asking about Hitler's deputy and personal secretary.

Again Eichmann said he knew nothing about him.

"But didn't they help you escape to Argentina?"

"That was a long time ago."

"But didn't some top Nazis help you?"

"*Ja*, but that was about ten years ago. Mengele and Bormann didn't help me then."

"What do you think your family will be doing now, seeing that you didn't come home last night?"

Eichmann shrugged as if he didn't care.

"Will they go to the police?"

"I don't think so. Maybe they'll think I had an accident and that I am now in hospital."

"Will they check out the hospitals?"

Eichmann shrugged again. "I don't know. I don't think so."

"Will your wife do anything? Maybe organize some sort of search?"

"I doubt it."

"Will she ask at your work place why you didn't come home?"

"I don't think so."

"Will your fellow Germans start looking for you?"

"I doubt it. They've got enough of their own problems. They won't want to involve the police in this."

We were pleased to hear him say this. We had been hoping that what he said was true. As events proved, the local German and ex-Nazi community did little to try and find out why he had suddenly gone missing. This was obviously good for us.

Suddenly Aharoni changed his tactics. "Why did you say your name was Ricardo Klement?"

"Because that was the name I've been using for the past few years. I even have documents made out to me under that name."

"So why didn't the rest of your family use that name?"

"What? Do you expect me to ask them to lie for me?" Eichmann asked as if he had been asked to do something really disgusting.

"But one your sons did call himself Klement." Eichmann shrugged. He had no answer for that.

"Why did you say you were Otto Heninger last night?"

"Because that was the name I used for four years immediately after the war when I worked as a lumberjack. I thought that as it worked then, it might work now." He smiled for a second, maybe thinking of his wartime career and then continued. "I managed to fool the Americans with that name and hoped it would work again if I used it now."

"So you don't think your family or friends will do anything about your sudden disappearance? They won't go to the police?" Aharoni repeated.

"I doubt it very much. They may ask a few questions locally but nothing more."

Several months later we learned that almost immediately after their father hadn't returned home that evening, Eichmann's sons, Nick and Dieter, had come to the conclusion that - for some reason - someone or some organization had kidnapped him. They had started a search in the area in which where they lived and of course found nothing. Then they began to remember a few apparently disconnected and unusual encounters that had happened over the previous three months: the two men wanting to buy land in the area, the car driver asking for specific directions and, of course, the whole story of delivering a birthday present from a friend.

Perhaps he had been kidnapped by some Argentinian Jews, or maybe even by the Israelis. They had talked about these possibilities in the past especially as they knew something about their father's wartime anti-Semitic activities.

They concluded that there was only one thing they could do. They went to see Carlos Fuldner, an old-time acquaintance of their father. He lived on the other side of Buenos Aires and had given Eichmann a job as a topographical engineer in his CAPRI company when he had first arrived in the country. Fuldner had then been and still was an important figure in the local ex-German community. He would surely know where their father was, or what had happened to him. After all, their father's first employer had been a friend of Argentina's past President Perón. He had been so influential that the Fuldner Bank at 374 Avenida Cordoba carried his name.

The next day Nick and Dieter went to see him at the bank and told him what they thought might have happened. They added that they thought the kidnappers, whoever they were, might also try and kidnap their mother and their little brother. Fuldner was less excited than Eichmann's sons. He told them that the truth might be less dramatic than what they thought and that their father had probably had some sort of accident on his way home from work. He reminded them how badly paved and lit was the area around their house. Perhaps their father had fallen over or had been hit by a passing car. He guessed that he was now lying in a hospital bed somewhere.

"Or a morgue," Nick had added.

Fuldner said that knowing how poorly organized the Argentinians were, "in comparison to us careful Germans," a day or so might pass before the hospital looking after their father would contact them. He advised them to go home and be patient. He was quite sure that they would soon hear about him. His advice had not satisfied Eichmann's sons and they had pressed him to make some discreet enquiries with the police. In the meanwhile, they told him, they would go to the Mercedes-Benz plant and ask a few questions there.

They were told, yes, he had left a little later than usual because of a last minute meeting but then he had taken his usual bus home. The sons then tried their luck at the San Fernando police station and the hospital but of course the people there could not help them. A day or so later they found his glasses frame, twisted and broken, near the 203 bus-stop but this did not offer any information as to their father's whereabouts. Had there been an accident? It was hard to tell. There was no blood on them. Had he been kidnapped? If so, by whom? They could not tell. They would have to wait two weeks to learn the truth.

Chapter Seventeen
Learning More About Eichmann

After the first two interrogation sessions, life settled down into some sort of normality - normal that is, if you can count living under the same roof with one of the world's most evil men as normal.

We each took it in turn to sit in his 'cell' and keep an eye on him as well as taking turns to guard the safe house. We were concerned that somehow some of the local Germans and ex-Nazis would find out where we were holding him and try and rescue him, even though *Tira* was in a relatively isolated spot.

In addition to our guarding duties, those of us who understood Spanish had the job of listening to the radio to hear whether Eichmann's name was mentioned. Fortunately it was not. All that our listeners heard was news about Argentina's President, Arturo Frondizi, the American election campaign between Kennedy and Nixon as well as other news and gossip about Argentina's approaching national celebrations.

"Is it good?" I asked one evening, "Is it good that we don't hear Eichmann's name on the radio? Maybe the authorities have found out what we've done but are too embarrassed to admit it publicly."

"Because he was a top Nazi and is now living here?"

"Exactly. His presence here can't be bringing much honor and glory to the country, can it?"

"That's true enough," Gat said. "So let's hope Harel gets his plans for getting us out of here moving as soon as possible. I'm getting sick of sharing my life with that Nazi creep. The quicker we're out of here, the better."

The others nodded. We had not joined the secret service to wait on the mass murderer of our people hand and foot.

What also made it harder for us to act as jailers was that we had received orders not to talk to him. Only Aharoni was allowed to interrogate our black-goggled prisoner while he lay on his bed, his leg shackled to the bed-frame.

Sometimes, during the first few days after we had caught him I would accompany Aharoni as he carried out his interrogation. Sometimes he would leave Eichmann on his bed; sometimes he would interrogate him while he sat bound to a simple wooden chair in the middle of the room. The idea, Aharoni explained, was that Eichmann would never know what was happening to him. Aharoni would sit there with a notebook in hand recording the questions and answers and I would sit behind him, a silent observer.

Eichmann was always calm and obedient. No, subservient would be a better word to describe his behavior. He would act like a dog trying to please his master. He never shouted or raised his voice against us or his fate and later when I talked to Aharoni about this and that I thought the spark had gone out of him, Aharoni replied, "Don't let him fool you, Haim. Just remember, a couple of days ago he refused to tell us his name."

"True, he kept insisting that his name was Ricardo Klement."

"Right, that and another couple of false names. No, my friend, we must not be taken in by this man. I'm sure that if he feels he'll be able to fool us, he will try it."

This happened the next day. Eichmann started complaining that he was feeling pains in his chest and wondered whether he hadn't suffered some sort of minor heart attack.

"I haven't slept well the past two nights," he whined. "Maybe you could remove the chains from my leg?"

Aharoni said nothing, but sent Dr. Elian up to check his heart and chest. He found nothing wrong and so our prisoner remained shackled to his bed for the rest of his stay in our safe house.

Over the next three days, under Aharoni's expert questioning, we began to learn something about Eichmann's past. He told Aharoni in great detail how he had escaped from Hungary as the 'Thousand Year Reich' came crashing down around him, both literally and metaphorically. He told us that it was during this period in the winter of 1944 that he had sought out his old

Austrian-born comrade, Ernst Kaltenbrunner, to help him escape.

"Why him?" Aharoni asked quietly.

"Because I thought he was my friend. I'd known him since 1932 when he first brought me into the Nazi party and also into the SS."

"And did he help you?"

"No. I was very disappointed in him. He told me to go away because he didn't want to be connected with me and my wartime activities. At first I couldn't believe that he, a man I'd thought of as a good friend and fellow Nazi and SS officer, would treat me that way. Like an unwanted dog. But I had no choice. I managed to escape on my own, both from the Americans and also from various weak-minded Germans and Austrians who were trying to buy forgiveness by handing SS officers like me over to the authorities."

"And so you called yourself Otto Heninger?"

"*Ja*, and also Otto Eckman and Adolf Barth as well," Eichmann added, volunteering information in an effort to curry favor with Aharoni.

"And what about the name, Ricardo Klement?"

"Ah, I started using that name when I decided to leave Europe and come here to Argentina. I knew that many Germans had come here after the war…"

"Don't you mean ex-Nazis fleeing here?" I couldn't help interrupting.

Eichmann looked over to where I was sitting and said nothing. Aharoni also looked at me and just put a finger to his lips. He looked at Eichmann again. "Tell me about Ricardo Klement," he said.

"As I said, I took that name when I came here after some friends in Lower Saxony had helped me make my escape plans."

"Wasn't it dangerous for you to contact your former SS comrades? One of them might have turned you in to the Americans or the British as some sort of bargaining chip?"

"No, no. There was no problem like that. We remained in touch through secret messages and disguised adverts and notices in the papers. There was also a man called Günther who helped me get in touch with a group connected to the Vatican."

Aharoni noted all this down, then turned to me and said in Hebrew, "H, we'll have to check up on all of this when we get home. But isn't it amazing how easily he's spilling the beans? I thought we'd really have to try and drag all this out of him."

"Maybe it's because he's had it all locked up inside him for too long and now he has to tell someone, you know, like a Catholic confession," I suggested.

Aharoni shrugged and turned back to face our prisoner who was sitting there in his striped pajamas quite comfortably.

"How did you stay in contact with your wife when you were in Argentina and she was still in Germany or Austria?"

"With Vera? Oh, that was easy. We wrote letters to each other and no-one suspected that Herr Klement was really me." He smiled his twisted smile at the memory as if to say 'Oh wasn't I clever? I outsmarted all of you.'

"So if changing your name was so successful, why didn't you change your wife's name and your children's names as well?"

Eichmann shrugged. "For some reason I wasn't able to do so then. There were reasons that I cannot remember now. So I told Vera and the boys what to say if ever anyone asked them about their names. Well, it worked up to now, didn't it?" And he smiled his crooked smile again.

"And where did you live when you came here to Buenos Aires. You didn't live on Garibaldi Street from the beginning, did you?"

Eichmann looked surprised. "How did you know that?"

Aharoni ignored the question. "Well, where did you live when you first came here?"

"On Chacabuco Street. Number 4261. I lived there for almost six years."

"And what did you do there? What was your job? Where did you work?"

Eichmann's chain from his leg to the chair leg rattled as he changed his position.

"I ran a laundry for a while but it didn't work out and I lost money from it."

"Why is that? You were used to running much larger organizations than a laundry, weren't you?"

Eichmann ignored the jibe. "The local Chinese," he said with a sneer. "Their laundry was much cheaper than mine. Their work wasn't as good as mine of course, but they beat us Germans. In the end I was forced to sell my laundry at a loss."

"And then?"

"Then I ran a rabbit farm for someone. I was the manager. But there was a problem. The farm was quite far from Buenos Aires and I could see my family only at the weekends. I wanted to see my four sons grow up. During the war I had been so busy…"

"Murdering Jews," I couldn't help adding.

He ignored me and continued. "I wanted to watch my boys grow up. I didn't want to miss that again."

"And that is when you moved to Garibaldi Street?"

"*Ja*. I didn't have much money after the laundry business collapsed; and land in that part of San Fernando was cheap."

"And that is why you built your own house there, because you didn't have much money?"

"*Ja, ja.*"

"But you didn't have any running water or electricity. Wasn't that a problem for a man with a wife and four children to live like that?"

Eichmann nodded. "*Ja*, it was at first, especially after we moved from Chacabuco Street where we had had those things. Vera wasn't very happy about it and we had a few arguments about this. But in the end she agreed with me especially after I said that as soon as I earned enough money…"

"From your work at Mercedes-Benz?"

203

"*Ja*, I would see about the running water and electricity. But of course, that never happened because you took me away," he said in a voice that accused us of messing up his plans.

"And why was your house registered under the name of Lieble and Fichmann?"

"First of all, I didn't want my name to appear on any official documents. Secondly, I wrote Fichmann so that if there were any problems I could say that it must have been an honest mistake."

"Honest? That's honest?"

Eichmann twisted his mouth and remained silent.

"Did you get any financial help from any of the other ex-Nazis living here in Buenos Aires?"

Eichmann shook his head. "No, not really. I didn't want to ask them and they didn't volunteer to help me. I think they didn't want anything to do with me."

"Why is that? Surely you were an important guy? Weren't you one of Himmler's right hand men?"

"*Ja*, but I think that what I did during the war made them distance themselves from me. Like Kaltenbrunner and the others. This, I thought at the time, was very strange. Kaltenbrunner had given me orders on Christmas Eve 1944 to leave Budapest and because I obeyed him, I was saved from falling into the hands of the Russians. If that had happened, I am sure they would have shot me on the spot, or tortured me. They did that with almost all of the top Nazi and SS officers they caught." He stopped and collected his thoughts. "And besides," he added. "I had also disobeyed Himmler's orders."

"What do you mean, disobeyed? Wasn't he your boss?"

"*Ja*. But when he told me to put a halt to the transportation and deportations from Hungary in the summer of 1944, I didn't obey. I kept it all going as before."

"Why? Hadn't he given you a direct order?"

"*Ja*, but from the time when I was in Budapest, I could see that the situation in the German army was beginning to break down and so I felt that I could afford to disobey orders and not be punished for doing so. And besides, although you called Himmler my boss, in a way he was like me. We were both top SS men who were subject to Hitler's orders. The Führer hadn't told me to stop my transportation activities so I felt I had every right to continue them whatever Himmler said. That was my duty. I had sworn to carry out the Führer's orders and that was what I was doing."

"Even though it meant killing millions of Jews, Gypsies and other non-Aryans as you called them?"

"But they were against the state. I was just doing my duty. I had sworn a personal oath to Hitler and I didn't feel free from it until the end of the war."

"And so for you, Hitler was your great leader?"

"*Ja, ja. Der Führer war infehlbar* – infallible."

By now, Aharoni and I had heard enough from this man. How long could you sit in a small room with a man you loathed, you hated for what he had done and for what he stood for? And besides, the sheer physical situation in the cell itself was miserable. The few items of furniture in the room were plain, depressing and minimal. An iron bed, a cheap wooden table, one chair and four plain off-white walls, only one of them bearing four cheap pictures of Argentina. The single light bulb glowed day and night and the windows were completely sealed. This was done for two reasons. The first was so that we could keep an eye on him all of the time. The second was that we wanted him to lose his sense of time. Aharoni had told me that when a prisoner is in such a 'timeless' state, not knowing whether it is day or night, it is much easier to cross-examine him.

After spending three days observing and listening to Aharoni interrogate Eichmann, I took a break one afternoon. While sitting in the back garden of *Tira* reading a trashy escapist novel, I felt a light tap on my shoulder. I looked up to see Malkin looking down at me.

"Had enough up there?" he asked, turning his head to the villa's second floor.

"Yes. There's a limit to how much you can hear that man justify himself and what he did."

"I agree. That's why to relieve myself from all that I've done some sketching. Here have a look at these."

He pulled out a few pages from the large pouch he often carried and showed me several of his sketches and pictures. I looked at them carefully. I hadn't known that my fellow agent was such a talented artist. It is true that, in the past, I had seen his sketches but I hadn't really paid much attention to them. Now I saw what he had been working on while the rest of us had been guarding, sleeping or just trying to pass the time. As I looked at the pages I saw Eichmann's face staring back at me, superimposed on a map of South America. Although our prisoner must have been wearing his goggles at the time, Malkin had drawn what his eyes looked like, based on the few occasions when he had been allowed to remove them. Malkin had sketched his head – complete with receding hairline and twisted mouth. It was uncannily accurate.

"Here, have a look at this one as well," said Malkin, pushing over a surrealistic picture of Eichmann. Wearing dark glasses, he was lying down on top of a long line of train wagons, each wagon filled with sad faces. The wagons were clearly a symbol of the power that Eichmann had used as a transporter of death, sending all these wretched people to the Nazi death camps. A picture of Hitler's face appeared above the train and in the sky the picture showed the classic symbol of the Ten Commandments with the Hebrew words *Lo Tirtzach* – Do not kill – engraved upon it..

"It reminds me of Picasso's *Guernica* ," I said, returning it to him.

"That's good," he replied. "Because that was the painting I had in mind when I sketched it. I'll finish it later using black, white and brown as the main colors."

He then showed me another two sketches which he also planned to complete later. One was of his sister, Fruma, murdered by the Nazis in Poland in the spring of 1941. The second was of his brother, Jack, who was killed in an accident in June 1949. Both of them looked terribly sad and withdrawn.

Two days later I had another interesting conversation with

Malkin, again in the back garden at *Tira*. I was sitting there reading and enjoying the weak winter sunshine when I felt a light tap on my shoulder. I looked up and saw Malkin standing there. It was clear that he wished to tell me something important.

"Haim, listen to this. I've just broken the rules and I've been talking to Eichmann. I know we're not supposed to but I felt that I just had to ask him a few questions."

"Like what?"

"I asked him what had made him do the things that he'd done?"

"And what was his answer?"

"*Ich hatte den Auftrag zu erfüllen* – I had a job to do."

"What? Just like that? 'I had a job to do,'" I repeated after a few moments. "Murdering millions of people was 'just a job to do'? I know he believed in following orders, but to call the world's greatest murdering machine 'a job,' is something that I cannot understand." I sat there immobile, my eyes closed. Immediately my brain was flooded with grim pictures of the Holocaust: of the little boy surrounded by Nazi soldiers; of the people in the extermination camps pressed against the barbed-wire fences, and of Nazi storm-troopers mocking a bearded old Jew as they sliced off his beard and side-locks.

Malkin's voice cut through my thoughts. "Haim, he claims he hadn't planned what had happened. It just worked out that way. You know, he said that he believed that had no control over any of this. 'I was just following orders.' That was his justification. Everything that he did, he said, was his duty and - as a good German soldier - he had no choice but to do his duty to his Führer and his country."

"Even if it meant killing millions of people?"

"Even if it meant killing millions of people," Malkin repeated. He paused to let these terrible words sink in. "And then he told me that I had to believe him when he said that he had nothing personal against the Jews. This of course I could not swallow. So when I asked him if that was really the case, why had he joined the SS? After all, he knew what they believed in, didn't he?"

"And what did he say to that?"

"He shrugged and said that everyone he knew then was joining the SS." He told me, "We all felt that under Hitler's great leadership fantastic things were about to happen and we all wanted to be a part of it. Remember," he went on, trying to justify his behavior, "I was one of the post-First World War generation. Someone who had grown up during the humiliating years following the Versailles agreement. Now in the thirties, we were living through the terrible Great Depression. Hitler offered, no, promised us a way out of all this darkness, and so of course we took it."

"And this was the man he called *unfehlbar* – infallible," I said. "The one he swore an oath to."

"That's right. All of our six million Jews died because of creatures like him upstairs. Him and Himmler and Goering and all the rest of them. They saw it as their duty to follow Hitler. They never questioned him, his rotten ideology and his methods. That's why we had to catch him and that's why we have to take him home to face his accusers."

"Right, and to tell the rest of the world about him," I added. "It's one thing to talk about extermination camps and millions of victims, but now in a trial when we'll concentrate all of this onto one man, it will personalize this evil. It will bring it all into a sharper focus. "

I paused for a few minutes and then asked Malkin, "Tell me, did he tell you all this freely or did you have to try and persuade him?"

"No no, he told me quite freely. It was as if it had all been bottled up inside him and had to come out." Malkin paused and then half-smiled. "Remember, Haim, he couldn't have told his wife or children much of what he had done, could he? They might have heard some of it from him or from elsewhere but I'm sure none of them knew any of the details or the numbers involved."

"Yes, I think you're right." I agreed.

"The irony is," Malkin continued, "that *dafke* he felt he had to tell it to a Jew, to an Israeli, the Israeli Jew who had actually caught him. He told me all this as though he wanted to please me, not especially with pride, just to put it on record, as it were. He even guessed, despite wearing his black goggles, that I was the one who had first stopped him on Garibaldi Street. The strange thing is that he isn't bitter. It's just like after being fifteen years on the run and looking over his shoulder all the time, he can now relax in a way. I think he expected his luck to run out one day - and now it has."

I mused over what Malkin had just told me and then I asked him what he thought about Eichmann as a person.

"Boring," was his immediate reply.

"Boring? What makes you say so?"

"First of all, I haven't noticed any spark of humor in the man, not even black or cynical. True, I wasn't expecting him to be a barrel of laughs, least of all while being chained to a bed and wearing those horrible goggles all day, but he hasn't commented at all about his present situation or about what he did in the past. He's just reported about it in a dry unemotional way. He's completely bland. Just like the image of the typical bank clerk or the petty civil servant."

"But, Zvi, that's the point. He wasn't a petty civil servant. He literally had the power of life or death over millions of people."

Malkin shrugged. "I know that, but his blandness, his inflexible way of thinking is I think his most dominant characteristic. The only thing that seemed to excite him was his children, especially his youngest one, Ricardo. He even told me that he loved children."

I exploded. "He said that? He said he loved children? So why did he send over a million Jewish children to the gas chambers?"

Malkin was silent. He had no answer. There was no rational answer to that question. "I don't know, Haim," he said at last. "I'm merely telling you what he told me. He kept saying that he didn't like the more brutal aspects of his job and that he couldn't stand the Nazi bully-boys either."

"Like Streicher," I muttered, referring to the editor of the Nazi newspaper, Der Stürmer, and the SA thugs.

"Yes, and those who acted like them. Eichmann even told me that he liked some Jews and that he even had some Jewish friends. He said that when he came to Palestine before the war, he preferred the Jews to the Arabs. He even claimed that he'd read Herzl's book, *Der Judenstaat* –'The Jewish State.'"

"Sure he read it," I added cynically. "As homework, so he could do his job better. That and learning Hebrew. So he could keep his infallible Führer happy."

Malkin shrugged again. "Yes, I guess you're right, there. But then, after talking to him about this, I asked him what he knew about Mengele, the doctor from Auschwitz."

"You mean 'the Angel of Death' ? Zvi also asked him about Mengele."

"At first he said that he knew nothing about him but when Zvi asked him again later, Eichmann said that Mengele had once offered him some free medical treatment."

"Ugh," I shuddered. "I don't think I'd like to receive any treatment from him. Haven't you read about the experiments he conducted on people at Auschwitz?"

"Yes, and that's why Harel is burning to get his hands on him. Nothing would keep him happier," I said, "than for him to fly back home with both Eichmann and Mengele."

Malkin smiled cynically. "You mean it took us fifteen years to catch Eichmann and now we have a few days to spare in which we can catch Mengele?"

"Well, that's what the boss would like," I said. "And that's what he's aiming for right now.

Anyway, Eichmann did give Harel his first tip-off. He said that Mengele had been living in a boarding-house run by an ex-German woman called Frau Jurman. He didn't know the address but was quite sure that it was here in Buenos Aires. All of this seemed to confirm what Harel had already known about

Mengele. Apparently the boss had been talking to the director of the *Shin Bet*, Amos Manor."

"Well, if that's so, Haim, where do we go from here?"

"I don't know. All I know is that Harel is going to talk to us tonight about trying to catch Mengele before we go back home."

And that is what happened.

That night Harel called us all together and said that he would like also to catch Mengele. If necessary, we would carry out an armed raid on his hide-out and, he added, he had asked Tel-Aviv to send him some more men as back-up for this operation.

"Are you sure this is a good idea?" someone asked. But before Harel could reply, Eitan said that he didn't agree with this plan. "Isser," he said. "You know the old Hebrew saying, 'Try to catch a lot and you'll end up catching nothing.' I suggest first we make sure we get Eichmann out of here and back home before we go for Mengele."

Harel's face showed that he didn't agree with this and he insisted that while we were here, we should try and grab Mengele as well. He told Aharoni to put more pressure on Eichmann and squeeze as much information as he could out of him concerning his fellow-Nazi.

In the end it all came to nothing. Eichmann could not or did not tell us much more about the 'Angel of Death' from Auschwitz and when we left Buenos Aires a few days later it was without Mengele.

Now all that remained was to finish off the week in the safe house and wait for our plane to take us back home. But this, as Harel predicted, was easier said than done.

Chapter Eighteen
Plans for Flying Home

The days in *Tira* passed slowly. Painfully slowly. All we wanted to do was to pack up and fly home. Apart from sitting around, talking, reading, and playing cards or chess, all we had to do was to carry out our various forms of guard duty. Basically we knew that our prisoner couldn't escape, and since he wasn't given any knives or any other sharp object, he had virtually no opportunity to harm himself. Apart from our own people, nobody came to or left the house and so all of our sentry style duties were carried out for the record; a task that had to be done.

One evening, after I had finished my shift sitting by the front window upstairs, Aharoni asked whether I would join him for a visit to Eichmann's 'cell' to get him to sign a letter saying that he really was Adolf Eichmann.

"What do you need that for?" I asked. "We know who he is and he's even admitted it."

"I know but Haim Cohen…"

"The Attorney-General?"

"Yes, he told Harel that we should get a written statement from him saying that he really was the man we wanted. I don't understand all the legalities here but Cohen said that such a written admission could prove important in a future trial."

"So don't we also need a written confirmation of guilt? Something about his actions and connections with Hitler and the rest of the Nazi top brass?"

"No, apparently not. The attorney-general told Harel that all that would come out in the trial. Anyway, two days ago I asked Eichmann if he was prepared to come to Israel to be tried there."

"Yeah, I'm sure he agreed to that," I muttered sarcastically.

"You're right. Actually he was quite violent, well, as violent as he could be considering he was chained to his bed. I've not seen him so agitated – not since we grabbed him. He insisted on saying that he hadn't committed any crimes and that he wasn't prepared to go anywhere with us. Then yesterday he

212

said that he'd changed his mind and that he was prepared to face a court."

"Why the sudden change?"

"He said that he was prepared to face a court and prove that he was only following orders – something that thousands of his fellow-Nazis had also done."

"And he agreed to do this in Jerusalem?"

"No. He swore that he didn't owe us Jews anything but he'd agree to face a court here in Argentina or in Germany. I told him that this was impossible as that wasn't the reason we'd grabbed him. I also told him that Argentina and Germany weren't interested in holding a trial like this."

"And what did he say to that?"

"Haim, he said that Austria would then be a good alternative. He told me that his family lives there and that he'd had spent much of his life there."

"I presume you told him that was also impossible?"

"Of course. I told him the trial would be held in Israel and that he'd better start getting used to that idea."

"And, since then, has he said anything about this?"

"Yes. Earlier this morning he told me that if he gets a fair trial in Israel and a chance to defend himself, then he'll agree to come back with us."

"Huh, as if he's got an alternative," I answered.

"Exactly. So if you want, come up with me now to his room and we'll get him to sign this statement for the attorney–general. Haim Cohen's prepared one for us so let's see what he," and he indicated our prisoner upstairs, "will do with it."

"But tell me, Zvi, just before we go, I've just thought of two possible legal questions. The first is: how can we in Israel put him on trial when our country didn't exist while he was committing his terrible crimes? And the second one is that since Israel didn't exist then, none of the people he murdered were Israelis."

"I've also thought about that and so I asked Harel what the answer was. He told me that he'd had several long discussions with the attorney-general and that it'll be all right in the end. It's a question of moral rights, not necessarily only legal ones. Besides," he asked, "who else would put him on trial? The Argentinians, the Germans and the Austrians won't agree to. It would be too embarrassing for them."

"Yeah, I guess you're right. And in any case, it will be the sons and the daughters and all those who survived who'll have the moral right to try him. I doubt whether anyone will be able to argue seriously with that point."

"That's just what the attorney-general said. So let's go upstairs and hope that he'll sign without raising any more objections."

We went upstairs and told Malkin he could take a break unless he wanted to stay. Saying that he'd be very pleased to take a break, he left. Aharoni then asked Eichmann if he had thought any more about signing the agreement about being tried in Israel.

"*Ja*," he said quietly without adding any reasons or explanations. "I will have my trial in your country."

Aharoni approached Eichmann, and took off the man's goggles. Eichmann shook his head and blinked in the light as he tried to focus his vision. It was the first light he had seen for a few days. I gave him the statement and he read it through twice, slowly and carefully. I could see his lips mouth the words as he held his head to one side. When he was finished he held out his hand for Aharoni to hand him a pen. I noticed it was a ball-point. Aharoni was taking no chances that our prisoner would try and stab himself with the first sharp instrument that he'd been given since he had been captured.

"What do I write for a date?" he asked.

"You don't. Just write Buenos Aires, May 1960."

"Are you sure I don't need to write today's date?"

"Just write what I told you."

It was clear that he had lost his sense of time and we were pleased about this. "Do you understand what you have just read?" Aharoni asked.

"*Ja*,"

"Then sign it here at the bottom."

Eichmann did so without showing any emotion and without saying anything else. It seemed to me that he had accepted his fate and that there was nothing he could do to change it in any way.

He was about to ask for something when, at a signal from Aharoni, I put the goggles back on him and then read the statement that Eichmann had signed.

I, Adolf Eichmann, the undersigned, declare herewith of my own free will:

Since my true identity is now known, I recognize that there is no sense in attempting to evade justice any longer. I declare myself willing to go to Israel and face proceedings there before a competent court.

It goes without saying that I will receive legal defense and I will try to put the facts of my final years of my office in Germany into the record without any embellishments, so that posterity will be given a true picture. I am making this declaration of my own free will. No promises were made to me, nor was I threatened in any way. I wish finally to find peace of mind again. Since I cannot recall all of the details and tend to confuse events, I request that I receive help in my desire to find the truth by having documents and testimony put at my disposal.

Adolf Eichmann, Buenos Aires, May 1960

I went downstairs and returned a few minutes later with Malkin who still had an hour left before the end of his shift guarding Eichmann. On his return, Aharoni and I left with Eichmann's signed statement to join the others who were trying to keep themselves busy during this endless week of waiting.

I walked past those who were reading or filling out crosswords and went to join Shalom Danny, sitting in a corner, complete with his inks, pens and brushes. If anyone in our team was irreplaceable, it was Danny. Like several others in the team, Danny had grown up in Nazi-controlled Europe. Hungary had been his own particular hell. As he sat there working out how to make a set of forged papers for Eichmann, he was thinking now the time had come for him to have his own personal revenge.

On the fifth evening of our enforced stay in *Tira,* Malkin came up to me. "Haim," he said, "I've been watching Danny work. It's such a joy. This man is brilliant. I wish I had his talent."

"But your work is also good," I said, and I believed it, too. I wasn't trying to be patronizing. "It's powerful. It's got character and I really like your *Guernica* style picture of Eichmann and the train carriages."

"Thank you, but my work isn't as fine or as precise as Danny's. I am telling you, Haim, that man is a genius. He can even make convincing copies of seals and documents in languages that he doesn't even speak, such as Arabic."

"I know, but if he's so good at his work and knows that everyone recognizes his talent, why does he walk about with such a long face all the time?"

"That's not hard to answer," Malkin answered. "He really wanted to be part of the team that actually grabbed Eichmann and not be just one of the backroom boys."

"But he's doing what he's best suited for. In fact, without him, I doubt if we could have got as far as we have."

"I know that, Haim, and that's what I told him yesterday. I told him that by forging all the necessary documents and passes for us, it's as though he's personally signing Eichmann's death-warrant."

"Did he accept that?"

"I think so. At least he smiled and said that he wanted revenge for what Eichmann had done to his family. He also said he'd hoped he'd be given a more active role, a more physical part, but now I believe he's now accepted what he is doing here."

"That's good," I said. "Because his next job is to make sure that we'll all have the necessary papers for our flight home which, for me, can't come soon enough."

"Don't worry, my friend. In a few days we'll be out of here and I know that Danny's already completed quite a lot of the papers we'll need. He showed me some of them and believe me, they're brilliant. Just brilliant."

"Well let's hope that our flight home and its planning will be just as brilliant. I've had enough of Eichmann and this place. I want to go home and see my family. Six weeks in Buenos Aires, especially being stuck in here, has been more than enough for me."

He gave me a supportive pat on the shoulder. "Cheer up. Harel's coming here tonight to give us the details of our flight home. Hopefully, by this time next week, you'll be back on your kibbutz feeding the chickens or milking the cows or whatever you do there. Me, I plan to spend my first few days of leave lying on the beach in Tel-Aviv and just being lazy."

"And painting."

"Yes, that as well," he said, smiling at the thought.

As Malkin had said, Harel came to see us that night and gathered us all together to outline the plans for our flight home.

"This is the idea," he began, holding a sheaf of papers bearing names, flight plans and a detailed road map of Buenos Aires. "As you know, we'll be flying home with our special passenger on an El Al plane. We're planning to leave here in a few days, on 20 May, late at night. We are going to make the minimum of refueling stops en route, probably two at most: one in Dakar, West Africa, and the other in Rome. I've gone over all this with Rafi, Avraham and El Al's chief pilot, Captain Zvi Tahor. If all goes to plan, we should reach Tel-Aviv sometime in the morning of 22 May. Is that clear so far?"

It was, so he continued.

"OK. So what I told you just now is the rough outline. Here are the details. As you may know, apart from one flight last week, El Al has never flown to Buenos Aires before. The reason for this second flight is to take back home the official Israeli delegation who were invited to take part in Argentina's 150th

Independence Day celebrations. Minister without Portfolio, Abba Eban, and General Meir Zorea are heading this delegation, so naturally there will be some other very senior officials and…"

"And Eichmann and us who'll be flying back with them," someone finished off his sentence.

"Right, but there are many problems that must be dealt with first. These can be divided into three sorts: technical, security and personnel. The technical problems include flight-plans, fuel, landing clearances, telex services and all the aircraft maintenance and other services that are a part of international flights. Especially long flights like this one.

"Security and personnel problems include choosing suitable people to make up the cabin staff, flight and technical crews. And there's the problem of dealing with our prisoner upstairs and seeing that he is properly catered for.

"Finally of course, there is the problem of getting Eichmann onto the plane without arousing any suspicions from anyone at the airport. We've arranged to have the plane parked some distance away from the other planes there but, nevertheless, we'll still have to pass through one or two security checks."

"Maybe we could drug him and stuff him into a box labeled 'Agricultural Equipment,'" someone sitting behind me suggested.

Harel shook his head. "Too risky and, besides, it's been done before."

"How about putting him inside a diplomatic bag?" I asked.

"No, Haim, not this time. This is what we're going to do. We're going to sedate him and then smuggle him aboard dressed up in an El Al uniform as though he's drunk or ill."

"But he'll need special papers and a passport for that," I said. "Even airline crews have to pass through immigration and customs, especially as we're going to have one or two refueling stops en route."

"Don't worry about that. That's what Shalom Danny is working on now, preparing the necessary papers and documents. In addition, someone from our own security services is flying out here, a fellow who looks quite a lot like Eichmann. So if any

218

questions are raised about who's arriving and who's leaving here, we shouldn't have any problems on that score. In the meantime, Captain Tohar is checking out whether we really do need to make a refueling stop in Recife, Brazil or whether we'll be able to reach West Africa in one go. He promised to let me know tomorrow."

Harel looked around and asked whether we had any questions or other suggestions. There were none and so we broke up into small groups to discuss our remaining few days in *Tira*. Now that Harel had given us some details about the flight home, the atmosphere in the safe-house was definitely better: we could now see the light at the end of the tunnel.

That night I went to the 'cell' with Danny to see about the details he would need for Eichmann's fake documents. I saw that they were nearly complete and all he needed now was a few photographs.

As we were about to climb the stairs to the second floor, Danny turned to me and said, "What I want to do is to tell him what he did to my family. It's time he heard the truth about what he did, and from someone who actually suffered as well."

But when the moment came for Danny to tell him, he could not. He just stood there, staring at Eichmann, now ready for his head and shoulders photo, dressed in a dark jacket and white shirt and tie on top of his striped pajamas. Danny stared at him for a full minute and Eichmann stared back at him. The German did not know who he was as this was the first time that Danny had been there in the 'cell.' There was no way he could have known what was going through Danny's mind, nor what had happened to him in the past. Danny then started shaking and it was only when he picked up his camera did he manage to control himself. As he began to adjust the lens, he opened his mouth to say something, but no words came out of his mouth. Again there was complete silence as the two men stared at each other. This was finally broken when Danny the photographer overcame Danny the Holocaust survivor. Telling Eichmann how to sit and pose, he took his shots. As soon as he had finished, with his camera in hand he whirled round and left the room as quickly as he could without saying another word.

He was still shaking when I saw him, his hands wrapped around a mug of coffee ten minutes later. "What happened up there? You looked as though you'd just seen a ghost and you still do. I thought you wanted to tell him something."

"I did, Haim, but when I saw that monster sitting there, even though he was dressed in half a suit, pictures of him in his black SS uniform kept flashing through my mind and I was struck dumb. It was too much. I couldn't say what I'd wanted to. I'm sorry." We sat there for a few more minutes in silence and then he said, "Come on, let's get out of here. Take me back to *Ma'oz*. I'll feel better there."

I drove him back and on the way tried to calm him down by telling him he was doing a great job by helping us through his forged papers to bring Eichmann to face his accusers. "Maybe some good will come out of all this," I said, but Danny shook his head and did not look convinced. I left him at *Ma'oz*, sad and shattered, and hoped he would be able to pull himself together and continue with his work.

Two days later after Danny had completed the 'Zeev Zichroni' papers, a minor diplomatic farewell ceremony took place on the tarmac at Tel-Aviv airport. Abba Eban, Meir Zorea and their official retinue were standing at the foot of the stairs by the El Al Britannia as the government's official photographer took his pictures of this occasion. Only a few people on board knew the real purpose of Flight 601. Abba Eban had been briefed earlier by Ben-Gurion, and Captain Tohar was also in on this secret. Despite the fact that most of the other passengers and crew had been kept in the dark for security reasons, co-pilot Captain Shmuel Wedeles had sensed that something unusual was happening. As soon as he saw El Al manager, Yehuda Shimoni, sit down and buckle himself up in the plane, he leaned over and asked him if they were going to bring back Eichmann or Mengele, or both. Shimoni put his finger to his lips and seeing this gesture, Wedeles assumed that he had guessed correctly.

Like many others connected to 'Operation Eichmann,' Wedeles was very pleased to be involved. His own family had been murdered in the Holocaust and his religious father had been forced to eat pork publicly before a pro-Nazi mob had set his beard on fire.

The Britannia, the 'Whispering Giant,' took off from Lod airport soon after everyone was aboard and set off for Rome and Dakar in West Africa. There a relief crew would take over for the next leg to Recife, the last refueling stop before continuing on to Buenos Aires. They were due to land at Ezeiza airport on 19 May in the afternoon. The passengers and technical crew felt excited about breaking new ground for El Al, while Abba Eban and the few other people on board in the know were also thinking about the importance of Flight 601, but from a different angle.

All went according to plan until the plane landed at Recife at seven in the morning on 19 May. There a surprise awaited them. This is how Captain Tohar described the scene later to me and the others.

"Our flight 601, El Al 4X-AGD, landed at Recife after a difficult approach and landing in which we just missed hitting a hilltop forest. After we had taxied to a halt for refueling, we found a whole lot of people there waiting for us. Naturally I became very anxious and wanted to know what was happening. We left the plane and saw that hundreds of people from the local Jewish community had come there to welcome us. They had come to witness and bless this special flight from Israel to South America. In addition, the manager of the airport, all decked out in the fanciest uniform he could find was also there, complete with his own retinue of officials and photographers."

"That was all you needed," I commented, "especially if you'd planned to make a quick and quiet getaway."

"Exactly."

"By the way, how did the local Jewish community know about the flight?" asked Malkin.

Captain Tohar shook his head. "I don't know. Perhaps there was a member of the community working in the flight operations department in the airport. International flights are listed publicly and so I can only suppose some sharp-eyed person saw this and then spread the word around.

"Anyway, however they knew, they insisted on holding some sort of reception ceremony and after that some of the passengers and crew went off to the terminal to buy some food and souvenirs. Naturally, knowing about our special passenger made me feel even more tensed up.

"Then I sent two of the flight crew to the central control tower to file a flight plan to Buenos Aires and to collect the necessary metrological information for the next leg. But when they got there, an armed soldier wouldn't let them in. My men didn't want to attract any attention so they quickly returned to tell me what had happened. I was wondering what to do when one of Abba Eban's men, a Portuguese-speaking diplomat, told me to be patient and he'd deal with the situation. Thirty minutes later he returned with an old man carrying a bag who told the soldier who had stopped us that he had to speak to the manager of the airport. He went off with the bag and lo and behold! the manager himself appeared a few minutes later."

"Magic," I said.

"Magic, my foot!" Tohar smiled. "Money. Three and a half hours after landing in Recife, we were on our way to Buenos Aires."

"So that's why you were late," Aharoni said. "We were so worried that someone had discovered what we were up to."

The captain smiled. "Anyway, all's well that ends well. We made a good landing here and Abba Eban gave an impressive speech in Spanish. I told most of the crew that they could go sightseeing in Buenos Aires – but only on condition that they'd be back at the airport by early evening to be ready for the flight home on the following day. I also told two of the plane's mechanics that they'd have to stay overnight with the plane in the Aerolineas Argentinas maintenance area. Naturally they were not very happy about not being allowed to see the sights of Buenos Aires par nuit, but orders are orders."

"Of course."

"Fortunately it had been arranged beforehand that the plane would be kept as far out of sight as possible and that was the situation soon after we landed."

That evening Captain Tohar had a meeting with Harel, Yehuda Shimroni, Aharoni and myself and we discussed the final details for smuggling Eichmann on board.

The El Al captain opened the meeting. Looking at Harel he said, "Isser, I will do anything you ask of me that is reasonable under the circumstances and that does not endanger my passengers and crew and of course, the aircraft. Also, please do not ask me to land at Recife again."

"Why not?"

"Because we cannot count on the Brazilian authorities there. All we need is another unexpected delay, especially with Eichmann on board."

Harel agreed and asked the captain to make doubly sure that all his crew would be ready to fly out early the next day. "I'm telling you, Zvi, my men here have all had enough of baby-sitting this monster here this past week."

Captain Tohar shook his head. "Sorry, Isser, but I cannot agree to that. My crew will need all the sleep that they can get. Remember, this is going to be a very long flight home and this will be the first time that most of them will have ever flown over the south Atlantic from west to east. And," he added, "this will be on top of just landing here after a long flight, so sorry, the earliest we'll be able to leave is on the twentieth, in the evening."

Harel saw that he had no choice and after a round of coffee and cakes, we sat down again to work out the final details. The meeting then broke up and Captain Tohar left to meet his crew at the 'Hotel Internacional' where they were staying for the night. There he told a select few about the true purpose of the flight. He also instructed his flight crew to prepare the necessary plans for a direct flight from Buenos Aires to Dakar. There would be no stops in South America once the plane had left Buenos Aires' Ezeiza airport.

That night you could have cut the tension in *Tira* with a knife. We were all desperate to board the Britannia and to bring to an end the holding of our ex-Nazi prisoner on foreign soil. In an effort to reduce our tension we went over our plans again and also returned the safe house to the condition it had been in before we had taken it over. The other team members in the other safe houses did the same. All unnecessary papers and clothes were torn up and burned and the rubbish was disposed of in different trash cans. During the early part of the evening, Eichmann spent his time sitting on his bed. He must have felt something was happening because he kept asking "*Was ist los*? What's up?" but, of course, none of us answered him.

Then just as I was about to start my last evening shift on guard, I heard a shout from the front of the house. Someone had been spotted lurking near the outside gate of our safe house.

"Haim, Moshe, run upstairs and get ready to hide Eichmann in the secret room!" Aharoni shouted. "Rafi's gone outside to check who's out there and what they're doing."

We ran up to Eichmann's 'cell' and were about to tie him up when Aharoni appeared at the door.

"False alarm. Rafi said there was nobody there. It must have been shadows or someone walking past very slowly. He's checked out all the outside walls and we're all right. I thought that maybe some of Eichmann's family or friends had found out where he was, but that's not the case. So you can leave him as he was."

That night we all went to bed late even though we knew the next day would be long and tense. The two questions on all our minds now were these: Would we succeed in smuggling Eichmann onto the plane? And would we be able to fly home to Tel-Aviv without any problems?

Chapter Nineteen
Adios, Buenos Aires

By the time the sun had risen on a bleak winter's morning in Buenos Aires we were all feeling very nervous. A few of us had slept well but most of us had not. My bursts of sleep had been punctuated with vivid dreams of blue and white airplanes and a black-SS uniformed Eichmann escaping, complete with the sneering face that typified this man. Although Shakespeare had written, 'Sleep that knits up the raveled sleeve of care,' I did not feel at all rested when I got up the next morning. To quote the Bard again, but in a different context, Eichmann had indeed 'murdered sleep.'

Convinced that I was one of the first to wake up, I went downstairs to make myself a cup of coffee only to find that most of the team were already sitting there in the spacious kitchen and front room. Judith Nessayahu was busy frying eggs and serving the typical Israeli breakfast salad of finely diced tomatoes and cucumbers together with some olives. I joined Aharoni, Eitan and Shalom at the kitchen table and, naturally, all our talk was about the forthcoming operation and the flight home.

We knew we would not be doing anything until the afternoon; and the enforced inactivity only served to increase our restlessness.

As the long drawn-out breakfast merged into mid-morning, other members of the team joined us in the kitchen. Those who didn't want to talk about what we were going to do that evening played cards or chess or read whatever books and newspapers that were at hand. I preferred to sit by the table and, like old soldiers from time immemorial, shared past experiences with Aharoni and Eitan about how we had foiled various enemies in Paris, Berlin and Vienna. Later, Shalom joined us and told us some jokes and how he had used them to 'soften up' the security guards at Ezeiza airport.

"Oh yes," Shalom said, his eyes smiling at the memory, "I told the guards a few stories about El Al and how everyone in Israel thinks that it is great that Argentina is celebrating its 150th independence anniversary."

"But hardly anyone in Israel knows about it," I said.

Shalom shrugged. "I know that, but it kept the guards happy. I told them that this year we in Israel would be celebrating our twelfth anniversary and they thought that this was kind of sweet.

"Anyway, to cut a long story short, I don't think we'll be having any problems getting through that part of the security system. We're all good friends out there now," he smiled impishly.

Needless to say, we hoped he was right but, in the meanwhile, we had to prepare Eichmann for the ride to the airport and the flight home. This meant dressing him up in an El Al uniform and then sedating him with enough drugs to make him feel groggy, but not so much that would put him out of action. In the event of anyone wanting to take a good look at him, he had to look as though he were suffering from a particularly nasty hangover. We also had to ensure that he looked like 'Ze'ev Zichroni,' the El Al flight navigator who stared out from the page on his fake passport.

And then just to make sure that it didn't look too strange suspicious that an El Al crew member of Eichmann's age and build had suddenly appeared as part of the crew leaving Buenos Aires for the flight home, Tel Aviv had sent us a man who looked like Eichmann. After his presence had been registered by the authorities, he was spirited out of Argentina using a different passport and papers. He flew home as a tourist on a flight out from Chile.

As we were going over the details of the evening's work for what must have been the hundredth time, Dr. Elian joined us.

"Are you absolutely sure about sedating him?" I asked.

The doctor nodded. "Yes, and I hope I'll be able to control the effects of the drugs. I'll make him weak enough so he won't have the strength to call out for help, but he'll still be able to walk,

walk that is, with two of you supporting him. Nevertheless, it might be useful to have a gag handy."

But this still left us two problems to deal with.

The first was airport security. While it was fun to listen to Shalom's stories and how he had charmed the guards at the airport, we also knew that there were other guards there whom Shalom had not been able to soften up. These would be the usual customs and immigration officials as well as the security men who had the right to board our plane if they suspected that anything irregular was happening. Perhaps they would say he was unfit to fly and would not allow us to take the 'sedated flight navigator' on board until he had sobered up.

The second problem was that we didn't know whether the Argentinian police knew anything about Eichmann's disappearance. Had his family informed them? And if so, would the police make the connection between the missing ex-Nazi and the drugged El Al crew member? We thought this was indeed a long shot, but experience had taught us that past missions had succeeded or failed due to such 'long shots.' In order to be as informed as possible, the Spanish-speaking members of our team had scanned all the local and national newspapers as carefully as possible. They also listened to the radio and watched the television news to see whether Eichmann's disappearance had been noted. Up to now, they said, it hadn't. But did this mean that his disappearance hadn't been reported or did it mean that it had, but that the authorities were keeping it under wraps?

In other words, we had no way of knowing the answers to these questions and would not know until we put our plan into action. It was this lack of answers and certainty that was making us all nervous that day.

Aharoni tried to calm our nerves by saying that - as far as he had had been able to discover through our network of *sayanim*, - Eichmann's family had not reported that 'Ricardo Klement' was missing and that his name had not appeared on any local police or hospital accident reports. He said that the family could not admit that Ricardo Klement was really Adolf Eichmann, an ex-Nazi who had entered the country illegally and had been living there, basing his life in Argentina on false papers.

"I'm guessing that the family might start an unofficial hunt for him, calling in old friends and maybe a few ex-Nazis to help out," Aharoni said, "but I really doubt whether they'll make a big noise. Because if they do, Eichmann's family will be forced to uncover a whole network of lies and deception and it will also make the authorities here look inefficient."

"By the way," I asked, half-way through yet another mug of coffee. "What happened to Harel's idea of smuggling Eichmann out of the country in a crate on board a ship – a back-up plan if the El Al plan doesn't work out?"

Eitan looked at me. "We do have a large crate waiting for us at the embassy here, in the cellar, but…"

"It didn't have any air-holes in it," Dr. Elian added. "I might be able to keep him sedated for a few hours at a time but without air he'll be dead pretty quickly."

"That's right," Eitan said. "So we drilled about fifty holes in the crate, not so big that you could look through them but just big enough to provide him with enough air. We also fitted some leather straps inside so he would be kept in a sitting position. Ah yes, we also labeled the crate…"

"Agricultural machinery?"

"No, Haim. That's old hat. Besides, if we had labeled it like that or anything similar, the customs officials may have opened it. So," and here his eyes twinkled behind his thick glasses, "we were more or less honest this time. We labeled it like this." And on a scrap of paper he wrote:

Diplomatic Post

From: *Israeli Embassy, Buenos Aires.*
To: *Foreign Ministry, Jerusalem*

"And then it would be loaded onto a freighter bound for

Israel?"

"Yes, either that, or we would load it onto a smaller Israeli ship and then transfer it to a larger Israeli ship outside Argentina's territorial waters. But," and here Eitan said this slowly, "we hope very much that we won't have to use this back up plan because that means we'll have to crate him up and…"

"Taking him back home will be a lengthy business," I said finishing off his explanation.

"Exactly. I'm not sure how long it would take but it would certainly be longer than a plane flight. In any case, there aren't any Israeli ships due to arrive here in the near future, so we are going to have to succeed with this evening's plan."

Everyone nodded in agreement and then Aharoni added, "And of course, with a ship, we 'd have more stops en route and each one of them could mean more inspections and all sorts of awkward questions. No, my friends, as Rafi has just said, we must succeed this evening."

"By the way," I said looking around, "Where are Avraham and Moshe? I haven't seen them this past hour. Are they upstairs with him?"

"No, they're at the airport. They are fixing up a secret compartment on the plane where we can hide Eichmann in case any police or airport officials come on board and start asking too many questions."

"Where will it be? In one of the toilets?" I asked.

"That's right. They're converting one of the first class toilets. They're putting up a false wall, but let's hope we won't have to use it. Then once they've finished with the plane, they'll meet up with Harel in one of the cafés on his list."

"Hmm," I muttered. "It's not often that the boss is around for the kill, is it? Usually he stays behind in Tel-Aviv and we report back to him."

"True, but this time this operation is very important for him. After playing down the capture of Eichmann at the beginning, he really wants it to succeed now."

"Don't we all?"

An hour later, I went upstairs with Malkin to prepare Eichmann for his flight to Israel as an El Al navigator. With a copy of Danny's photo of our 'passenger' next to him, Malkin applied some make-up to Eichmann's face and dyed his hair. Then he drew a few lines on his face to 'age' him.

Finally he told Eichmann to remove his pajamas. "*Warum –* Why?"

"Because you've been promoted from being our prisoner to becoming an El Al crew member," Malkin said cynically. "Now strip off and put on this shirt, tie and uniform."

Five minutes later the transformation was complete. From looking like a pale nobody, Eichmann now looked like one of El Al's senior members, the gold sleeve rings of rank showing up brightly on the dark blue uniform.

"And now for the hat," Malkin said, leaning over to put it on the head of our new 'navigator.' "Yes, you look much better with this one rather than with that horrible SS death's-head one you used to wear. Hmm," he added, standing back to admire his work. "Yes, wearing a Jewish star on your cap definitely suits you. Don't you think so, H?" he asked me.

"Definitely, much better."

"Good. Now Mr. El Al navigator, sit down and put these sunglasses on." Eichmann did so.

"There, that's better. Now you really look the part. What do you think, H?" Malkin asked. "Do you agree?"

Just as I was about to say 'yes', Dr. Elian knocked on the door and came in, complete with his black leather medical bag. He nodded to Malkin. "Tell him to roll up his sleeve. I want to give him an injection."

Malkin told him and Eichmann rolled up his sleeve as the doctor was loading his syringe with the sedative. Suddenly our 'navigator' pulled back.

"I don't need that," he said quickly, pointing to the syringe. "I won't make any noise. I promise." His body language and voice were like that of a small boy promising to behave in front of his strict father.

"Don't worry," Dr. Elian said, looking distinctly unimpressed. "It's nothing. It won't hurt. It will just help to keep you calm."

"But I'm not nervous," Eichmann pleaded.

"No matter. I've received orders you're to receive this," the doctor said as I smirked at the irony of his last statement.

Dr. Elian took Eichmann's outstretched trembling arm, inserted the needle and quickly pumped in the sedative. The effect was almost immediate. Eichmann slumped forward, but then raised himself groggily and looked at us as I adjusted his sunglasses which had fallen half-way down his nose.

Then I went downstairs to tell the others that Eichmann was ready.

"Right, so if he's drugged and dressed," Eitan said, "Go back upstairs and bring him down to the car. He'll sit in the back between you and Dr. Elian. And make sure you pull his cap over his face and make it look as if he's trying to grab some sleep."

This we did and just as Aharoni switched on the engine, Eichmann looked up drunkenly and in a slurred voice asked us not to give him any more injections. He promised he would keep quiet and behave himself.

Aharoni looked around from the driver's seat and adjusted his rear-view mirror so that he could keep an eye on his special passenger as well as on the road. He waved to Malkin and Judith Nessayahu. They would be staying behind to finish tidying-up *Tira* and hold the fort if anything unexpected happened.

Malkin opened the garage doors and the gates of the outer walls and we were off. We had planned to meet the rest of the team in two other cars near the airport As usual we split up to drive to the airport via indirect routes as a precaution against being followed. We arrived at our pre-arranged meeting place and our three-car convoy drove the last mile to the airport without any problems.

"How is he? Did he resist when you jabbed him?" Y. who had been staying at the *Ma'oz* safe-house asked.

"No," I replied. "Dr. Elian said he's all right now, drowsy, but he's able to walk with some help from us."

Now, all together again, we drove to the airport perimeter fence. We followed it for half a mile and then stopped at the entrance gate to the maintenance area where our plane was waiting. Just as we were about to pass through, a security guard suddenly came out from his booth and waved to us to stop. It was at this point that our sleepy passenger started moving about in the back seat and appeared to be waking up from his drugged sleep.

"Keep him quiet!" Eitan hissed to Dr. Elian and me as the guard walked over to us. He signaled Shalom to wind down his window and was about to ask him something when he smiled.

"*Hola*! Pablo," Shalom called out. "It's us, the El Al crew. Didn't you recognize me?"

"Oh, hi, Israelis," the guard smiled recognizing Shalom and he turned to raise the red and white barrier. He looked in each car very casually and waved us on. Making sure that we kept out of the floodlit areas, we drew up at the foot of the steps to our plane. Captain Tohar was waiting there for us and gave us a quick thumbs-up. Just as he did so, an airport security man suddenly appeared out of the shadows and started walking towards us. We could hear his heavy shoes crunching on the light gravel on the tarmac.

"Get him out of here!" Rafi whispered urgently to Captain Tohar. "Or take him over to the other side or to the back."

The captain waved in a friendly way to the security man and casually led him to the back of the waiting Britannia.

"Quick, now let's get him on board," Eitan said quietly. "Surround him and help him up the steps. Now, now before that cop or whoever he is comes back."

We didn't have to be told twice. We hustled Eichmann up the stairs, his feet half-dragging and banging on them as we kept an eye open for the security man to reappear. Then we sat him down in a pre-arranged window-seat in the first class cabin. We each breathed a sigh of relief. It was just after eleven o'clock that night and everything had gone according to plan. I thought to myself, 'so far, so good.'

While we were congratulating ourselves, Harel was sitting at his temporary command-post in the airport restaurant waiting for the Britannia to taxi over to the runway. He gave orders for all the rest of the team to get on the plane, and then grabbing his own bag and trying to look like a well-travelled businessman, he quickly followed them on to the apron.

It was now midnight and we were all pretty jumpy. The plane was ready, the cabin and flight crews were in position and our team and passenger were all seated and buckled into our seats. What was delaying our take-off? Had someone tipped of the authorities at the last moment? Captain Tohar had told me that he hadn't had any problems filing his flight plans and had received the NOTAMs – the Notices to Airmen – and as far as he could see, everything was in order.

I looked out of the window at the airport's bright terminal lights half-expecting to see some police cars come racing up to the foot of the plane. The minutes ticked by and we all sat there looking at each other. From time to time we glanced at Eichmann sitting there, sedated and slumped down in his seat by the window, his peaked uniform cap covering his face.

"What's up?" I whispered, as though anyone outside could hear me.

Harel shrugged. For once he had no answer but tried to remain calm as he pulled out a newspaper and started reading it. If necessary, he had said, he could use it to cover Eichmann if anyone unwanted came aboard.

What neither Harel nor I knew at the time was that one moment after Captain Tohar had completed his pre-flight checks and obtained the necessary clearance to fly to Recife, he had received a radio message from the Ezeiza control-tower.

"El Al, hold your position. There is something wrong with your flight plan to Recife."

Later Captain Tohar told us that everyone on the flight deck froze on hearing this. Had the authorities found out about

Eichmann at the last moment? Had they discovered that the flight plan to Recife was a bluff and that we were not really going to fly there? Could El Al just ignore the control-tower's request and take off without receiving official permission?

The flight crew had a quick discussion and as a result, Captain Tohar, who realized that they could not ignore the control-tower and simply take off, sent Shaul, his senior navigator, over to find out what the problem was. "Check out what's going on over there and make it fast. If I don't hear from you in ten minutes, I'm going to take off without you."

Looking out of the windows, all we could see was Shaul run over to the base of the control- tower and then disappear inside.

"What's the problem?" Shaul asked. "Why are you delaying our take-off? Won't we miss our slot?"

For an answer, the controller for the night shift handed a flight document over to Shaul. "Two things," he said. "The first is that you haven't written on this form what your alternative route is and…"

"Pôrto Alegre," Shaul answered immediately, knowing that this was not true.

"And one of the members of your flight crew has forgotten to sign this flight plan. I cannot let you go without his or your signature."

Shaul quickly scribbled his name at the bottom of the document, breathed a sigh of relief, shook hands with the controller and raced back to the plane.

Breathing heavily, he took his place on the flight deck and told the others what had happened.

They all breathed a sigh of relief. Maybe now they could take off before anything else happened.

Shaul turned to face his captain. "Were you really going to take off without me if I wasn't back in ten minutes?" he asked.

Captain Tohar tried to look fierce and then smiled. "Since when does an Israeli officer leave one of his men behind?" he said and clapped his navigator on the back. "Now get on and do what you are paid to do and let's hope we'll be out of here in a few minutes."

Despite what had happened, the atmosphere on the fight deck was still tense as Captain Tohar radioed the control-tower for permission to take off.

"This is the El Al flight from Ezeiza to Recife. May we proceed?"

"Affirmative."

Suddenly the sound of the quietly purring engines grew louder and we started moving slowly forward down the runway. We held our breath. We in the passenger cabin didn't know what had happened on the flight deck. All we could do was ask ourselves whether we could now take off - or were we being moved to another area in the airport for some unknown reason?

The revving sound of the engines grew louder and from my seat by the window I could see and feel that we were gathering speed. Then with a final noisy boost of sound, our Bristol Britannia charged down the runway, lifted up into the dark night skies and banked around the airport below. Suddenly, the bright lights of Buenos Aires disappeared behind me and I found myself looking over the black waters of the Rio de Plata below. We were off on our historic flight back to Israel.

Chapter Twenty
The Flight Home

A few minutes after leaving Ezeiza, Captain Tohar called out over the loudspeaker system that we had left Argentina's airspace and that now we were on our own.

"We've done it!" I shouted out and unbuckling our seatbelts, we all got up and hugged and began congratulating each other.

"Done what?" an El Al steward asked me. "What's all the noise about?"

I pointed to where Eichmann was sitting slumped in his seat. "You see that man there? That's Eichmann. We're bringing him home to stand trial for what he did during the war."

"You mean Adolf Eichmann? One of the top Nazis? The one who's been hiding all this time?"

"Yes," I almost shouted. "We've got him at last!" I was about to add something when Adi Peleg, the El Al security chief, held up his hands for us to keep quiet. It was clear he had something important to say.

He looked around for a moment, coughed to clear his throat and began. "You've been accorded a great privilege. You are taking part in an operation of supreme importance to the Jewish people. The man with us," and here he stopped and pointed to where our sedated 'crew member' was now leaning against the inside of the aircraft cabin, oblivious to what was going on around him, "that man with us on the plane is Adolf Eichmann."

As the news sank in to those who had not been in on the secret, there was a moment of stunned silence. But suddenly, like flood waters crashing through a broken dam, the air was filled with cheers, questions and even sounds of crying.

"Hooray! We've got him!"

"Are you sure? Are you sure that's him?"

"I thought something like this was going on, except I thought that that guy may have been Mengele."

As the noise died down, I noticed one of the stewardesses was sitting on her own, her head bowed down and shaking.

It clear that she was crying and that she could not control her tears. I heard her repeating to herself, "It can't be true. I don't believe it."

I moved over and sat down next to her. "What can't be true? What don't you believe?"

She looked up at me and wiped her eyes. "You know I'm from Hungary, don't you? Well, at the end of March1944, the Nazis entered our suburb in Budapest and rounded up all the Jews who were living there. Then they marched them through the city to the banks of the Danube near the parliament building and shot them and threw their bodies into the river. Just like that. I was the only one of my family to survive."

"How?"

"I was quite young at the time and I was small for my age. Somehow I managed to slip away and hide in the rubble of a ruined building. I remained there for nearly a week. I didn't come out, not even at night as there were Nazi patrols and Arrow Cross men prowling around."

"Arrow Cross? The Hungarian Fascist Party?"

"Yes," she nodded.

"So what did you live on for that week?"

"I was lucky. I found a few bottles of lemonade and some bags of carrots and potatoes in the rubble. Then when all of that ran out, I sneaked out one evening and managed to join a group of partisans. I swore that if I ever had the opportunity of taking revenge on any of those responsible for what happened, I would do so."

She stopped, wiped her eyes again and then looked up at me. "And so you see. God must have heard me, for now I am part of the team bringing him," and she pointed to our passenger, "back to Israel to stand trial for what he did. I am so happy about this; I'm overwhelmed. Now it seems as though my family will be avenged in some sort of way." She looked up again. "Please leave me now. I must sit here alone for a while. I need some time to take this all in."

I moved away knowing I would be hearing many similar stories in the future. I also knew that by having played my part in this operation, I would be helping many people who had suffered because of this terrible man. Helping to bring Eichmann back to face his accusers would, I hoped, enable many of those who had lost their faith in humanity have it restored. If not completely, then in part.

I walked along the aisle to join our team and the El Al crew members who were not busy.

After the initial cheers, the general mood was now quiet and thoughtful. People were discussing what we had done and how this shrunken, blindfolded man by the window had been responsible for so much suffering and death less than twenty years earlier.

"That's really him? I can't believe it," a steward kept saying to himself. "He doesn't look as though he had the strength to hold a rifle, let alone fire it."

"He didn't," I told him. "He used his pen to sign all those orders – who was going to die and who was to be sent to the camps. He was much worse than the regular *Wehrmacht* soldiers. It was he who gave the soldiers the orders to kill as he sat there in his comfortable office in Berlin or Budapest or wherever."

Although we did not know it at the time, the mood in the cockpit was equally somber, but for different reasons. Since Captain Tohar had told Harel that he had had decided we wouldn't stop over at Recife to refuel, as soon as we left Argentina's airspace we immediately headed east over the South Atlantic. This meant that we would have to fly over 4,500 miles non-stop from Buenos Aires to Dakar. There would be no emergency landing-place en route if we ran out of fuel. Our flight would last for about thirteen hours. This was a daunting thought for the captain and his flight crew. They knew that three years earlier a similar type of plane had flown over 5,700 miles non-stop from New York to Tel-Aviv, but that plane had been considerably lighter. Apart from a skeleton crew, it had carried no passengers and very little food. All the seats had been removed as well as any other internal fittings and its cargo-hold was also empty. It was therefore no wonder that as our plane flew over the inky black waters of the South Atlantic all of the flight crew were keeping a very sharp eye on the plane's fuel gauges.

Fortunately, our grimmest thoughts came to nought. Thirteen hours after taking off from Buenos Aires, with red warning lights flashing in the cockpit, Captain Tohar began the procedure for landing at Dakar. The same thoughts were now going through everyone's minds. How would we be received there? Had news of what we had done and what we were now doing been radioed to the West African authorities? Would we be diverted to another airport and, if so, did we have enough fuel left for this?

Suddenly I felt a mechanical whirring vibration as the landing wheels were lowered. "Shut off two engines," the Captain ordered. "We must save as much fuel as possible," he added as the control tower and other airport buildings came into sight.

Back in the passenger cabin, Dr. Elian had given Eichmann another injection and Yaacov Gat had moved over to sit next to him. The chief cabin steward extinguished all the first class cabin lights and drawn the dark curtain over to block out any other lights.

We taxied to the refueling station and waited. What sort of reception would await us? The normal procedures for refueling and checking for an aircraft making such a stop - or would we be invaded by the airport authorities? The side door was opened to allow two health inspectors aboard. They were both smiling and one was carrying a large clipboard.

"Everything all right?" they asked, giving a cursory look around inside. There were no obvious clues as to who the sleeping 'crew member' really was. A few minutes later they left. "Bon voyage. Have a good flight," they said as they were gently ushered to the door. As soon as this was secured, a huge collective sigh of relief was heard. We had overcome that hurdle. Now all that remained was to complete the refueling and for the flight crew to complete the flight plans and all the other necessary paperwork.

Eighty minutes after landing at Dakar we took off again. However, despite the feelings of relief that Dakar was now behind us, Harel warned us that we still had a long way yet to go.

"Be prepared for another long flight," he said. "It won't be as long as the one we've just done, but Captain Tohar has told me that we still won't be able to take any short cuts to get to Rome."

"Do you mean we won't be able to fly straight north to Rome?" Shalom asked.

"That's right. First we're going to have to fly north over the extreme west coast of West Africa until we hit the Mediterranean. Then we'll continue via Gibraltar, southern Spain and France. However, we can't take any short cuts over the Med because we don't want to risk any sort of encounter with the Egyptian air-force. After all," he smiled grimly, "this plane would make a good shooting target for them. Or they could force us to land at one of their bases."

"Do you mean a repeat performance of what the Bulgarians did to an El Al flight five years ago?"

Harel nodded, remembering how all the fifty-eight passengers and crew had died when an El Al Constellation had strayed into Bulgaria's airspace.

Apart from those who took it in turn to keep an eye on our 'passenger,' the rest of us dozed off or looked out of the windows, chatted in small groups or read. I was asleep when Aharoni shook me by the shoulder. "Haim, wake up. We're nearly home. We should be landing in Tel-Aviv in about fifteen minutes."

"What?" I asked groggily. "Aren't we supposed to be stopping in Rome first?"

"Yes, we were, but then Captain Tohar saw that we had enough fuel to fly straight home. It seems that we had some good tail winds behind us."

I shook my head to wake up properly and then looked out of the window. The sun was up and I could see the blue waters of the Mediterranean below. I went to wash my face and have a shave and, looking into the small mirror, I decided I had had enough of airplanes for quite some time. Over twenty-four hours of enforced inactivity was too much for me. I was impatient to land and I knew that the other members of the team were also feeling the same way.

"Look, there's Tel-Aviv," Aharoni called out and I breathed a sigh of relief. Soon we would be on terra firma and could hand Eichmann over to the police. Now that we were about to pass on the responsibility of looking after him to another authority, a sudden feeling of relief came over me. For the first time in almost two weeks, the team and I would not be responsible for this ex-Nazi's safety and welfare.

Just then I heard and felt the rumbling that came from below as Captain Tohar lowered the landing gear and a few minutes later the 'Whispering Giant' landed. It was ten past seven in the morning, 22 May. We taxied to the terminal where the cabin crew and some of our team left the plane. Harel stood by the door and personally thanked each person and also reminded them not to say a word to anyone, family included, about our special passenger. He then returned to the office he had set up in the first class cabin. I remained in the plane, together with Eitan, Aharoni, Shalom and a few others and kept an eye on Eichmann who was still sitting there, slumped in his seat. Apart from one or two trips to the toilet, he had remained there for the whole journey from Buenos Aires - handcuffed, goggled and silent.

It was at this point that two customs officials came aboard. I told Harel and he got up to inform them that this was a special diplomatic flight and that there was no need for the usual customs inspection. Scratching his head, the older official nodded and told the younger one to drive him back to the office and I pulled the plane's door closed.

The mobile staircase was moved away and Captain Tohar taxied the plane for the last part of its journey, to the El Al service area where we would be far away from any prying eyes in the terminal. When we pulled in to the large hangar we found two people waiting for us. Mordechai Ben-Ari, the deputy head of El Al, and Moshe Drori, the man who had been in charge of our operation's logistics.

After a brief chat in which Harel warmly thanked Ben-Ari for all his help, the deputy director returned to his car and drove back to the terminal. Then Harel turned to face Drori.

"Isser, where is he?" asked the logistics man.

Harel pointed up to the stairs to the plane and then followed Drori into the first class cabin where I was sitting next to Eichmann.

"That's him?" Drori asked. "The man who murdered millions of Jews? Somehow I thought he'd look so powerful, so frightening. But this guy looks so ordinary, so run of the mill."

Harel nodded. It was not the first time he had heard this reaction and, no doubt, he would be hearing it many times in the future. He looked at Drori. "Where are you going to take him now? Tel- Aviv? Jerusalem? Your special place in Jaffa?"

Drori shrugged and looked uncomfortably at his boss. "I don't know."

"What do you mean you don't know? You've had nearly two weeks to think about it."

"I know that," stammered Drori. "But I was waiting to hear from you what I should do with him."

For once Harel was speechless. "Haim, Zvi, wait here. I'll go with Drori and sort this thing out. Now let's go." And they left the plane leaving us to think what would happen to the logistics man once his boss had sorted out this problem.

Two hours were to pass before a large minibus with blacked-out windows pulled up at the foot of Britannia's steps. It was followed by a large black car and from our position we saw Harel get out of the car and then come aboard. Shortly afterward, Eichmann was taken off and bundled into the minibus and driven away to a secret detention center in Jaffa.

Now, for the first time in over a month, Aharoni and I were free of worrying about the man who had proudly declared, "I'll jump laughing into the grave happy at having exterminated five million Jews!" This feeling of relief, of a huge weight being removed from my shoulders, was enormous and it was only when we had handed Eichmann over to the police did I fully realize what I had been through these last few weeks. I could feel myself growing again. Growing physically and spiritually. Our mission had been to catch Eichmann and to bring him back here. This we had accomplished and now I was going through an unprecedented mixture of emotions: on the one hand, there was the joy of having caught him and, on the other, was an undeniable feeling of anticlimax.

What would my next mission be? However, now was the time for the Israeli judicial system to take over.

That night I received permission from Harel to take a few days' leave, a "well-earned leave" he had said, and drive home to my kibbutz in the south. There I was greeted by my wife and children who knew they could not ask me where I had been and what I had been doing. It was very hard to keep silent about it all, but, in a way, I had become used to this way of living. I had a feeling that once the capture of Eichmann became known, my wife would guess where I had been and start asking questions. But until then she had to be satisfied with "I've been working for the government, doing things abroad which I can't talk about."

I guessed it would not take long for the word about Eichmann's capture to get out and I was right. In 1960 Israel had a population of just over two million and, at times, it seemed as though everyone knew everyone else. Inevitably, someone involved in the operation, perhaps one of the El Al cabin crew who was not trained to keep secrets, would inadvertently open his mouth and then the whole country would know.

In the meanwhile, Harel drove to Jerusalem and asked to have an urgent meeting with the Prime Minister. Being the head of the *Mossad* and the other secret services, this request was granted immediately. Wasting no time on small talk, a social convention that neither of these men liked or was good at, Harel got straight to the point.

"We've got Eichmann."

Ben-Gurion ran his fingers through his famous mop of white hair. "Where is he?" he asked.

"Here in Israel. In the detention center in Jaffa. If you want, we can deliver him to the police straight away."

Ben-Gurion was quiet. He did not react at all. Finally he looked up and asked, "Are you absolutely sure it's him?"

"Yes. Absolutely."

"How did you identify him?"

Harel thought for a moment. This conversation was not going the way he had envisaged. He had expected a more enthusiastic reaction. Instead, he was being interrogated in a distinctly cool way.

"We found marks and scars on his body that proved he was our man. And besides, he admitted to us, both orally and in writing that he was Adolf Eichmann."

The Prime Minister leaned forward and put his hand on Harel's shoulder. "That's all I wanted to hear, Isser. *Kol havod*. Well done! You and your men have done a great job, a great job indeed. But can you just imagine putting this man on trial in front of the whole country, no, in front of the whole world and it turned out that he wasn't Adolf Eichmann?"

Harel smiled quickly at hearing this and Ben Gurion continued. "Tomorrow I want two people here, people living here in Israel, to identify him formally. They are to be people who have seen him personally in Europe. Is that clear?"

Harel nodded and turned to go. The meeting was over.

As soon as he returned to his headquarters in Tel-Aviv, he began to organize a search for two such people. He had his staff look through the *Mossad* files to find two Jews who personally come into contact with Eichmann when he was serving as the all-powerful *Obersturmbannführer* in Nazi-controlled Europe. Two men were found. They were Moshe Agami and Benno Cohen. Agami had been the Jewish Agency's representative and had had dealings with Eichmann in Vienna, and Cohen had served as a chairman of a German Zionist organization. Both of them had survived the war and now both of them were brought to Camp Iyar, the detention center where Eichmann was being held. There, together with Ephraim Hofstetter, one of the early investigators into Eichmann's whereabouts, and now the deputy chief of Bureau 06, the special office set up to prepare the future Eichmann trial, they positively identified Eichmann.

"Are you absolutely sure?" Hofstetter must have asked each man at least half a dozen times. "Yes, yes." They were both absolutely sure. The man they had just seen in the interrogation was no other than the evil man they had spoken to over twenty years earlier. Then they had bargained for the lives of the Jews that Eichmann had been determined to annihilate.

As soon as Harel had received a written report on these short but dramatic meetings, he rushed over to the Prime Minister's office. There in a terse conversation he confirmed that the man they had caught over two weeks earlier in the dark in Garibaldi Street was none other than Adolf Eichmann.

As soon as Ben-Gurion heard this, an order was sent to the center in Jaffa and Eichmann was taken out of his cell. He was bundled into the back of a windowless police van and driven the short distance to where Judge Emmanuel Halevi was in court. With no members of the press or the public present, the judge asked Eichmann to identify himself.

"I am Adolf Eichmann," the prisoner answered immediately.

"Then I charge you with genocide, the mass killing of the Jewish people. You are to be remanded in custody for fourteen days."

As soon as the judge had finished, Eichmann was whisked out of the courtroom and returned to his cell.

At four o'clock on 23 May, Prime Minister David Ben-Gurion stepped up to the rostrum in the old Knesset building in downtown Jerusalem and waited for silence. It took a few moments for the traditional hum of discussion to die down in the parliamentary chamber and then he delivered the following message:

I have to announce in the Knesset that a short time ago one of the greatest of Nazi criminals was found by the Israeli security services: Adolf Eichmann, who was responsible, together with the Nazi leaders for what they called the 'Final Solution of the Jewish Problem' – that is, the extermination of six million Jews of Europe.

Adolf Eichmann is already under arrest in Israel and he will shortly be brought to trial in Israel under the Nazis and Nazi Collaborators (Punishment) Law of 1950.

I was sitting in the public gallery next to Harel, Aharoni and a few others from our team. We waited for the reaction. There were a few moments of complete silence as the members absorbed the significance of Ben-Gurion's words. Then all sorts of reactions broke out. Some cheered but others remained silent. Some moved around, talking to everyone they could while others remained still.

Some looked pleased but others sat there crying. Were they crying out of pure emotion or were they crying in the same way that the El Al stewardess had cried on the plane? I could not tell, but I knew I would never forget the scene that was being played out in front of me. As the noise continued and as the reporters rushed out to the bank of phones especially installed for them, we *Mossad* men quietly left the chamber and got into our cars parked on King George Street and drove back to Tel-Aviv.

It was also soon after Ben-Gurion had made his announcement that Harel phoned Haim Yitzhaki, his man in Cologne, and told him to inform Prosecutor Fritz Bauer about what had happened.

Some time later when I met Yitzhaki on home leave in Tel-Aviv, I asked him how the prosecutor, the man who had urged Harel to go after Eichmann, had received this information.

"I arranged to meet him in a restaurant in Cologne," Yitzhaki began. "And I must admit, the old prosecutor looked at me rather doubtfully. I could see that he was expecting to hear some bad news; that something had gone wrong with our plans. Had Eichmann had escaped? Or hadn't he been in Buenos Aires when we'd arrived there? So you can imagine the joy, the happiness he felt when I told him that all had gone according to plan and that now Eichmann was sitting in an Israeli jail waiting to stand trial.

"I'm telling you, Haim, even though Fritz Bauer is a big man, he jumped up, knocked his chair over and gave me a big bear-hug right in the middle of that restaurant. I could feel his tears on my cheeks, but they were tears of happiness. Tears to say that justice had been done at last. Everyone in that restaurant was looking at us but that didn't matter. I suppose they thought that I'd just told him that this old man had become a grandpa again or that he had won first prize in the lottery. In any event, it took him a good few minutes to calm down and all the time he kept smiling and muttering, "*Wunderbar, das ist wunderbar,*" to himself.

"We finished our coffees and then shook hands and left the restaurant. As is second nature to us *Mossad* people, we immediately set off in different directions and when I looked around after a few seconds, he had already melted into the crowds of people outside on the sidewalk."

If anyone had paid any attention to me that evening as I walked back to the office, they would have noticed that I was smiling. Smiling with happiness. Not only had we caught Eichmann and brought him back here – some might say 'smuggled' rather than brought – but we had vindicated an old man's long-delayed hopes of justice being carried out. An old man who had personally suffered because of the Nazis - a man who represented the best face of the judiciary system.

Chapter Twenty-One
The Trial and Aftermath

My part in the catching of Eichmann and bringing him back to Israel was over. Nearly a year was to pass before I saw him again. This was on 11 April 1961 in Bet Ha'am, the People's House, a large public building in downtown Jerusalem. 11 April was the opening day of his trial, Criminal Case No. 40/61, a trial that was to continue until 14 August 1961.

As I was sitting there in the public gallery, a sudden silence descended over the seven hundred and fifty people who had been talking quietly as Eichmann, escorted by two policemen, was brought into the courtroom. He was made to sit in a specially constructed bullet-proof glass booth as one hundred armed police and guards surrounded the building. I saw him seated in the front of the booth with two guards wearing light khaki uniforms who sat right behind him. Immaculate in a dark suit, a white shirt and a striped tie, he was also wearing black thick-framed glasses. His sharp appearance was spoiled however as he kept wiping his nose with a large handkerchief.

As I sat there waiting for the judges to make their entrance, I couldn't help but overhear some of the remarks of the people who were sitting near me.

"That's the Nazi killer? The clerk in our bank looks more dangerous than he does."

"He looks so ordinary."

"Huh! That's the man who killed my family? I never would've believed it."

"He looks like my neighbor, the one who wouldn't say boo to a goose."

"Look at that smirk on his face. It's disgusting."

Several minutes later, the three judges walked into the courtroom and took their places facing the accused. Chief Justice, Moshe Landau, opened the proceedings in Hebrew. This was translated to Eichmann through a headset that he was to wear throughout the length of his trial.

"Are you Adolf Eichmann, son of Adolf Karl Eichmann?"

"*Jawohl*," Eichmann replied, leaning into the microphone in front of him.

"Are you represented in this trial by Dr. Robert Serviatus and by Mr. Dieter Wechtenbruch?"

"*Jahwohl*."

"Good, then I will begin by reading the indictment." He cleared his throat and began. "You are accused before this court in terms of an indictment containing fifteen counts. I shall read the indictment to you and this indictment will be translated for you into German. This is the indictment against you on behalf of the Attorney General.

"First Count. Nature of the offense: Crimes against the Jewish People. Particulars of the offense: a) The Accused, during the period from 1939 to 1945, together with others, caused the deaths of millions of Jews; the Accused, with others, were the persons responsible for the implementation of the plan for the physical extermination of the Jews, a plan known by its title 'The Final Solution of the Jewish Problem.'"

Judge Landau then entered into the specific details of this Count which included details of the mass deportations and the establishment of extermination camps at Auschwitz, Chelmno, Belzec, Sobibor, Treblinka and Majdanek, among others.

Following the reading of this grim list, the judge outlined the various Nazi operations, which led directly to the deaths of Jews in the Ukraine and Belorussia as well as the brutal deportation and transportation of Jews in cattle trucks to the above camps from Germany, Austria, Italy, Bulgaria and Belgium.

After the judge had read out this Count, he asked Eichmann for his plea.

Holding his head to his side, Eichmann leaned over to the microphone and impassively said, "In the sense of the indictment, no."

He was to repeat this phrase after having heard each of the following fourteen Counts read out to him.

If the First Count were not horrendous enough, the judge continued reading out the details of the Second Count. Here Eichmann was accused of compounding the crimes of mass deportation and transportation with the establishment of forced labor camps.

Count Three dealt with mass arrests, torture, beatings, social and economic persecution of Jews together with the passing of the infamous 'Nuremberg Laws.' These, said the judge, had been specifically designed to deprive all the Jews of their basic civic and human rights.

Count Four referred to the Nazi plan known as 'The Final Solution' and the enforced sterilization of Jews living in Nazi-controlled Europe. Count Five expanded on some of the details outlined in the first Count.

Count Six added more about the Nazi Crimes against Humanity and Count Seven was concerned, among several other terrible clauses, of dealing with the destruction of the Austrian Jewish community beginning in March 1938. This Count also dealt with the plundering and mass looting of Jewish property throughout the war.

Count Eight dealt with the Nazis' anti-Semitic rule in Axis countries, and Count Nine concentrated on what the Nazi regime had done to the Jewish population in Poland.

In a similar way, Count Ten referred to the Nazi rule in Yugoslavia, and Count Eleven charged Eichmann with how the Nazis had dealt with the Gypsy population in Nazi-controlled Europe. Count Twelve referred to the infamous massacre at Lidice in Czechoslovakia, and Count Thirteen referred to Eichmann's own personal membership of the Nazi party. This was compounded in Count Fourteen when Eichmann was accused of being an active member of the SS.

The final Count referred to Eichmann's actions as a leading member of the Secret State Police – the infamous Gestapo.

It took Judge Landau nearly an hour to read out the indictment and during all this while, everyone sat there in complete silence. The size and scale of the crimes committed by this apparently insignificant bureaucratic-looking man, sitting there in his glass booth just a few yards in front of us were impossible to take in. But we were not allowed much time to dwell on this because Dr. Servatius, Eichmann's defense attorney, was now standing up to forward an objection to these legal proceedings.

"This court," claimed the large crew-cut lawyer, flown in from Germany specifically for the trial "has no right to try my client. The judges, as Jews and Israelis, cannot be unbiased and I therefore call for an international tribunal to hear this case. This court," he continued, looking around, "is not competent and the proceedings here under the Nazis and Nazi Collaborators (Punishment) Law cannot be held here. Neither the accused nor the alleged victims were citizens of the State of Israel when these alleged acts were committed."

As he declared his objections, I began to wonder if what he was saying would carry the day. Back in Buenos Aires, we had also discussed these legal points. Each point Dr. Servatius mentioned was true. The State of Israel had come into being three years after the end of the war and not one of the witnesses and accusers was technically a citizen of that state when Eichmann had committed these crimes.

I looked around and saw that many of the people sitting near me were also looking extremely worried. Would Eichmann escape justice due to a legal technicality? It didn't seem fair or moral.

However, I had no time to think about this as Eichmann's defense lawyer was now expanding on his objections to the trial.

"This state has a vested interest in the outcome of this trial," Dr. Servatius continued, his heavy German accent being clearly heard all around the courtroom. "I challenge the principles of the Nuremberg Tribunal which are being exploited here today: that crimes have been created where none had previously existed. My client," he added, turning to look at the impassive man sitting in the glass booth behind him, "performed acts of state and, as such, the state was responsible for them, and not the individual who carried them out. One state cannot try another and my client does not represent the state of West Germany."

The defense lawyer paused for a few moments to let his words sink in. Then breaking the silence and heavy atmosphere of the courtroom he continued. "In any event, West Germany is paying reparations to Israel. This should be enough. If you look around, you will see that this trial is being covered internationally by the press and the television. This means that due to the impact of international pressure my client stands no hope of receiving a fair trial. This man," Dr. Servatius said, turning again to point at Eichmann who, for the first time seemed to be showing some interest in the proceedings, "was merely a receiver of orders. He was a minor figure. He was not a leader."

And," he added. "If all of the above is not enough, my client was brought to this court, to this country, illegally and under duress. Later I will call upon Captain Tohar and Yehuda Shimoni of the Israel national airline, El Al, an airline which is financed by the Israeli government, to prove my last objection."

Just as I had felt concern with the way in which this case had opened, I saw that many of the people sitting there were feeling the same. Their whispered questions between themselves reflected this anxiety.

"Is it possible that the German lawyer may be right?"

"Will Eichmann get off before the trial even begins?"

"Is it true that he can't be charged as Israel didn't exist then?"

But we were not to feel anxious for long. For just as Eichmann's defense lawyer sat down, Dr. Gideon Hausner, the balding Israeli attorney-general stood up and faced the man we had worked so hard to bring to justice. When you saw him, physically, seated in the courtroom, the European-born Israeli jurist was not an impressive figure. But when he stood up to take his stand I felt that he was going to make history. I was right.

Standing there at his table he moved in closer to the three microphones and pointed at the accused, at Adolf Eichmann, the ex-Nazi *Obersturmbannführer*, one of the chief instigators and executioners of 'The Final Solution.' The attorney general's black cloak was lifted like a huge bird's wing as he raised his arm and pointed at Eichmann, now facing him through a glass panel.

"When I stand before you here, Judges of Israel, to lead the Prosecution of Adolf Eichmann, I am not standing alone. With me are **six million accusers**. But they cannot rise to their feet and point an accusing finger toward him who sits in the dock and cry: "I accuse." For their ashes are piled up on the hills of Auschwitz and the fields of Treblinka and are strewn in the forests of Poland. Their graves are scattered throughout the length and breadth of Europe. Their blood cries out, but their voice is not heard. Therefore I will be their spokesman."

I left soon after this dramatic rebuttal of Dr. Servatius' opening words. I felt that this trial would go the way the Prime Minister and the judiciary wanted and hoped it would bring some comfort to Eichmann's living victims. I felt sure that it would bring a just verdict and that the world now had the chance to see how terrible and widespread this man's work had been. I hoped that this trial would act as a precedent and that in future no-one would be able to murder and torture innocent people and think that they could escape unpunished.

The trial continued until mid-August. Tens of concentration camp survivors testified against the mild looking man in the glass booth. Many of them broke down in tears as they recalled what they had suffered twenty years earlier. Over fifteen hundred documents were produced to prove Eichmann's complicity in 'The Final Solution.'

Despite Eichmann's claim, "I never did anything great or small, without obtaining in advance express instructions from Adolf Hitler or any of my superiors," he was found guilty on all charges.

Four months later the court was reconvened and on 11 December 1961 Adolf Eichmann was sentenced to die for what he had done to the Jewish people during the Holocaust. He submitted an appeal. This was studied and rejected, as was his appeal for clemency.

Six months later, on 1 June 1962, two years after we had seized him in Buenos Aires, Adolf Eichmann was hanged. I learned about this when I was sitting on the patio of my kibbutz home reading the evening paper. It said that the death sentence had been carried out the night before in Ramle jail. He had refused to eat a last meal but, instead, had drunk half a bottle of red Israeli Carmel wine. When his confessor, Reverend Hull, asked him if he had repented, Eichmann had replied, "No."

Unrepentant to the end, his body was cremated and an Israeli naval patrol boat took his ashes out to sea and scattered them over the Mediterranean beyond the limit of Israel's territorial waters.

This would prevent the erection of any future monument for him; and no country would serve as his final resting place.

After I had read this, I sat there staring into space without seeing anything for a long while. I thought about what I had done to help bring this monster to face his accusers. Technically, justice had been served. This man had committed many unspeakable crimes and now he had paid for them. But was I pleased with the final results? I did not know. I did not know whether hanging him had been the most suitable punishment. I began to think it was too quick. Many of his victims, both living and dead, had suffered for many years and would continue to suffer. Would it not have been fairer, more balanced, to let him rot in an Israeli jail for the rest of his life? There he would have learned that the Jewish people, those who had survived his murderous Nazi regime, the people he had tried to literally wipe off the face off the earth, together with their descendants were now living and breathing. They were now rebuilding their lives and, at the same time, they were building up their new country, Israel, day by day.

254

Where Are They Now?

Zvi Aharoni

Born as Hermann Arendt in Frankfurt, Germany in 1921, Zvi Aharoni emigrated to Mandatory Palestine in as a young boy. During the Second World War he served in the British army and later spent twenty years working for the *Mossad*. This included hunting ex-Nazis such as Adolf Eichmann and Josef Mengele. After retiring from the Israeli secret service, he became a businessman in Hong Kong and then spent his last years in Devon, south-east England. He described his role in tracking and catching Eichmann in *Operation Eichmann: The Truth about the Pursuit, the Capture and the Trial.*

Fritz Bauer

(1903 – 1968) Born in Stuttgart, Germany, Fritz Bauer studied law and became the youngest recipient to receive his doctorate in law. He had joined the Social Democrat Party by 1920 and when the Nazis came to power, he was arrested by the Gestapo and dismissed from his legal position. In 1935 he emigrated to Denmark and eight years later moved to Sweden. He returned to Germany in 1949 and became the District-Attorney in Hesse in 1956. He held this post until his death in 1968.

He was a co-founder of the Humanistic Union and as one of the chief instigators in tracking down Adolf Eichmann, he supplied the *Mossad* with much useful information.

David Ben-Gurion

Originally named David Gruen, Ben–Gurion was born in Plonsk, Poland in 1886 and emigrated to Ottoman Palestine in 1906. After working for some time as a farm laborer, he became involved in politics and formed the first Jewish trade union in

1915. Exiled by the Turks during the First World War to the USA, he helped found the American branch of the Jewish Legion. On his return to Mandatory Palestine, Ben-Gurion became the Secretary-General of the General Federation of Jewish Labor – the '*Histadrut*' – and later, the political leader of the Palestinian Jewish community – the '*Yishuv*.' In May 1948 he declared Israel's independence and became the country's first Prime Minister and Minister of Defense. Always a controversial and colorful character, Ben-Gurion retired from politics in 1963 and in order to set an example to young Israelis, spent his retirement at Kibbutz Sde Boker in the Negev. He wrote many books and died in 1973 aged 87, a man who symbolized the country he had worked so hard to establish.

Shalom Danny

The brilliant *Mossad* forger of papers and documents died of a heart-attack three years after 'Operation Eichmann' in 1963.

Rafi Eitan

Born in 1926 in Kibbutz Ein Harod, Mandatory Palestine, Rafi Eitan served in the *Haganah* and the *Palmach*. During the Israeli War of Independence, he served in Intelligence and later became responsible for co-ordination between the *Shin Bet* and the *Mossad*. Apart from 'Operation Eichmann,' Eitan was also responsible for halting the delivery of German arms to Egypt (1964-1966) and later worked on the planning of the Israeli air attack on the Iraqi nuclear reactor in 1981. Later he worked for the Ministry of Defense and then became the Minister for Pensioner Affairs. However, he lost his seat in the Israeli parliament (*Knesset*) after three years in 2009. Today he devotes much time to his hobby of sculpting.

Yonah Elian

The doctor on the team responsible for catching Eichmann

was born in Romania in 1923. He arrived in Israel after the Second World War and later became one of the country's leading anaesthetists. In addition to his role in sedating Eichmann, Dr. Elian worked with the *Mossad* on several other operations. His skills were highly praised by Rafi Eitan, the leader of the 'Operation Eichmann' team. Dr. Elian died in 2011 aged 88.

Tuvia 'Tadek' Friedman

(1922–2011) was born in Radom, Poland and became one of the most well-known Nazi-hunters. He managed to escape from the Radom concentration camp in 1944 and later worked for the Allies in catching Nazi and SS officers. After arriving in Israel, he served with the *Haganah* and then worked as the director of the Israeli Institution for the Documentation of Nazi War Crimes. He contributed information to the *Mossad's* dossier on Eichmann and recorded his anti-Nazi activities in his book, *The Hunter*. He died in Haifa, Israel aged 88.

Ya'acov Gat

This *Mossad* agent was born in Romania and despite his being sent to a forced-labor camp during the Second World War, he survived and came to Israel via a British internment camp in Cyprus in 1948. He joined the *Shin Bet* secret service two years later and spent the next twenty-three years there. On his retirement, he worked as the treasurer of a private security company.

Isser Harel

The *Mossad* director and spymaster was born in Vitebsk, Russia in 1912 and emigrated to Mandatory Palestine in 1930. After taking part in the Israeli War of Independence, he founded and ran the *Shin Bet* secret service before taking over the *Mossad* as well. Apart from running the Eichmann operation Harel gained fame in 1956 by being the first in the West to obtain a copy of the Soviet Communist Party chief, Khrushchev's secret speech which denounced Stalin. Two years after catching Eichmann, Harel was back in the news when he located Yossele Schumacher, the Orthodox Jewish boy, who had been kidnapped in Israel and smuggled to New York by his grandparents. Many people in the Israeli security establishment criticized Harel for this saying that this matter was not one, which concerned Israel's national security. He resigned from the *Mossad* in 1963 and later joined the 'National List,' Ben-Gurion's political party. Harel wrote several books about his time in the *Mossad*, including *The House on Garibaldi Street*, his own description of 'Operation Eichmann.' Harel died in 2003 aged 91.

Gideon Hausner

The Israeli Attorney-General who made the famous opening speech for the prosecution at Eichmann's trial, "I am not standing alone. With me are six million accusers..." was born in Lemburg, Austria-Hungary in 1915. At the age of twelve he emigrated to Mandatory Palestine and later studied law at the Hebrew University, Jerusalem. During the War of Independence he served in the *Haganah*. Soon after he was appointed Attorney-General in 1960, he became the chief prosecutor at Eichmann's trial. He served as Attorney-General for three years before going into politics where he remained until 1981. He served as Minister without Portfolio for three years from 1974 and was also Chairman of the Yad Vashem Holocaust remembrance Museum in Jerusalem. He wrote two books about justice and the Holocaust and died in 1990 aged 75.

Lothar Hermann

The man who supplied the first accurate account as to where Eichmann was living was born in Germany where he studied law.

This half-Jewish lawyer fled to Argentina before the Second World War started, after he had spent one year in the Dachau concentration camp. There he had been severely beaten up which resulted in him losing his eyesight. Together with his daughter, Sylvia Hermann, he gathered information on where Eichmann lived and this information eventually ended up in the hands of Dr. Fritz Bauer, the German-Jewish prosecutor. This led to the chain of events which resulted in the capture of Adolf Eichmann and his being brought to Israel to stand trial. It then took Hermann over ten years to receive the $10,000 reward for supplying the information which led to Eichmann's arrest. He died in Argentina in 1974. His daughter, Sylvia, who had acted as his 'eyes' left Argentina for the United States where she lives today.

Zvi (Peter) Malkin

The *Mossad* agent who actually caught Eichmann in Buenos Aires was born in Germany in 1927. He and his family fled to mandatory Palestine in 1936 in order to escape the rising tide of Nazi anti-Semitism. Like many in the 'Operation Eichmann' team, he served in the *Haganah* before joining the *Mossad* where he served for 27 years. He became the Chief of Operations and apart from catching Eichmann, he helped uncover the Soviet spy, Israel Be'er who had penetrated the Israeli secret service during the early years of the State. Like Rafi Eitan, Malkin was also involved in preventing the Egyptians from obtaining German arms in the 1960s. Malkin left the service in 1976 and was awarded the Prime Minister's Medal of Honor. He wrote five books including *Eichmann in My Hands*. He devoted his retirement to painting and died in New York in 2005.

Avraham Shalom

Born in Vienna in 1928, he moved to Mandatory Palestine in 1939. He joined the *Palmach* in 1946 and fought in the Israeli

War of Independence. He joined the secret service in 1950 and remained there until he was forced to resign over the '300 bus' affair in 1986 in which he was accused of having overall responsibility for the deaths of two unarmed terrorists. He spent his last six years in the *Shin Bet* as its director. In 2012, he recounted the part he had played in the country's security in the documentary film, *The Gatekeepers*.

Moshe Tabor

(1917–2006) The *Mossad's* expert safe-cracker was partially motivated by revenge when he worked with the 'Operation Eichmann' team in catching Eichmann in 1960. The Nazis had murdered his family in Lithuania and this resulted in Tavor volunteering as a member of the revenge squads which hunted down and killed many SS men toward the end of the war. He died in 2006 after many years service in the Israeli secret service.

Zvi Tohar

Born in 1915 in Berlin, the El Al pilot had escaped from Nazi Germany and later learned to fly with the RAF. Bringing Eichmann to Israel, was not the first time that he had been in the news. In 1957 Tohar piloted El Al's first non-stop flight from Tel-Aviv to New York. One year later, even though one of his airliner's eight landing wheels was missing, the El Al captain managed to make a smooth landing at New York's Idlewild (now Kennedy) airport.

Simon Wiesenthal

(1908-2005) Together with Tuvia Friedman, Simon Wiesenthal became one of the most well-known Nazi-hunters. He was born in Austria-Hungary and studied architecture. He spent the Second World War in several concentration camps and barely survived the experience. He became a Nazi-hunter immediately after the war and provided photographs of Eichmann to the *Mossad*. He became a secret *Mossad* operative and wrote several books and articles about his wartime and Nazi-hunting experiences. He devoted much time to working at the Jewish Documentation Center in Vienna and died in 2005 aged 97. He was buried in Herzliya, Israel.

Eichmann Family

After Adolf Eichmann was flown to Israel in 1960, His wife, Vera and her youngest son, Ricardo, spent the next few years moving between Germany and Buenos Aires. She finally settled down in Osterburken, Germany and never accepted her husband's guilt or execution. Her youngest son, Ricardo became a professor of archaeology in Germany, and although he recognizes his father's terrible past, he does not speak much about him. His two other brothers, Dieter and Nick (the one who first accidentally revealed where Eichmann lived) returned to Germany, and like their other brother, Horst, who remained in Buenos Aires, are convinced that their father was, to use his excuse, merely carrying out orders.

THE END

Acknowledgements

I would like to thank three people who made this book possible. The first is my ever-vigilant editor, Marion Lupu, whose sharp eyes and editing skills were truly essential for the writing of this book. The second is Avner A., the initiator and curator of the Eichmann 'Operation Finale' exhibition, an exhibition that was held in April 2012 at *Beit Hatfutsot*, 'The Museum of the Jewish People,' on the Tel Aviv university campus. Not only did he encourage me with this project but he also supplied me with many of the relevant details concerning this whole story. The third source of help was my old college and motor-cycling friend, Patrick Nethercott, who read the manuscript and advised me on several points, especially those connected with the German language and Germany in general.

Bibliography

Operation Finale:The Story of the Capture of Eichmann, Exhibition catalogue, Published by Bet Hatfutsot, The Museum of the Jewish People, Tel-Aviv, Feb. 2012.

Zvi Aharoni & Wilhelm Dietl, *Operation Eichmann*, John Wiley & Sons, Inc., New York, 1997

Michael Bar-Zohar & Nissim Mishal, *Mossad: The Greatest Missions of the Israeli Secret Service*, CCCO/HarperCollins, New York, 2012

Neal Bascomb, *Hunting Eichmann: Chasing down the World's Most Notorious Nazi*, Quercus, London, 2009

Tuviah Friedman, *The Hunter*, Doubleday & Co., New York, 1961

Martin Gilbert, *The Holocaust: Maps and Photographs*, The Jerusalem Post, Jerusalem, Israel, 1978

Isser Harel, *The House on Garibaldi Street: The Capture of Adolf Eichmann*, Corgi Books, London, 1975

Walter Laquer, *The Terrible Secret: Suppression of the Truth About Hitler's "Final Solution"*, Penguin Books, Middx., UK, 1982

Nora Levin, *The Holocaust:The Destruction of European Jewry 1933-1945*, Schocken Books, New York, 1974

Peter Z. Malkin & Harry Stein, *Eichmann in My Hands*, Warner Books, New York, 1990

Dan Raviv & Yossi Melman, *Spies Against Armageddon: Inside Israel's Secret Wars*, Levant Books, New York, 2012

Stewart Steven, *The Spymasters of Israel*, Ballantine Books, New York, 1980

Walters, Guy, *Hunting Evil*, Bantam Books, New York, 2010

Elie Wiesel, *Night,* Hill & Wang, New York, (1958), 2006
Useful website: *36 Questions & Answers about the Holocaust*

If you enjoyed this novel by
D. Lawrence-Young try:

Anne of Cleves: Henry's Luckiest Wife

It is winter 1539. King Henry VIII is galloping through the night to Rochester to meet Anne of Cleves. She has just arrived in England and is destined to be his fourth wife. He has seen her portrait – a portrait of a sweet, demure and innocent young woman. The impatient and lovesick king must see her before their marriage. But this rushed and unplanned rendezvous is going to shock them and their country both and lead to some completely unexpected and fatal results.

In D. Lawrence-Young's well-researched novel we learn of the strong emotions and the deadly politics when a bitterly disappointed Tudor king's romantic plans go badly awry.

Catherine Howard: Henry's Fifth Failure

This historical novel has it all: sex and romance, violence and war, infidelity and intrigue.

Catherine Howard, the Duke of Norfolk's niece, is raised in the very free atmosphere of her grandmother's palace. Here she becomes aware of her own sexuality and the exciting effect she has on the men at court around her. She is also an unknowing part of her uncle's devious plan to obtain more influence with the king - he pushes her onto the newly-divorced and lovesick King Henry VIII who is looking for a fifth wife.

Meanwhile, John Butcher has become a guard in the dreaded Tower of London. He guards the king, witnesses the executions of Anne Boleyn and Thomas More and takes part in the fighting in Ireland. However, when he returns to London, his meeting with Catherine Howard, the king's fifth queen, produces unexpected and dramatic results.

In D. Lawrence-Young's second Tudor novel we learn how Catherine Howard's passionate nature mixed with the murky, deadly politics of the Tudor court and a furious king produce a classic story of passionate love, disappointment and revenge on a royal scale.

About the Author

D. Lawrence-Young has been teaching and lecturing on drama, history and English for many years. He is happiest when researching Shakespeare, English and military history. He has edited *Communication in English*, a best-selling English language textbook, and has also written over a dozen historical novels, which have covered British, Australian and Israeli topics. He has also written three novels based on the life of Shakespeare.

He has contributed many articles to *Forum*, a magazine for English teachers and also to *Skirmish*, a military history journal. He is the treasurer of the Jewish History Society in Jerusalem and also Chairman of the Jerusalem Shakespeare Society. He is a published (USA) and exhibited (UK and Jerusalem) photographer. He plays the clarinet badly and is married and has three children and three grandchildren.

CPSIA information can be obtained at www.ICGtesting.com
Printed in the USA
BVOW04s2230131114

375100BV00023B/240/P